ATTENTION!

BEFORE YOU READ THIS BOOK, PLEASE DOWNLOAD THE FREE SUPPLEMENTAL WORKBOOK

DOWNLOAD INSTRUCTIONS:

The Conscious Intelligence Supplemental Workbook is available for download at
www.EricErenstoft.com/Workbook

Or by scanning the code below

CONSCIOUS INTELLIGENCE

Master Your Circumstances
Master Your Life

ERIC ERENSTOFT

DISRUPT TSQ MEDIA

DISRUPT TSQ MEDIA

Copyright © 2020, 2010 by Disrupt TSQ Media
Copyright © 2020, 2010 by ElevateID.org
Copyright © 2020, 2010 by Eric Erenstoft
Copyright © 2020, 2010 by E. Erenstoft Enterprises, Inc.

All rights reserved, including the right to reproduce this book or portions thereof in any form whatsoever. For information email your request to Connect@ElevateID.org with Subject Line: Disrupt TSQ Media, Subsidiary Rights Department, Permissions.

Conscious Intelligence is a registered trademark filed through The United States of America Patent and Trademark Office, USPTO.

For information about special discounts for bulk purchases, please contact Disrupt TSQ Media sales at Connect@ElevateID.org.

The Disrupt TSQ Media speakers bureau can contract authors and thought leaders to speak at our sponsored, curated live events. For more information or to book an event, contact the Disrupt TSQ Media speakers bureau at Connect@ElevateID.org or visit our website at www.EricErenstoft.com/invite-eric-to-speak/ and provide details in the fields provided.

10 9 8 7 6 5 4 3 2 1

Printed in the United States of America.

ISBN: 978-1-7343868-0-6 (Hardback)
ISBN: 978-1-7343868-1-3 (Paperback)
ISBN: 978-1-7343868-2-0 (eBook)
ISBN: 978-1-7343868-3-7 (Audio Book)

Library of Congress Control Number: 2020904975

Cover and Workbook design by Seareign Designs
Interior design by Melissa Vail Coffman

DEDICATED TO
My familial soulmate, hero, and guardian angel
Dr. Bunni Tobias, Ph.D. aka: Mom

NOTE TO READERS & DISCLAIMER

E. Erenstoft Enterprises, Inc., ElevateID®, www.ElevateID.org, Disrupt TSQ Media, in association with Eric Erenstoft and affiliates (referred to herein as ElevateID® and Affiliates) together represent a content-based company that has made a substantial investment in protecting its intellectual property. This book, as well as the related websites, web presences, recorded media, social media, videos, literature, and collateral material, are all copyright protected. Only ElevateID® and Affiliates have the exclusive right to train, perform publicly, and present from the content of the book and aforementioned related material. This means ElevateID® and Affiliates do not allow others to implement the tangible expressions of the book, or anything substantially similar without permission.

Moreover, the terms ElevateID®, The Genome of Elevated Consciousness®, The Invisible Distinctions®, and Conscious IntelligenceTM, are common law and registered trademarks owned by ElevateID® and Affiliates. ElevateID® and Affiliates, therefore, ask that you respect their intellectual property rights and not use the book and aforementioned material in any manner that would infringe ElevateID® and Affiliates' intellectual property rights. ElevateID® and Affiliates would joyfully consider working with your organization in licensing and implementing the book concepts. Please contact us at connect@ElevateID.org.

DISCLAIMER: The material, content, and intellectual property in this book, associated websites, and all literature and collateral (collectively referred to herein as ElevateID® IP) is not intended or implied to be a substitute for professional medical advice, diagnosis, or treatment. All content, including text, graphics, images, and information, contained on or available through ElevateID® IP is for general information and illustrative purposes only.

While every effort has been made to adhere to accuracy and presentation of facts, ElevateID® and its Affiliates make no representation and assume no responsibility for the accuracy or completeness of the data or information contained in any of ElevateID® IP. You are encouraged to confirm any information obtained from or through

ElevateID® IP with other sources, and review all information, especially regarding any medical condition or treatment with your physician.

NEVER DISREGARD PROFESSIONAL MEDICAL ADVICE OR DELAY SEEKING MEDICAL TREATMENT BECAUSE OF SOMETHING YOU HAVE READ ON OR ACCESSED THROUGH ELEVATEID® IP OR ANYWHERE ELSE.

ElevateID® and its Affiliates do not recommend, endorse, or make any representation about the findings, efficacy, appropriateness, or suitability of any scientific research, externally, internally, or otherwise, nor do they present, represent, or claim any scientific findings of their own. ElevateID® and its Affiliates did/do not conduct any scientific research and present no findings, claims, or representations. Reference to ANY science, physics, methodologies, research, or terminology, including but not limited to elevated consciousness, genome, DNA, grieving process, singularity, Divine are referred to anecdotally and/or used solely as conceptual, abstract, theoretical, illustrative, figurative, euphemeus, connotative, allegorical, symbolic, or metaphorical expressions.

The material is subject to copyright and is restricted. Any unauthorized use, whether expressed, implied, likeness, or misleading representation, is strictly prohibited. Any stated or implied endorsement by ElevateID® and its Affiliates of a commercial product, process, or service or used in any other manner that might mislead is strictly prohibited. ELEVATEID® AND ITS AFFILIATES PROVIDE NO ADVICE AND ARE NOT RESPONSIBLE OR LIABLE FOR ANY ADVICE, COURSE OF TREATMENT, DIAGNOSIS, OR ANY OTHER INFORMATION, SERVICES, OR PRODUCTS THAT YOU OBTAIN FROM ANYBODY REPRESENTING OR CLAIMING SOURCING FROM ELEVATEID® IP.

Unless otherwise explicitly stated, all information, text, recordings, electronic images, or any other media contained in any and all ElevateID® IP is the intellectual property of ElevateID® and its Affiliates.

Any/all information generated, created, sourced, expressed by ElevateID® and its Affiliates is subject to change without notice, is periodically being updated, and does not always carry a revision date.

CONTENTS

ACKNOWLEDGMENTS xiii

INTRODUCTION. xvii

SECTION I: AN INTRODUCTION TO CONSCIOUS INTELLIGENCE

CHAPTER 1: What Is Conscious Intelligence? 1

CHAPTER 2: The Invisible Distinctions (IDs): The Building Blocks of Conscious Intelligence 19

SECTION II: THE CONSCIOUS INTELLIGENCE PARADIGM

THE BASE DISTINCTIONS

CHAPTER 3: Distinctions of Communication 31

CHAPTER 4: Distinctions of Freedom and Imprisonment 49

CHAPTER 5: Distinctions of Personal Power. 71

CHAPTER 6: Distinctions of Personal Sovereignty 101

CHAPTER 7: Distinctions of Advancement, Productivity, and Leadership 141

THE CENTRAL DISTINCTIONS

Introduction to the Central Distinctions. 171

CHAPTER 8: The Anchors of Love 175

CHAPTER 9: The Shades of Love 189

THE ELEVATED DISTINCTIONS

Introduction to the Elevated Distinctions 205

CHAPTER 10: The Call To Serve 209

CHAPTER 11: Charity | Service | Moral Obligation 221

CHAPTER 12: Social Justice and Change 237

CHAPTER 13: Essential Life Force, the Divine, and Certainty 253

CHAPTER 14: Distinctions of Absolute 265

CHAPTER 15: Determination. 277

CHAPTER 16: Happiness | Purpose | Bliss. 287

CHAPTER 17: Execution 307

SECTION III: THE CONSCIOUS INTELLIGENCE PERSPECTIVE

The Conscious Intelligence Perspective. 315

CHAPTER 18: Full Circle 319

CHAPTER 19: Afterword—My Final Thoughts 327

Appendix 331

Endnotes 333

ACKNOWLEDGMENTS

We are a part of all we have met

My collective work, exploration, investigation, research, and studies on Conscious Intelligence is in part accredited to the culmination of the many experiences, challenges, triumphs, and guardian angels I have met on the circuitous path that has become the tapestry of my life.

Formulating The Genome of Elevated Consciousness® and what has become The Conscious Intelligence Paradigm, proved to be my Mount Everest. It has been the most grueling and equally rewarding endeavor pouring every cell of my (B)eing into this platform and area of study. And while I did not employ a single ghost writer, I am grateful for the collaborations with key colleagues and editorial staff that played a significant role in refining the dense, vertical, thick manuscript geared more for doctorate journal-level consumption into one that is accessible to everyone, regardless of their age, background, or diversity—encompassing all age ranges, education levels, professions, races, religions, sexual orientations, and lot in life.

I am deeply grateful to the many teachers, gurus, servicemen and women, friends, family, and colleagues—and the divine—as well as the monsters, bullies, ill-willed, horrific people that, to this day I believe knew not what they did—All who have forged me into the driven, resilient, creative—and flawed, humbled, and imperfect human being that has become uniquely, *Me*.

Acknowledgments

I OFFER MY DEEPEST GRATITUDE TO:

First and foremost, my biggest fan, inspiration, familial soul mate, and Guardian/Arch Angel, Dr. Bunni Tobias, aka.: Mom.

Sheltering Angel: Lisa Wuerth Siefert.

Mentoring Angels: Joseph Campbell, Carl Gustav Jung, Stephen Covey, Dr. Wayne Dyer, Alan Watts, Lau Tzu, Sun Tzu, Martin Luthor King Jr., Shel Silverstein.

David Wolpe, Rick Warren, Ms. Robinson, Karlene Counsman Von Szeliski, Valerie Gianatti, Randy Kent, Trudy Beck, Ms. Morrison, Dr. Terrence Kite, Dr. Sattler, Russell Gough, John Michael Vincent, Robert Washburn, Bill Arndt, Guy De Fabriti Shaw, Vincent Chase, Jodi B., Cassie K., Gene Oliver, Milton and Emily Trager.

Coaches: Mr. Marcus, Schiezel, Corso, Azevedo, Grizz, Fry, Hooks, Bonnie Adair, Clay Evans.

Senseis: Kazuo Chiba, Ichero Shibata, Pablo Vazquez, Terri Teshiba, Sara Nielsen, Gloria Nomura, Rhonda Hutley, Robert & Bernard.

Yogic Arts: Vinnie Marino, Jesse Schein, Kumi Yogini, Aree Khodai, Liz Arch, Rachel Jackson, Heather Dawn, Erika Schnicki, Sean Gray, Calvin Corzine, Shiva Rea, Mia Togo, Joan Hyman, Sarah Ezrin, Chad Hamrin.

Aerial Arts: Jonathan Conant, Ryan Schneider, Dean Chapman, Randy Lamb, Dayna Thompsen, Richie Gaona.

Musical Artists: James Hetfield and Metallica, Tori Amos, Loreena McKennitt, Liz Story, Eddie Vedder, Chris Cornell, Annie Lennox, Cat Stevens, Hans Zimmer, John Williams, Mozart, Vivaldi, Need To Breathe, Sarah McLachlan, Lily Wilson, Kari Kimmel.

Rebecca & Thomas, Abe & Rose, Anne, Rose, Addie, Celia, Sam & Bernice, Mickey & Julie, Amy, Hilary, Sheldon. Jeff & Patti Memler, Susan Mahoney, Nancy, Penni, David, Jon Kuz, Moo, Michel Joy Del Re, John Goodman, Lara and Dr. Iris Rosenfeld.

Jennifer D. Kenning, Allison Dickey, Pam Lazzarotto, Natasha Gaffaney, Elise Lampert, Jason (Turbo), Kevin Koster.

Jen Kushell, Lori S, Vicki M, Arthur I, Sharon H, Melissa C, Michael U, David A, Matt R, Ted W, Bryan S, Jessica P, Harry N, Rosalinda O.

*I've spent my entire life
questioning everything around me.*

~Eric Erenstoft

INTRODUCTION

I was the annoying kid that asked, "Why?" incessantly. So many of my conversations with teachers and other adults went like this:

Me: "Why is this the way it is?"
"Well, Eric, because…so and so…"

Me: "Well, why that?"
"Because…such and such."

Me: "Okay, so, if that's the case, then why that???"
"Oh, for Pete's sake, Eric, go look it up!"

… *So I did.*

A FAVORITE PHYSICS PROFESSOR validated my entire *childhood* in a single lesson. He said, "If you have something substantial and want to see what makes it tick, and you can't get to the guts of it, get a bigger hammer!" When I learned that this is the basic and essential premise of physics, I was hooked—especially since, as a youth, I loved breaking open televisions and other electronics to tinker with their cool inner workings.

Incidentally, my mom, a child psychologist, validated my entire *adulthood* in a single lesson: "Know the rules so well that you know when to break them." She understood too well the pros and cons of following the rules and when to paint outside the lines. She understood how left unchecked, sometimes the world and its conventions can paint you into a corner.

The Conscious Intelligence Paradigm presented in this book is a direct result of a lifetime of striving to understand how everything works and why people are the way they are. I followed my interests wherever they led me, across subject matters and world continents, through social sciences and hard sciences, business and entrepreneurialism, martial arts and the yogic arts, philosophy and psychology, spirituality and philanthropy. I began to see that by becoming keenly attuned to how perspectives are formed, how we project them out into the world and back to our own selves, that we can dramatically shift the course of our life. When we gain the ability to observe our own perspective and understand what shapes it, we become able to deconstruct the flawed *paradigms* we formulate. When these *frameworks* are flawed, they get in the way of our own happiness, success, and balance. Conscious Intelligence has much to do with elevating perspective—shedding light onto it—and shifting.

My work deconstructs Conscious Intelligence, distilling it into its elemental components—*distinctions*. The work frames these distinctions into a paradigm, *The Conscious Intelligence Paradigm*. The Paradigm acts as a navigational guide to illuminate and access Conscious Intelligence. When these key distinctions, called Invisible Distinctions, are illuminated, we become conscious of them, able to respond powerfully to our circumstances, and poised to bring about optimal results.

As a seeker, I have always questioned how things work. So powerful is the notion that two of the most influential people in my life taught me to break things. Both my physics professor and my mother taught me the subtle distinction that breaking things *open* in a quest to discover their true essence sits in stark contrast to merely breaking things. Interesting, don't you think? This *notion* inspired an essential question that remains inside of me still today:

> *How do we approach things begging to be broken?*

A New Century Demands a New Consciousness

IN THIS BRAVE, NEW 21ST CENTURY, we are experiencing the expansiveness of innovation, technology, communication, and globalization—and with this expansion, unlimited possibility. We are getting more, it's coming faster, and we're demanding it right now! The economy and the markets are broadening worldwide, transacting in real time, and continuing to expand exponentially, all while being monitored on a device sitting in the palm of our hand. Much of the power formerly held by the few is now within the grasp of the many. Big data analytics, media, news, shopping, investing, and entertainment now are all highly individualized. Today, *we* are the field reporter, the news anchor, the whistleblower, the product reviewer. Technology has created more economic output than the world has ever seen.

Extraordinary, right? Not so fast! As with anything so powerful, we have to maintain perspective and not forget that technology is a tool, a machine, not to be mistaken for its operator: *you* and *me*. Because this sea of change is moving faster than our human ability to adapt to it, we are often left feeling as if we are in a pressure cooker. In this age of real-time, on-demand, instant-messenger, same-day delivery, we often find that our communication is reduced to speaking in sound bites. We are spending less time listening before our fingers are tapping away at a response. The volume of information flow today can feel like we are drinking out of a fire hose. It thrusts us into overwhelm. News is negative, because that's what trends and what drives profits. Facts and statistics are crafted, angled, and distorted for strategic gain. Politics feel toxic. The environment is suffering. Amidst this world of globalization, we have an increase in polarization, terrorism, opioids, gun violence, public health and education issues, as well as the breakdown of our natural tribal societies. Human relationships are suffering from the lack of face-to-face interaction. We are witnessing frays in the real-world fabric of human connection *despite* being connected 24/7.

Is this age drawing us closer together, or are we experiencing a widening chasm that leaves us feeling more distant, divided, and in disarray? Is all this change empowering or overwhelming? Why are we witnessing a strong compulsion to blame and an equally strong aversion to accountability? Why do we often feel we are just coping rather than moving ahead? Will we fall slave to technology or ascend to become its master?

How do we approach a system that is begging to be broken?

In framing The Conscious Intelligence Paradigm, I set out to illuminate a pathway to how we can experience the world with greater clarity, perspective, and, yes, consciousness. This Paradigm, (derived from the *Genome of Elevated Consciousness*, my research, thesis, and body of work), facilitates opening the key channels of communication between one another and with ourselves. It helps us navigate our circumstances with clearer connection, so that we can approach business, productivity, relationships, communication, and ourselves much more powerfully and purposefully.

All of my studies, influences, and experiences have added to my understanding of Conscious Intelligence. While my formal education placed me on a track to become an orthopedic surgeon, I moved on to study business, communications, and the arts. I have spent my life devouring philosophy, psychology, physics, and theology; poets, existentialists, nihilists, Taoists, Buddhists, pragmatists, and every other *-ist* I could find. My study and fascination with Far Eastern philosophy came to life when I moved to Japan to live and work professionally for a time and studied the culture, trained for my Black Belt in martial arts, and became a practitioner in the yogic arts—just as Western philosophy came to life when I moved to Europe to live and work professionally for a time and studied art history, architecture, and theology.

When I wasn't at sports practice during my primary school years, Mom immersed me in the performing arts, taking me to the theatre, symphonies, concerts, and ballets. She brought me along to doctorate lectures on psychology, philosophy, astrophysics, and alternative medicine. I'm pretty sure she made friends with the Ph.D.s in engineering and computer science while she pursued her doctorate in psychology just so she could *offload* me and my insatiably curious mind for five minutes so she could steal away to study. I'll never forget being whisked down to the computer labs to program and play games with professorial students. This was a hoot in the 1970s, as computers filled entire rooms!

On the more *unconventional* side, her mind expansively curious and always open, she dragged me along regularly to psychics, channelers, astrologists, healers, and to lectures such as Jerry Jampolsky's *Love Is Letting Go of Fear*, where he spoke on his books based on *A Course in Miracles*. My brother and I had a field day with that one! The next time we ticked off my mom, finding ourselves being chased around the house, her belt in hand, we'd offer back in desperation, "Come on, Mom, love is letting go of fear!"

Of everyone and everything mentioned, I would say there are three luminaries in particular who focused these points of light into a laser: Carl Gustav Jung, Joseph Campbell, and Stephen Covey. There is a truth to their work that resonates to all corners of my universe, a truth that connects us all—the *collective unconscious*, the *archetypes* and *The Power of Myth* threaded throughout the human psyche, and the powerful habits we can develop to shape the life we can live into. To me, these elements illuminate our human circumstances; they frame the predicament that all humankind has witnessed throughout the millennia, endured, questioned, celebrated, warred over, destroyed, and rebuilt.

No matter where we are on earth, what age we are, our lot in life, or our heritage, we are all connected by circumstances that the entirety of humanity uniquely shares. I believe it is our calling to seek out and discover this ethereal connection…the connection to each other, to the earth and all of her splendor, and to the expansive sky that reaches beyond our scope, out into the universe.

It is this vision, this yearning for connection—and masochism, definitely crazy, delirious masochism—that motivated me to frame *The Genome of Elevated Consciousness*, and from it, this *Conscious Intelligence Paradigm*. It is my offering to you—along with my hope that it will serve to illuminate in you what I have strived to illuminate over the course of my life.

SECTION I

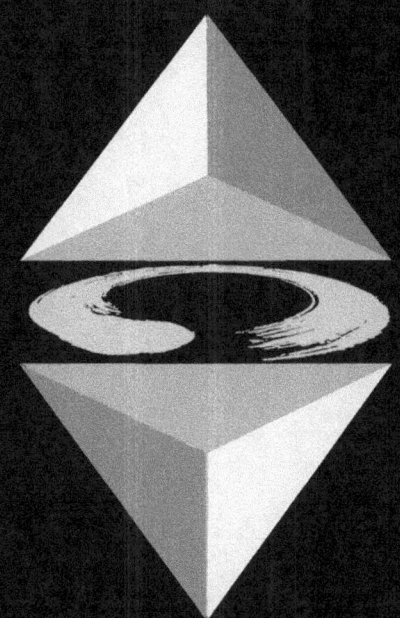

AN INTRODUCTION TO CONSCIOUS INTELLIGENCE

CHAPTER 1

What Is Conscious Intelligence?

Conscious Intelligence is the ability to gain mastery over our circumstances. It is the attainment of clarity and perspective within our circumstances to bring about optimal results.

It is perspective that elevates us far above our circumstances without placing us an inch above anyone else.

INHALING THE MOST COLOSSAL BREATH my five-year-old lungs could muster, I submerge, weightless, gazing upward towards the surface. Sunbeams penetrate the clear blue water and radiate across my face and body, continuing their dance across the pool bottom. I am in my happy place…pure bliss.

The world pauses as if holding its breath along with me…until suddenly, I am whisked skyward. I giggle with exhilaration as a friend of my father launches me high into the air, sending me soaring and then plummeting down in a cannonball splash. I surface, giggling louder, begging him to do it again.

The scene is a backyard pool party, hosted on a beautiful Southern California summer afternoon. The kids swam and played while the adults stood chest-deep, cooling off with an adult beverage. I'm all wound up, excited to play with my new friend. I splash him and he retaliates, splashing me back harder. I nudge him. I taunt him. I beg relentlessly, "Launch me into the air again!" But now, he doesn't respond.

Moments pass. I prod him multiple times, unsuccessfully. So, I employ a new tactic: a covert underwater mission to ambush his leg. Eventually, a large hand clutches my head as if palming a basketball. I grin underwater, beaming. Mission accomplished! I have his attention again. Only oddly, instead of drawing me up, his large hand pushes me downward, holding my head firmly under the water. Several moments pass. Several more. And more...

Adrenaline jolts through me like electricity, detonating me into a flailing panic. I reach out, grasping for anything that can help pull me to the surface. There's nothing, nothing but terror. The giant's grip is unwavering, and I am not strong enough to resist and break free. My underwater screams expend precious oxygen as my lungs fill with water. People are all around, but no one can hear me. My life is literally in another man's hand.

The cerulean blue water turns to black abyss. I can't fight anymore and give in. Then comes the hardest lesson, the shame—my discovery that when drowning, it's common for one's body to go into shock, lose control of bodily functions, and go limp.

Only then does the monster finally hoist me back up to the surface.

I remember the muted hum of obscured voices and commotion as I lay strewn on the pool deck. I am coughing violently, choking up water incessantly, and sobbing helplessly. It's quite a scene for my father and his new wife. My adult playmate stands over me, his eyes glaring into mine just long enough to assure that the truth of this incident will remain between us. His demeanor then softens as he feigns concern, taking credit for rescuing me. I feel ashamed. The incident is never mentioned again, and the memory submerges into the depths of my psyche.

We are all products of our circumstances and experiences, whether chosen or not, some that we create and some that others create. They shape us. They frame our thoughts, beliefs, perceptions, sensations, memories, and conditioning. They impact us. Some can cause us to resist change and limit progress, some become biases, some expose us to areas in life we didn't know existed, some become hardwired within us, and some fall to the wayside of our awareness—But ALL of them influence the decisions we make moving forward.

Our circumstances are not only the situation around us; they are the situation *in* us.

They are also the situations that got us here—but how they affect where we are going is entirely up to *us*.

A major distinction that emanates from Conscious Intelligence is that—We *are not our circumstances*. We are not defined by our circumstances. Our circumstances are not us. Our response to any given situation stems from the way we approach that situation.

> *We cannot always control our circumstances, but we can control how we conduct ourselves within our circumstances.*

The Conscious Intelligence Paradigm provides a means to illuminate perspectives surrounding the nature, causation, and dynamics of our circumstances. From the biggest decisions of our lives to the seemingly inconsequential, this Paradigm can inform and drive our conduct, how we observe, listen, process, engage, act, speak—essentially, *how we respond*. If assimilated, it can guide us to respond optimally.

For most of us, there is a moment. It is a moment when we discover that we are vulnerable—where we realize that, for the first time, there exists a choice of not or never again. It is the decision we all face when something we are interested in, curious about, or obliged to do exposes us to peril. This might be school, work, a hobby, dating, sex, or perhaps a near drowning. Maybe we fell off our bike, were made fun of at school, were rejected by the *one*, discovered our parents are flawed, were told we are not deserving, worthy, or good enough, or were unfairly robbed of an honor, award, or promotion.

Any moment when we discover we are not invincible or that the singular, positive result we expected isn't all-but-certain after all, we are faced with a crucial decision: Do we dive back into the parts of our lives where we pulled the ejection handle? Do we return to the place we considered safe, where danger reared its ugly head, where security was corrupted, where we were let down, betrayed, violated, leaving us instead vulnerable to hurt, disappointment, and fear? Do we get back on that bike, date again, expend the back-breaking time and effort? Do we take the risk…again? Or do we avoid any chance of conflict, uncertainty, shame, or shortcoming, and instead choose not or never again?

Our world is peppered with countless, seemingly trivial choices. While they are happening, these apparent, insignificant moments can instantly become peak moments that shape our entire world. How these moments occur to us and how we interact with them has everything to do with how our circumstances unfold to become the lives we live into.

> It's the time a friend pushes us off the sideline, onto the field, where we discover that our life takes on a whole new direction.
>
> It's realizing that, alongside the fragility of life, priceless moments exist where we would give anything to share just one more moment with a loved one who perished too soon.
>
> It is the time we fall off the proverbial cliff, and instead of plunging to the canyon floor, we take flight.
>
> It is the chance meeting of our future spouse, boss, or best friend that changes the trajectory of our lives entirely.
>
> Only when we reflect on these moments do we realize they are infinitely more than what we could have known at the time.

> *Change is inevitable. Growth is optional.*
> *~John C. Maxwell*

Immediately following the pool incident, I avoided the water for a time. I was running this non-resolving equation in my head:

> *In what was once the sanctuary to my most peaceful bliss now lurked the terror of a horrific death.*

I longed for a way to relieve this torment, but the only shelter I knew—the water—was now cohabitated by the very source of my anxiety and near demise. We often avoid the circumstances we fear, the people, places, and things with which we've had bad experiences. It's our human condition to be shaped by these collective experiences. Who would blame me if I never went back?

Except…I grew up near the ocean and was surrounded by water. All of my friends played at the pools and surfed at the beaches. I was either going to get back in or miss out on everything. Not only that, but the water called to me. I can't really explain what I mean, except to say that I just knew that the water embodied boundless wisdom, serenity, and life—and now I knew it also embodied humbling power. The water was sacred, and as if she insisted, was my salvation. As I learned later, the ocean in archetypal perspective symbolizes the collective unconscious—the medium of cleansing, re-birth, and transformation.

As a child, I was not yet conscious of the powerful life choice I was actually facing, one that would forever affect my life. You see, this instance was an ember that touched off a fire in the area of my soul where my personal crown of thorns resided—a perfect storm of tinder where three internal weather systems were converging. Being deeply sensitive and possessing copious amounts of empathy and compassion, I remember wishing upon myself the transferal of others' pain as if I had a superpower that could take it all away. At age five, I vividly remember my mom's face the first time I exhaled this admission to her. She happened upon me while I was visibly in my head, which was not in itself unusual, except this time observing me in deep inner struggle. Initially, her crinkled face reflected the clinical one she'd make while seeking to understand a patient; then, in the magical moments following, her face softened to match mine as I watched her deeply "get" my inner ordeal. In those ensuing moments, I observed the strong lioness who was my mom falter briefly, revealing the very same heartache—in a similar effort—as she tried to take mine away.

The second of the storm systems was my longing to fit in and to be accepted by others; I was tormented by the feeling that I was different, which led to my susceptibility to be bullied and picked on. The third was an absence of the proper guidance in my life to stand up and protect myself. Quite often I found that my personal plight was left to chance, remedied only on the seldom occasion that someone was there to intervene and come to my rescue. The weighty burden of vulnerability left me unprotected from the afflictions of shame.

As fate would have it, I was ushered back to the water's edge. Unaware of the near-drowning incident that occurred while visiting my father, Mom enrolled me in the Harbor View Dolphins swim team—probably because there were no Ph.D. engineering professors within arm's reach to whisk me off her hands for a while! The push was uncomfortable; I bore a new appreciation for the water, but I went along with it, and the fun and joy eventually resumed its place back at the helm. I discovered this one swim stroke, *the butterfly*, that none of the kids wanted to do because it was so difficult. Whenever the need arose for a butterflier, which was pretty much all the time, I volunteered, rarely unchallenged, and as a result, got to fill the spot at all the competitions. As it turned out, the butterfly's rugged training had an interesting byproduct: it conditioned me well for common freestyle, especially in grittier environments like water polo and swimming in the ocean. All the while, I just wanted to partake in all the fun! By high school, I began setting varsity records and, to my surprise, my team and coaches honored me with the accolades of "Most Dedicated" and "Most Valuable." Then the accolades began to elevate to "All-State" and "All-American." I made the USA National Junior Water Polo Team, the feeder into what becomes the USA Olympic Team.

Through this all, the idea of others feeling helpless and alone as I did that one dark day in the pool persisted. It haunted me. Once again, I felt that compulsion to take away others' pain, to prevent anyone else from feeling as I had that day. One day, that five-year-old's deep desire for conciliation came full circle: Two men appeared on the pool deck and invited me to join a specialized team. A team that saves lives. I tried out, entered the gruelingly competitive academy, and emerged an ocean rescue responder through Laguna Beach Fire Department and, years later, with LA County Fire Department. Now drowning has since become a subject I am all too familiar with and am an expert in, *literally*.

Through this all, the water gave me life, focus, sanctuary, inspiration. It gave me mentors in the form of coaches and battalion chiefs. I developed friends and found a community. And yet, I could have chosen *not*, all those years ago, without even recognizing that there was an alternative.

> *Conscious Intelligence is the ability to gain mastery over our circumstances. It is the attainment of clarity and perspective within our circumstances to bring about optimal results.*

While very simply stated, when unpacked, this concept has a multitude of layers and profound depth. Everything we do, everything we are up to, involves circumstances.

> *When we observe the multitude of circumstances we encounter, we begin to truly understand the vast scope of what Conscious Intelligence means.*

So many of us go through the actions of life not thinking about or questioning our circumstances. We are like pinballs, passively bouncing off flippers and bumpers, rolling up ramps or down holes. Oftentimes, no inquiry is made into even seeking alternative perspectives. As a result, few resources are acquired to help us expand our minds to consider the spectrum of choices that exist.

> *Conscious Intelligence adds to the dimensionality of our circumstances by broadening the perspective we can bring to our circumstances. We learn, grow, and evolve—And when called for, it inspires us to change.*

The word *inspire* means "to breathe life into." Are there areas of your life that require more breath? You see, breathing is automatic; we can do it without even thinking about it...or we can override our autonomic nervous system and commandeer our breathing. Until we are aware, the act of breathing is automatic, and so our options are limited. But we have a choice. Once we become conscious of our breathing, we can make choices. We can hold our breath, breathe more rapidly, breathe deeper, etc. What's amazing is that our bodily functions respond in accordance. When we combine this with the doctrine that:

> *We are not our circumstances*
> *We are not defined by our circumstances*
> *Our circumstances are not us*

...we can begin to see why mindfulness practices, yogic arts, martial arts, and meditation all center around breath.

Independent of what is going on around us (or in us), we have the ability to control our breath. If we calm our breathing, for example, our heartbeat slows, our adrenaline quantities lessen, and our body calms as a result. If we imagine ourselves in a stressful situation (or subject ourselves to the stress of a situation), the opposite occurs. Our body and internal functions follow our breath, and our mind can facilitate all of it. Gaining perspective over our circumstances and, in the process, gaining our composure has a powerful effect on how we will ultimately fair within the circumstances. Breath is the essential food of life. If you don't believe me, try holding it for a while. In sync and mindful of this, we can guide ourselves from a life of fear and anxiety to serenity and grace.

In the same way, becoming present to our expanded scope of choices in any given circumstance facilitates the guiding of our circumstances to an optimal outcome. Enhancing our ability to seek, gather, and formulate alternatives is what it means to access Conscious Intelligence. When we are given the tools to expand the consciousness in our lives and circumstances, as well as to expand our awareness of available alternatives, we can make powerful choices that lead us to better environments, relationships, emotional and physical health, and balance.

Every day, we experience people acting out of pure emotion: anger, fear, jealousy, excitement, delight, longing, desire. While this spectrum of emotion naturally elevates us as a human race, it is a double-edged sword and can also manifest a polar opposite effect. There exists no such thing as a correct emotion in a circumstance, but there *is* such a thing as approaching circumstances without being clouded by emotions, be it ours or someone else's. Decoupling emotions from a circumstance in order to see the circumstance more clearly is a powerful component of Conscious Intelligence.

> *When we access our Conscious Intelligence, we draw from a perspective above the circumstance, diminishing the risk of being constrained by any myriad of emotions coursing within the circumstance.*

Applying Conscious Intelligence is not a state absent emotion; it does not mean abstaining from having emotions. After all, emotions are part of being human. We can apply a principle brought to light by Viktor E. Frankl: "Between stimulus and response there is a space. In that space is our power to choose our response. In our response lies our growth and our freedom." If we think of the stimulus as upstream in timeline, and the response as downstream, accessing an elevated perspective upstream poises us to respond optimally downstream. This is also a powerful component to Conscious Intelligence.

> *The elevation of consciousness is a process.*
> *When it is cultivated and employed,*
> *it moves us towards our highest expression.*

Transactional Thinking

YOU MAY NOT BE FAMILIAR WITH THE TERM "Transactional Thinking," but we've all seen it. It is cause/effect thinking. Transactional thinking says: *Do this, get that. Think and Grow Rich*, do these six things and earn seven figures; subscribe to this diet and lose thirty, forty, even fifty pounds; follow these ten steps and you'll find ___ (fill in the blank: *success, financial freedom, purpose, happiness, love*, etc.).

> *Ahhhh, yes, the allure of getting more by doing less—*
> *the magic pill, the Golden Goose, the Midas touch,*
> *the big secret only successful people know…*

There is no shortage of experts *prescribing* the answer, claiming to have *that one map* they think we should follow that will set us on our way to the Promised Land. Bookstore shelves are swollen with best-sellers acclaiming these transactional promises, and the landscape is replete with prescriptions from so-called experts telling us what path to take to attain these desired things. Conscious Intelligence isn't accessed by that way of thinking.

While transactional thinking is natural, is supported by the laws of physics, and is our common human experience, some things require a different approach. We are wired to default into transactional thinking: Cause/Effect, Action/Reaction, Stimulus/Response. We put our hand in a fire, we get burned. The sun rises, we wake up. We drink coffee, we get a jolt of energy. Our knee is tapped, and our leg jerks, but…*not everything is transactional in this world*.

Here's when this way of thinking becomes problematic. When we begin to conflate the way we view areas of our life such as our values, happiness, purpose, accountability, generosity, service, love…into binary, transactional *things*, we place a stranglehold on our ability of experiencing their highest expression. In doing so, we deprive ourselves and others of the deeper dimensionalities they possess.

Conscious Intelligence follows an entirely different paradigm and way of thinking: that of *illuminating* or shining a light on, rather than *prescribing* or telling you, what path to take. Why? Because its very nature expands perspective that facilitates discovery within the areas of our lives that cannot be fully realized by merely executing a transaction.

Prescription versus Illumination

THERE EXISTS A DISTINCTION BETWEEN prescription and illumination, just as there exists a distinction between giving someone a map with instructions versus equipping them with a compass and a powerful headlamp. Inspiring is a teacher who guides a student in a way that makes the student feel as if they made the discovery themselves. As timesaving as a map might seem and on occasion can sometimes be, a deeper and lasting understanding comes from making the trip ourselves.

*The only enduring way to shift consciousness
is to choose powerfully for ourselves
rather than be told what to do by somebody else.*

Illumination expands perspective while prescription narrows it. Here's that human nature thing again: when we are told to shift direction, i.e., when something is *prescribed,* we are often more prone to resist than if we are given a light that we can shine on the broader and deeper perspective, letting us clearly see it for ourselves so we can choose for ourselves. Who am I—who is anyone, really—to tell you what path is the right path for you? We all possess Conscious Intelligence; what this Paradigm offers is a brilliant light to access it. To access Conscious Intelligence is to expand our perspective, create a clearing, and facilitate any necessary course adjustments so we can set a heading towards our True North.

Solving Problems versus Labeling People

"I believe in solving problems, not labeling people." Remember my mom? As a child psychologist, she used this phrase all the time—in fact, it became a trademark of her entire life's work. She worked with all kinds of children and their parents—gifted, challenged, at risk, disabled, missing limbs, with extra limbs, autistic, blind, deaf, with Down syndrome, cerebral palsy, epilepsy, ADD/ADHD, kids on the spectrum (before it was even called that), and many others whose diagnoses had yet to be discovered. Growing up, I played with all of these kids, all of the time.

Were you ever told not to stare, that it's "not polite"? I never once heard this on my play dates with Mom's kids, not until much later out in the world. Good thing, as my curiosity was far too audacious anyway. As a child, I'd walk up to these kids and say, "Hi, I'm Eric! So, what's your story?" I had watched as my mom interacted with them like any other child, so I did the same. In retrospect, I guess the greeting was really forward compared to what they were used to, but I didn't know any different.

I soon learned that they regularly encountered people who were uncomfortable, disingenuous, or worse. When they saw no sign of that with me—and saw, rather, just a kid like them—they'd answer with delight and tell me everything about themselves. Then they'd ask, "So what's wrong with YOU?" We'd laugh for several moments… *and then I'd tell them*: I felt like kids my age didn't understand me, that inside was this deep desire to feel accepted, that I wanted people to like me…and that this left me vulnerable. And in this honest communication, I discovered these kids weren't so different from me at all. Perhaps their differences were more visible for the world to see, but that didn't mean I didn't have plenty of crippling insecurities hidden deep within myself.

And then…we'd play! Absent any notion of being different, we got on just like any other kids. Absent fear, our frankness and honesty with one another created a dynamic that celebrated our differences rather than polarized us.

It's interesting how fast we can judge or avoid others out of fear because they appear different or unfamiliar. But, when we delve in and sincerely seek to understand, we discover that we share much more similarity than differences. It's all a matter of perspective.

> *I chose to stare into my friends, not at them,*
> *and play with them, not avoid them.*

We all have challenges, formally diagnosed or not, visible or not. Mom's directive was simple: If we wanted to fit in and be treated like everyone else, we had better be accountable for our challenges. Otherwise we'd become imprisoned by them. We either had to own our own challenges or risk leaving the door open for the world to define them for us, projecting its own fears, judgments, and labels onto us.

It's no great surprise that we often avoid people and situations that make us uncomfortable. It's a human impulse, developed in the most primal areas of our brain: *to fear the unknown*. Our instincts can compel us to keep our distance, dismiss, or disparage. In our cave days, this kept us safe because we were trying not to get eaten. It kept us safe, but it kept us small. It kept us isolated. It kept us insular. That's not the world we live in today; we evolved and learned what we could do through collaboration, and tribes emerged. Yet, behavior today is increasingly resembling those primitive days. As a result, the disconnect has us missing out and experiencing a new form of cognitive dissonance.

We are not only missing out; we are missing the point.

> *What's behind that wall, that border, that organization?*
> *What's behind that religion, that facial expression,*
> *those eyes?*
> *We don't know what we don't know.*

Because we all see things differently, the world is a much more interesting place. Our diversity does not have to lead to divisiveness. Here's that word again: *perspective*. When higher perspective is lost, we witness breakdown, reactivity, and blame. This condition creates a minefield of volatility, and what results is our instinct to react rather than to rationally respond. Even the most trivial of interactions has us shutting each other out. More dangerously, we shut ourselves *in*. Instead of progressing, we cope; instead of thriving, we place ourselves in survival mode.

We possess the ability today to look deeper into things than ever before. Because we can, we are called to recognize that sometimes perspectives, paradigms, and conventions beg to be broken in order to allow new thinking to emerge, to evolve, to elevate our human race. Tension and stress, whether out in the world or deep within us, demand addressing. This begins with us breaking things open, starting with ourselves. To do so requires attaining clarity. It involves investigating our own perspectives and the responses these perspectives elicit.

Resistance

CHANGE IS THE ONLY CONSTANT IN LIFE. It is not only natural, it is a law of physics and a cornerstone of our earthbound existence. Along with change, we commonly experience this thing called resistance, which shows up as an attachment to fixed ideas we have. This resistance sources from a lack of information: either we didn't learn something, we mis-learned it, we misconceived it, or our fear had us neglect it along with the consideration of an alternative. Clinging to such notions often does not serve us and can ultimately lead to suffering.

Resistance is fueled by fear, and therefore is overcome in a few different ways. One way is to propel forward, realizing that the fear behind us is more agonizing, dreadful, and terrifying than the fear in front of us. Another way is to allow ourselves to be curious. Curiosity does much to wipe out fear because its very nature inspires illumination. At the end of the day, it benefits all of us to be more curious—curious with intention—so we can evolve our perspective and elevate our consciousness.

Because resistance is sparked by fear, it can also be alleviated by removing what fuels it. Eliminating the drag is as helpful as boosting the drive—just as when we are on a fitness regimen, losing weight is as beneficial as gaining muscle, for example. Removing the resistance that weighs us down helps us facilitate change. It moves the fulcrum favorably towards the tipping point. You see, gaining perspective is as much about removing impediments as it is about opening our minds to allow new perspectives to flow in.

Discovering Our Path to the Summit

> *I remembered one morning when I discovered a cocoon in the bark of the tree, just as the butterfly was making a hole in the case and preparing to come out. I waited a while, but it was too long appearing, and I was impatient. I bent over it and breathed on it to warm it. I warmed it as quickly as I could and the miracle began to happen before my eyes, faster than life. The case opened, the butterfly started slowly crawling out and I shall never forget my horror when I saw how its wings were folded back and crumpled; the wretched butterfly tried with its whole trembling body to unfold them. Bending over*

> *it, I tried to help it with my breath. In vain. It needed to be hatched out patiently and the unfolding of the wings should be a gradual process in the sun. Now it was too late. My breath had forced the butterfly to appear, all crumpled, before its time. It struggled desperately and, a few seconds later, died in the palm of my hand. That little body, I do believe is the greatest weight I have on my conscience. For I realize today that it is a mortal sin to violate the great laws of nature. We should not hurry, we should not be impatient, but we should confidently obey the rhythm of people and things.*
> ~ *from* <u>Zorba the Greek</u>, *by Nikos Kazantzakis*

A GROUP OF FRIENDS decide to summit Mount Everest. Well aware that few in the world have ever managed this monumental feat, they dive deep into research, get into the best shape of their lives, raise funds, and spend thousands of hours studying and training on the technical aspects of the climb. Along the process, they climb other mountains as part of their training and encounter extraordinary people—some who are blind, missing limbs, have terminal illnesses—but all have the same conviction and goal: *Everest*. This becomes an epic journey they all share.

Together, countless seasons later, at last, they summit Everest. They laugh, they cry, they embrace; they savor the precious moments at the top, marveling at the significance of their accomplishment. Just then, as they begin their descent, a *specialized* helicopter arrives at the top. An elegantly suited man disembarks. He takes in the view, snaps a few selfies, high-fives the pilot and crew, and hops back onto the helicopter.

One year later, there is a special cocktail reception, a reunion for those who have summited Everest. Everyone is sharing their inspiring stories and extraordinary accomplishments in the year since—how their injuries, failures, resiliency, perseverance, and courage during the feat tested their will, built their character, and gave them courage. Then, into the reception walks the man who summited Everest via the helicopter. He begins circulating, mingling and reminiscing, sharing and viewing others' photos—*a fellow Everest alumnus*.

You might be thinking, "Seriously? Who is this guy?" He didn't train or work to make the trek, bust his tail, endure the treacherous conditions, invest months or years preparing, sacrifice time away from his family, suffer oxygen deprivation, overcome mental challenges and personal failures, push through the fear, the injuries, the hardships, the sacrifice...nor did he give himself the opportunity to feel the *connection* to the earth, sky, wind, snow, and people encountered along the journey...

It is our human nature to seek shortcuts, to find the easy way, to cut corners. We are always endeavoring to reduce our workload, mask discomfort, sidestep responsibility, get there faster. What of experiences like this one? The man summited Everest, didn't he? He had photos identical to the rest of the group to prove it. But there's something else at play here, isn't there?

I had the opportunity to work in the fashion industry where I travailed alongside some of the most beautiful people in the world. I witnessed a range of techniques fashion models employed for maintaining their figures and physiques. Some followed sensible diets or were vegetarian. These models avoided junk but allowed themselves to cheat once in a while. They exercised daily, used sunscreen, and drank plenty of water. Some refrained from caffeine, alcohol, excessive sugary drinks, and made an effort to get to bed early. Others smoked, ate junk food, drank alcohol, popped diet pills, used cocaine or other stimulants, skipped meals, and partied all night. Some resorted to starving themselves, becoming anorexic and bulimic. Both groups kept their figures and looked stunning on camera, fit the clothes, and earned boatloads of money. But how do they look now? Guess which ones are still healthy, glowing, and gorgeous, and which are either weathered, sickly, or dead. Over time, one can see the different lifestyles manifest in broad daylight—when skin hangs on bones versus looking toned and alive. Is it always advantageous to take shortcuts? Do they always pay off?

> *There is a distinction between taking the path less traveled*
> *versus hitching a ride,*
> *Between making a path more efficient*
> *versus cutting corners.*

Elevating consciousness takes work, and it isn't a one-time, one-and-done kind of thing. Like trekking to a summit, The Conscious Intelligence Paradigm provides tactics, skills, techniques, insights, approaches that make our trek more efficient and adroit. There exists a distinction between making the trek efficient versus cutting corners. Accessing Conscious Intelligence is not a shortcut, nor does such a journey want for one when approached from an elevated perspective. Think of it as a lifetime of cultivation. I have spent much of my life aggregating, organizing, and consolidating The Conscious Intelligence Paradigm so that it could be framed in a clear, concise, and organized anthology. Applying its principles is something only you can do. While I will walk the path with you and guide you, I cannot walk it for you. This is *your* trek and *your* summit.

Knowledge is only a rumor until it is in the muscle.
~ Papua New Guinea proverb

If knowledge and awareness were the only factors required to elevate our consciousness, then this book would need only to be a laundry list of vocabulary definitions resembling a cursory table of contents. It would be that helicopter ride that just drops you at your perceived summit. But this is not the way it works, not the way we humans experience life, and despite what many may misconceive, not truly what we humans seek. Knowledge and awareness are but singular bits of information while wisdom and consciousness are multi-dimensional networked states of being.

Here's the point: A major distinction exists between simply being aware and in the cultivation of elevated consciousness. While the possession of knowledge and information is an important step, it is only the first step. Merely knowing something doesn't snap the necessary muscle system immediately into shape, just as knowing how to do an arm curl doesn't snap our biceps instantly into rock hard Popeye arms. Something much more is at play, and your senses will be honed to feel the difference; they likely have already started.

Noblesse Oblige

> *With great power comes great responsibility.* ~ *Voltaire*
> *You've been given much, much is expected.* ~ *Luke 12:48*

MAKE NO MISTAKE: elevating consciousness does not make life easier or put one's life on cruise control. Rather, it propels us into a higher orbit, carries with it an ever-higher moral obligation, and increases the potency of our power to make an impact. With such power, the highest levels of responsibility become requisite: this is *noblesse oblige*, the inherent responsibility of those fortunately gifted with more to take an active role in elevating others. More power employs more resources, and having more resources increases our influence in the world. How we implement our power in the world ultimately determines our impact and how we will be defined by it.

It will always be incumbent upon us to facilitate change in our lives. If we don't, life will eventually do it for us, like a wave that we can choose to either ride or sit and watch until we get clobbered by it. This fact will never change. What *can* change is us—either by our doing or by that which is done to us—and the velocity with which we can change is, to a large extent, up to us.

My hope is that the comprehensive insights outlined in this book will help illuminate your path to productivity, performance, happiness, success, and deeper purpose, all while diminishing fear, increasing curiosity, and, as a result, facilitating the harmony that so often is desperately lacking today, both in the world around us and within us.

The underlying framework of this platform, The Conscious Intelligence Paradigm, is an organized and structured set of elemental distinctions designed to illuminate Conscious Intelligence. It provides the behavioral insights and tools that let us cultivate a path to the life we endeavor to live into. Its intention is not to take on the philosophical or literal interpretation of what consciousness is. It merely serves as a conduit to expand our perspective. As a result of the insights that we gain, we become better poised to respond optimally to our circumstances.

CHAPTER 2

The Invisible Distinctions (IDs): The Building Blocks of Conscious Intelligence

The mind is everything.
What we think, we become.   ~Buddha

THE KEY TO ACCESSING CONSCIOUS INTELLIGENCE is the ability to identify and differentiate between what I call *Invisible Distinctions*. These Invisible Distinctions illuminate the differences between certain ideas, beliefs, or perspectives that, when confused or conflated (as they often are), lead to miscommunication, conflict, and breakdown. When we can identify and understand these key distinctions, we attain clarity around the entirety of our circumstances. What results is a keen ability to draw from perspective *above* our circumstances to elicit a more conscious course of action *within* our circumstances.

> **Distinction**: A significant and notable difference between two things that may otherwise seem similar.

> **Invisible**: Not in one's frame of sight; unseen. In terms of the Invisible Distinctions, "invisible" pertains to that which we don't readily see.

The concept of distinctions is central to The Conscious Intelligence Paradigm. In general, a distinction can be obvious, such as the distinction between a *cup* versus a *mug*, or can be complex and more elusive, such a*cknowledge* versus *wisdom*. Obviously, it's the latter we're focused upon here. I call them *Invisible* because we often don't think about or notice the nuance within them, and yet they inform how we see the world, how we perceive things, and how we interact with others. Invisible Distinctions influence how we formulate our ideas and our values, and they are the basis of how we shape our thoughts. They determine how we process our environment, consciously and subconsciously, and how our circumstances ultimately impact us.

These powerful distinctions embody every element of how we can elevate our consciousness with respect to business, productivity, relationships, communication, leadership, and entrepreneurialism, to create a conscious life we are inspired to live into.

Why Is It So Important to Make Distinctions?

THE INVISIBLE DISTINCTIONS bring to light modalities in the way we view the world and in how we articulate our thoughts. They make visible the often-overlooked subtleties that bear a profound effect on our everyday lives. They provide key insights into our psyche, the way we think, and the way we communicate. Breakdowns often occur when we unconsciously weave back and forth between different ideas as if they are one and same. This conflating of two or more completely separate concepts commonly results in misunderstanding, ambiguity, miscommunication, and breakdown. Making a distinction helps to clear the gridlock of bungled communication so we can avoid breakdown.

A powerful analogy can be drawn with cancer. When a cancer cell is introduced into an otherwise healthy tissue, it will infect the healthy cells around it. These previously healthy cells then metastasize and divide, thus passing along the mutation and perpetuating the mistake...all of which results in the destruction of healthy tissue and quite often the death of the original host organism. When an Invisible Distinction is conflated, a mutation of communication thwarts the intended outcome. What results is breakdown and, like cancer, the suffering of a similar fate.

Said another way, when we input flawed instructions into our navigation system, we veer off-path to an unintended destination. Communication failures stack up like piles of rubble in the middle of the road. Soon this rubble pile becomes the new normal, and we navigate around it, eventually no longer even being conscious that it is there—or that we have the power to clear it away. As more and more rubble accumulates, the path itself becomes a junkyard, an impediment that we and others find increasingly challenging to traverse. We become sidelined and isolated from the flowing super-highways of progress and actualization.

There are far too many of these types of breakdowns in the world today—of these conflations and bungled communications. They toxify relationships, politics, business, community, faith, and, most importantly, ourselves—and the devastating effects are pandemic. As they stack up, they appear insurmountable. We experience them as confrontation, dead ends, and ultimatums. Unchecked, they become a delivery system for shaming and blaming.

Divisiveness in this world is greatly attributable to the conflation of distinctions. The phenomenon narrows one's view of the world, obscuring and shaping their beliefs, teachings, perceptions, and environment. The affliction leads them to believe this is actually the way the world *is*. And, it is...*to them*.

> *We do not see the world as it is;*
> *we see the world as we are.* ~Talmud / Nin

We sink into overwhelm and our power appears to diminish. Only when we identify and develop an ear for these discordant notes, to borrow from a musical reference, can we correct them so that the sweet melody within can freely flow.

When we understand the differences and make the distinction, we effectively align our intentions with our actions. We also better limit breakdowns so we can optimally achieve the intended result. Rather than stumble, we can dance; and those around us—our organizations, families, communities, friends, significant others—can benefit and enjoy the music along with us.

Trimming the Turkey

HERE'S AN ANECDOTE I like to use to illustrate how when something strange persists for long enough, it becomes first normal and then, eventually, invisible.

A new bride has just prepared the Thanksgiving turkey for her husband, having followed the specific recipe and instructions given by her mother, passed down through the generations. It included everything from the prep, brining, herbs, and stuffing to procedures such as trimming off each end prior to baking, *exactly* as her mother always did.

The husband adoringly reports that the turkey is phenomenal and tenderly asks, "Why do you trim off the ends? They are the best part."

The bride responds, "I don't know. This is the way Mother and Grandmother have always prepared it."

They both awkwardly smile lovingly at each other and enjoy their succulent dinner.

A few years later, the couple and their now eight-year-old daughter visit Grandmother for Thanksgiving dinner. Grandma is preparing none other than the famous family turkey. Helping Grandmother prepare the meal, the young mother and daughter observe Grandma trimming off each end of the turkey. Having never asked why and still mystified by this aspect of the recipe, the granddaughter finally asks, "Grandma, why do you trim off the ends?"

Grandma laughingly responds, "*Darling, this is the only way it will fit into my tiny, old oven!*"

Many of the distinctions that will be discussed shortly are exactly this kind of invisible. The conflating of distinctions that have become invisible is like a tradition of perpetuated misperceptions. Subtle yet significant, once the Invisible Distinctions are identified, they can be introduced into our consciousness and, from there, employed.

The Power of Language

> *Your beliefs become your thoughts.*
> *Your thoughts become your words.*
> *Your words become your actions.*
> *Your actions become your habits.*
> *Your habits become your values.*
> *Your values become your destiny.* ~Gandhi

THE TRANSLATION OF THOUGHTS AND EXPERIENCES into words is crucial in how we (and others) show up and participate in our lives. Language formulation in the brain is created first through experiencing a thought, then by our probing our minds to formulate words, and then by articulating the thought into verbal expression. It is during this succession, from inception of a thought to the formulation of verbal expression, where language is at risk of becoming flawed, defective, or misconceived. Miscommunication in our cognitive processing results when language is incorrectly translated and then implemented into action (or mis-action). It is a mutation, akin to the introduction of a cancer cell into an otherwise healthy body as mentioned earlier. Being aware of how powerful language is can have a profound effect on what ultimately shows up in our lives.

> *Change our mind, and the world will show up differently.*
> *Change our narrative, and we will show up differently*
> *in the world.*

Whether spoken out loud or voiced internally, words are powerful. A base principle of Conscious Intelligence recognizes this impact. *Words matter*—not only in a literal sense, but also because they can land entirely differently than intended based on one's association to and experience with them.

This section addresses not just what we say or write, but also the specific moment that a thought is formulated into words. Anytime we speak of *language* or *words,* what we are referring to is both inner thought *and* the outward expression (written or verbalized) of these thoughts. Once we formulate words in our heads to define our thoughts, there is very little distinction in our minds whether these words are spoken out loud or remain silent in our head. Both incarnations affect the world around us either way.

Many of us have little awareness of the profound effect that commonly used words and phrases have in our everyday lives. Our words impact our lives and the lives of others. Our language informs the life we live into, often while we remain unaware. In fact, *especially* when we are unaware. Intentional or not, what we think or say plays a major role in how we define ourselves and how we are defined by others. Words formulate our actions; the impact of our actions define us out in the world. How we express ourselves through language constitutes a significant part of this. It is instrumental in defining us, *one way or the other.*

Charged Language

ONE SIMPLE WAY to narrow the risk of unintended consequences is to eliminate "charged" words from our vocabulary. Charged words pose a high risk of being misinterpreted or negatively received. I use the term "charged" because certain language can be evocative and inflammatory due to the unusually high multitude of meanings associated with it. When words are charged, they can conjure up negativity and bias and trigger unintended, visceral responses. A triggered person literally can add their own soundtrack or story to the current circumstance by juxtaposing a relational experience from the past that is otherwise unrelated. Like a song, phrases can evoke memories: good, bad, and ugly. By simply eliminating charged words, we can reduce risk of breakdown and unintended complications. Cleaning up our language is, in a way, like picking up litter that has washed ashore, making everyone's time on the beach much more pleasant.

Here are some examples of disempowering, charged words (not nearly a complete list). Can you identify why they usurp energy, risk generating unnecessary tension, and are deflating in everyday life circumstances?

Make me feel:	You make me feel; he makes me feel.
Hate:	I hate.
Sucks:	That sucks; you suck.
Need:	I need to; you need to.
Problem:	I have a problem; you have a problem.
Have to:	I have to; you have to.
Must:	I must; you must.
Should:	I should; you should.
Try:	I'll try.
Can't:	I can't; you can't.
Doomed:	We're doomed.
Screwed:	You screwed up.
Idiot:	You're an idiot.
Stupid:	You're stupid

Hate

THE WORD "HATE" is a supercharged word that engenders very deep relational meaning. Think about where this word is used, especially today: war, divisiveness, hate crimes, intolerance. People standing around chatting, suddenly hearing the word "hate" from a nearby conversation, will actually stop their own conversations to listen to what comes next out of the hater's mouth.

Do you know someone who uses this word excessively about even seemingly mundane things? *I hate that actor. I hate that color on you. I hate my boss! I hate working here. I hate when you do that . . .* The speaker of such words may shrug their shoulders and say, "Hey, I was just being passionate and expressive. So, sue me!" Right? Such an attempt to make light is definitely one's prerogative; this speaker clearly thinks of the word "hate" as a relatively benign expression of passion. But consider the fraternity of *actual* haters that share the use of that word the world over. Like smoking at a gas station, even if alone, we're still placing ourselves in peril, polluting our bodies (and the environment), and weakening our minds. It pollutes, so why do it? We all possess deep, visceral, reactionary relationships to certain words, phrases, and preconceptions that we use (and misuse). By eliminating as little as one word, we can change the entire relationship that we and others have to a circumstance.

> *Words matter. Negatively charged words*
> *emulate the person who speaks them.*

So often, the use of charged language unwittingly stacks the circumstances out of favor. Do we really wish to have such an association? Why risk using a word commonly associated with making people recoil or that have a powerful, psychological stigma to them? Using charged words is similar to risking injury by refusing to wear a seatbelt—why stack the cards against you unnecessarily by choosing language with higher instances of injury and misinterpretation? Breakdown in communication is far more common than getting into a car accident, and if we consistently refuse to buckle up, the result sooner or later *will* be devastating.

Failing to take conversational responsibility for extremely incendiary words risks unfavorable reception from those we would otherwise like to attract. This is not advocating correcting others; it is an emphasis on the importance of correcting *ourselves*. Eliminating charged language cultivates a more powerful and productive environment. Like removing toxins from the air we breathe, eliminating—or at the least reducing—charged words eradicate them from our consciousness and psyche. Over time, we no longer even miss them. Distinguishing between the subtleties that needlessly charge language can facilitate the cultivation of more inspiring communication and will shepherd a circumstance to a more positive outcome.

Ethical Responsibility, Misuse, and Exploitation of Words

An ethical line is violated when one misleads, slanders, gossips, publicly embarrasses, spreads rumors, smears, disgraces, or dishonors another. Such an act is not an "oops," a hand slap, or "I did a bad thing"; it is profoundly depraved and toxic and inflicts enduring damage—damage that cannot be entirely repaired or taken back even if proven false—despite being revealed to be inaccurate. Any conciliatory attempt at this point is of little consequence because the words are already out there. The genie is out of the bottle; the damage is resolute. One cannot force another to unhear it, forget it, or ignore it; the mental imprint simply remains and persists, even if the actor has recanted, repented, and/or apologized.

Distinction versus Definition

THE CONSCIOUS INTELLIGENCE PARADIGM framework is constituted by what I have termed The Invisible Distinctions as already mentioned. So, it is profoundly important that we delve a bit deeper still, to identify succinctly what a distinction is and is not.

Distinctions are not definitions. Distinctions are not black and white nor are they typically open and conspicuous. Quite often, dictionary definitions of The Invisible Distinctions make little or no distinction at all, or, the definitions presented are so broad, that again, what results is that no distinction is made at all. Distinctions are nuanced and more appropriately illuminated in their multitude shades of gray.

While some of the Invisible Distinctions can appear clear and dramatic, others are profoundly more subtle. The intention here is not to create semantical nitpickers of language and communication, but to focus on the deeper universal distinctions that carry significant gravity in the relevance of our lives. As you read through the Invisible Distinctions, please be mindful that the language has been selected very intentionally.

The Structure of The Conscious Intelligence Paradigm

THE PARADIGM IS DIVIDED into three main categories: Base Distinctions, Central Distinctions, and Elevated Distinctions. This organization serves two purposes: first, as we trek from Base to Elevated, we advance upward and elevate consciousness. At the same time, Conscious Intelligence is also rooted and grounded from its Central Distinctions, perfusing like oxygenated blood out into its extremities, just as every movement we humans make is initiated from our core center. The Central Distinctions are the life blood, the pulse, and the structural integrity that bind and connect the Paradigm, and they are the source of vitality that drives Conscious Intelligence. Everything that follows streamlines your access to Conscious Intelligence.

> *Once illuminated, the Distinctions can't be un-illuminated.*
> *They are like a bell that can't be un-rung.*

You can think of advancing from Base to Elevated Distinctions like the progression of language. Language has the ability to advance from prose to poetry, from literal to figurative, from denotation to connotation (that is…literal to metaphorical and conceptual, etc.). In the way that poetry, for example, reveals more than the black and white of its words, so too does the Conscious Intelligence Paradigm advance the distinction of language from a literal manner to a more conceptual manner, to reveal the subtle shades of otherwise cloaked distinctions, and to illuminate The Conscious Intelligence Paradigm.

It is here that our journey begins…

SECTION II

THE CONSCIOUS INTELLIGENCE
PARADIGM

THE BASE DISTINCTIONS

PRODUCTIVITY
Leadership & Advancement

SOVEREIGNTY
Locus of Control

PERCEPTION
Perspective

} **BASE DISTINCTIONS**

CHAPTER 3

Distinctions of Communication

*Between what is said and not meant,
and what is meant and not said,
most of love is lost.*   ~Khalil Gibran

COMMUNICATION IS FAR TOO OFTEN MISUNDERSTOOD, not only in conversations between us but also in the conversations we have with ourselves. Often, we are not alone in a miscommunication calamity. By conflating communication, we often create unintended circumstances, like a miscommunication fender-bender riddled with road rage and reactivity. We find that the road we originally paved with good intentions is suddenly at risk of becoming the location shoot for the next *Mad Max Road Warrior* film. The carnage embroils others, and the collateral damage diverts focus ever further away from a viable solution.

As the Invisible Distinctions permeate the more powerful, cognitive centers of your brain, subtleties that seem tiny and insignificant will become pronounced. When our ears are trained, when we understand such distinctions in our words, we are better equipped to formulate the choices we make in communication. The ability to detect language nuances, miscommunication and ambiguity, whether from our mouth or another's, intentional or unintentional, is central. It is compulsory if we are to elevate perspective and gain command of our circumstances.

The first thing I wish to establish is clear communication with *you* about the Invisible Distinctions, beginning with the understanding of two main terms: *communication* and *miscommunication*.

Communication is a process by which information is exchanged—via words, sounds, signs, symbols, and behaviors—in order to convey information to one another. I will add also to ourselves as well, because we are in constant dialogue with ourselves.

Miscommunication is the failure to convey information, such as ideas, thoughts, feelings, and responses, successfully.

With this in mind, let's begin with the Distinctions of Communication.

ID 1: Miscommunication versus Disagreement

MISCOMMUNICATION *IS NOT* DISAGREEMENT. These two things are confused regularly. The distinction seems simple, yes? But have you really thought about it? How often do we exit a confrontation that results in uncleared space—meaning we walk away without resolution or consensus—and chalk up the conflict to disagreement? Even in the most civil of disputes, we use phrases such as *yeah, we just don't see eye-to-eye on this* or *we agree to disagree*...and these examples are among the most benign of scenarios. More often, it's not nearly this civil.

While it is common that the parties miss seeing eye-to-eye in conflict, often this is not due to disagreement. It happens because the parties *aren't even communicating*! And if we aren't communicating effectively, there's no way to even know if we agree or disagree. Effective communication is *required* before it is possible to disagree.

> **Disagreement** means lacking agreement, i.e., lacking harmony, accordance, and the sharing of the same belief, opinion, feeling, and/or position.

When miscommunication happens, there is no possibility for disagreement regarding the issue at hand because neither party actually understands what the other is telling them. It's like one person speaking Chinese, the other speaking German, and both just throwing up their arms and exclaiming in their own language, "Naaaah, we just don't agree."

What often results is that the parties process the circumstance as a disagreement: "We just don't see eye-to-eye." Communication breaks down, the parties depart in haste and disgust, and they have *no idea* what actually just happened. They aren't in a state of disagreement; rather, they failed to effectively step on the field to communicate in the first place. How can two people disagree when it hasn't been clearly established what either is trying to express? Neither has afforded the other the opportunity to disagree.

This type of scenario may sound petty and semantic on the surface, but it is not. Breakdowns due to the conflating of this distinction run rampant in everyday life. Miscommunication is, by far, the most common culprit in the demise of relationships. This includes the one we have with ourselves, and it extends beyond to family, community, organizations, religious institutions, cultures, and world nations, not to mention political parties. Communication problems are cited as being the most common factor leading to divorce (65 percent), followed by the inability to resolve conflict (43 percent).[1] One need only to pick up a newspaper to observe miscommunication spanning the entire globe.

That which hinders your task becomes your task.

The misuse of communication, both intentionally and unintentionally, is so pervasive that it is impossible to escape contact with it in some form in our everyday lives. We are inundated with all forms coming from all directions, especially today, making it much more challenging to process and distinguish. A wise teacher once told me, "That which hinders your task becomes your task." Miscommunication means breakdown in communication. When we mistake miscommunication for disagreement, even daily squabbles are destined to result in carnage ranging from a marriage breakup to a nation breaking up, from getting fired from a job to warring nations firing not so good things at each other.

Only when clear communication is established can it be possible to disagree—

Real disagreements are fewer and further between once miscommunications are identified. Only when the miscommunications are cleared up can the work towards sorting out actual differences commence. Identifying communicational forks in the road can most effectively assure maintaining a desired course setting. It can better assure keeping the parties seated side-by-side on their journey to a much more desired destination.

SUMMARY | ID 1

We cannot disagree if we are not even communicating.

This situation is like one person speaking Chinese, the other speaking German, and both just throwing up their arms and exclaiming in their own language, "Naaaah, we just don't agree."

Only when clear communication is established can it be possible to disagree.

Miscommunication is, by far, the most common culprit in the demise of relationships. Communication problems are cited as being the most common factor leading to divorce (65 percent), followed by the inability to resolve conflict (43 percent).

ID 2: Objective (Fact) versus Subjective (Story)

MUCH LITERATURE EXISTS about the distinction of *objectivity* versus *subjectivity*, also called *fact* versus *story*, or what *actually* happened versus *what I made it mean*. Whatever we call it, this is about our inner narrative, what I like to call *adding our own soundtrack*.

We are surrounded by examples of this distinction, whether in a court of law or on the playground, at Thanksgiving dinner or a social outing. We all know that if something occurs and twenty people witness it, we could get twenty different stories and interpretations of what happened. The media loves to play on such drama. (And it's not just modern-day drama made popular with soap operas and episodic television; we are prone to it in our genetic programming; it's threaded throughout historical tradition from the plays of Shakespeare to ancient mythology).

For example, we open on a high school class taking an exam. A prepared student is focused, sitting at their desk working away. Nearby sits a student who is unprepared, fidgeting, eyes darting around the room. Suddenly, the unprepared student "accidentally" drops their pencil under the prepared student's desk. As the prepared student kindly bends down and retrieves the pencil, the unprepared student steals a glance off the other's paper. The teacher looks up, sees both students leaning over, interacting with each other, and gives them both a fail grade.

Clearly, objective facts and subjective stories exist in any circumstance. The ability to distinguish between these is key for us to gain an elevated perspective. Said slightly differently, knowing when we are in our own story narrative as opposed to when we are in the space of true objectivity is key to accessing the Conscious Intelligence with respect to our circumstances. In the above example, the *objective facts* are:

- The prepared student was acting in kind gesture, retrieving their neighbor's pencil, which had rolled under the desk.
- The unprepared student was peeking at the neighbor's test.

However, *the subjective story* from the teacher's point of view was that both of the students were cheating. While drama has its place in our popular culture and entertainment, it can be profoundly disruptive within our inner narrative and in our everyday life. It can lead to bias, false conclusions, and tragic decisions.

Imaginary Conversations

IMAGINARY CONVERSATION IS A TERM used to describe a fictional conversation entirely contrived by substituting of one's own internal story in place of facts. While commonly it is an attempt to make sense of appearances in a set of circumstances, it is instead a contrived projection lacking facts pertaining to the actual circumstance. To add insult to injury, quite often, they occur while the real person is standing *right there*. When one's inner voice behaves as if it is having a *real*, factual conversation with the other person, only without the real facts or other person's knowledge, we are in the midst of an imaginary conversation. While we can all stand to embrace our inner neurotic, we can all also endeavor to keep it under wraps or risk conflict and breakdown.[2]

Here are some colorful examples of an imaginary conversation (IC) showing the fictionally contrived story as opposed to the facts as experienced from the *actual* person's perspective (Fact):

IC: "I noticed you ordered take-out. I'm sorry that my cooking does not meet your standards."

Fact: "Umm, I never said your cooking was not good. I rather enjoy it. I just thought you might want to take the evening off being that we both worked fourteen-hour days today."

Fact: "Hey, look! That's my girlfriend's friend I was telling you about! Come on, I'll introduce you!"

IC: "Nah, I don't think it's a fit; she doesn't look trustworthy."

Fact: "You haven't even met her yet."

IC: "Yeah, but she looks like my ex-girlfriend I caught cheating with my roommate in college."

Fact: "Thank you for the detailed presentation. You opened our eyes to several things we didn't consider. We will discuss this with the partners and get back to you."

IC: "So basically, don't call us, we'll call you? Is there something I said or didn't address that otherwise would have earned your business?"

Fact: "Actually, the presentation was so insightful that it made us aware of a larger issue beyond what we considered. To heed your advice and to do this correctly, it will require a larger budget than we anticipated. So we are elevating this and championing *you* with a proposal to get more money to hire your firm to do the job as you brilliantly proposed."

An imaginary conversation is the product of our mind dredging up and transposing a mis-filed experience from our past into the present circumstance. We've all done it from time to time. Our mind invents a fictional narrative which we project as the other's thoughts—except it is not coming from or even being conceived by the other person. *Voilà!* We become the proud parent of an imaginary circumstance manifested and contrived completely in our minds, born into the real world. What results is obscured reality viewed through a fear-inspired, fogged lens.

When we are talking to someone (real) who is, at the same time, having an imaginary conversation with *us* (the imaginary us, not the actual us), we discover we are ensnared in an entirely defensive posture. We can argue and protest, maintaining *we never said that! That's not what we meant!* They may appear to be talking to us, but it's as if we aren't even in the room. They're having a conversation in our direction, but the words purportedly coming from us aren't ours. Then, convinced the other person is possessed, we do something like throw up our arms, grab a few garlic cloves, and burn sage.

How can we dismantle this ticking time bomb?

Despite our best intentions, when someone is having an imaginary conversation, the risk is heightened that the conversation may very well leave a mess anyway. While we can become hell-bent on straightening it all out right then and there, in the heat of it, we have been trapped in an unsolvable puzzle with extra pieces that don't belong. We are roped into the moment because we care and are fueled by the conviction and desire to resolve the miscommunication. Until the other is present, listening and not just speaking, we are often left contending with the simplest, most innocent misunderstandings. Until we can remove the pieces that have no business being there, we can expect a whole lot of ugly to persist. Problematic as this is, it is full of emotional triggers; it consumes precious time due to all of the cleanup and brings out the worst in us.

Defusing an imaginary conversation requires the same remedy that would also prevent one to occur in the first place: *more transparent communication*. Cultivating an environment where a question can be asked and answered versus a story being contrived can prevent the breakdown. Seeking understanding by asking "why" you ordered take-out versus contriving a narrative that you don't like my cooking helps illuminate the facts and prevent a story from being created by the absence of information.

We can minimize our chances of a train wreck by checking in during conversations where higher risks of ambiguity exist—and, when we see such a circumstance heading south, endeavor to pause and resume it later. If we are already waist-deep in the imaginary conversation, identifying that the communication in the moment is already failing can keep us from redoubling our efforts when we have lost sight of our aim. Remaining grounded, seeking perspective, and revisiting the conversation later when cool heads can again prevail are examples of employing our Conscious Intelligence.

SUMMARY | ID 2

What actually happened versus what we made it mean.

Objectivity versus subjectivity is also called fact versus story; it is what actually happened versus what we made it mean. Knowing when we are in our own story narrative as opposed to true objectivity is key to maintaining perspective, keeping a level head, and not creating our own narrative to a circumstance. Veering from facts with a subjective lens can obscure the motives and lead to breakdown, misunderstanding, and failure to effectively communicate.

Checking in during conversations where higher risks of ambiguity exist is a good idea, and when we see such a circumstance heading south, it can be advantageous to pause and resume it later.

ID 3: Physical Reality versus Conceptual Reality

Be cautious of inadvertently dismissing the existence of something altogether just because it can't be physically touched.

CONCEPTUALIZATION IS SOMETHING we humans all commonly utilize to understand, explain, and perceive the world. This includes things that are intangible, that we cannot see, touch, or detect with our *physical* senses. They include time, dreams, unicorns, ideas, plans, yet-to-be-built products, theories, world peace, or the Divine.

Language itself is, in fact, conceptual, contrived by us humans as a means to more effectively communicate and optimize our chances to survive, evolve, and interact. Four and a half billion years ago, there was this wet stuff covering 71 percent of the earth. Not until about one hundred thousand years ago did we come up with language and thus a name for it: "*Water*." But there are over five thousand known languages today, so *water, eau, agua, aqua, mizu, wasser, and mayeem* are all expressions through language of that same wet stuff. The point is that water, love, light, wisdom, compassion, fear, shame, and courage, to name a few, existed long before we invented the means to express them in language.

Throughout the distinctions that frame Conscious Intelligence, it will be paramount to recognize and distinguish what it means when we are speaking conceptually. While physical and conceptual reality are both real, distinguishing between the reality of something physically tangible and the reality of a thought or concept is essential. Special care not to inadvertently dismiss altogether the existence of something just because it can't be physically touched, is required. Comprehension of this distinction is key to understanding how something can live in conceptual reality.

We think and speak conceptually all the time, often without even being conscious of doing so. The distinction between physical and conceptual reality in terms of communication can mean the difference between the consideration of another's perspective and the straight-out dismissal of it. Our unique experiences, cultures, educational backgrounds, generational upbringings, and religious beliefs all inform the vastly different ways we process the world, formulate opinions, and develop our affinities and preferences. Our ability to conceptualize or imagine things, without a doubt, distinguishes us as evolved human beings.

We can disagree with another's perspectives, ideas, theories, or beliefs, but outright dismissal of these perspectives, ideas, theories, or beliefs is divisive, shallow, and can be dangerous. When we are not encouraging the cultivation of space where perspectives can be aired, our views risk becoming narrowed and we are prone to become closed off from each other. To narrow one's views so much that other ideas and perspectives aren't even considered has been proven throughout history to lead us into darkness. Why would anyone do that, especially in this age of innovation, technology, disruption, and infinite creativity?

The evolution of our human capacity of conceptualization has allowed us to imagine, communicate, and actualize vastly complex ideas throughout history. We can create feature films about a human riding a dragon or about time travel in a DeLorean. We implement language, mathematics, and storytelling to materialize the technological devices of today and tomorrow, likely one you are reading from right now if not from a physical book. Conceptualization has allowed us to create useful instruments: the wireless telephone, computer, GPS navigator, and phonograph we can hold in the palm of our hand; the tool a surgeon uses to perform a surgery without even making an incision; an airplane completely invisible to radar, or radar itself, are some examples.

While the examples will take on critical subject matter as we progress, we can make a simple example to illustrate. Take a *unicorn*. We can conceive one without it being physically real. How do we know this? Because you know what I am talking about: that horse-looking animal with the singular horn. We can describe, draw, or imagine a unicorn, a dream, a black hole, or world peace. We can conceive this whether it is, or will ever be, physically real or tangible—whether we ever fully understand it or whether we can (or can't) actualize it.

Conceptualization is the "plan" part of "Plan the work, work the plan"; the "work" part is the doing, the actualization of the concept. Humans employ their imagination, dreams, symbols, models, art, and visualizations—all unmistakably real, but not physically tangible.

For us to intentionally create anything, we initially must conceptualize what it is we wish to actualize.

Disruptors, visionaries, entrepreneurs, inventors, architects, artists, filmmakers, technologists, physicists, ALL are called to envision a possible reality before it can become physically so. They live and thrive vacillating between both physical and conceptual realities. In fact, their livelihood *is dependent on* the ability to toggle between the two as defined by the principle scope of their work.

Several of the distinctions that follow will call on you to employ your ability to conceptualize as we illuminate Conscious Intelligence.

SUMMARY | ID 3

Two realms of reality.

Physical reality is our *physical* world—the stuff we can see, smell, hear, touch, and/or taste.

Conceptual reality is a realm that is *beyond* our 5 faculties just mentioned.

Horses are physically real; unicorns are conceptually real, but only imaginary. The concept allows us to make the distinction between the different types of reality. Just because it is not tangible, physically real, or adherent to the laws of physics does not dismiss something as nonexistent altogether. When these two realms are conflated, the incidence of communication breakdown is high.

ID 4: Need versus Want

THERE ARE VERY FEW THINGS in this world that we actually *need*. Think about it for a moment: we need food, water, air. The remaining and vast majority of things often associated with "need" fall more appropriately into the category of things we would like to have, that we enjoy, or that enhance our lives—not into the category of things we actually *need*.

Oh heavens! Not us, but someone we know, is aghast because the food server hasn't brought out the ice water with a slice of lemon as quickly as we want. Someone we know is whining about having to take a cold shower because their sibling just finished showering and the water heater isn't working fast enough. A work associate is complaining after hitting every red light on the way to pick up coffee this morning and then couldn't find a parking spot.

We can only hope that those agitated people catch a glimpse of the faces of the billions deprived every day of sufficient drinking or running water (not to mention heated water or coffee!). We can only hope that those agitated people catch their own tongues, pinch themselves, and are soberly reminded that theirs are *First World problems*. More than one billion people in the world live on less than one dollar a day. In total, 2.7 billion struggle to survive on less than two dollars per day.[3] The amount we paid for our coffee this morning could feed an entire family for a week in far too many households in the world today.

> *Ok, I get it—sometimes the definition of the word "need"*
> *is a bit exaggerated...*
> *Where are we going with this?*

We can't get too far into a conversation about need before mentioning psychologist Abraham Maslow. In the early 20th century, around the same time every telephone call was connected by hand at a switchboard with live operators, Alexander Fleming's penicillin treated its first patient, and scientists created the first ever nuclear bomb, Maslow developed a humanistic approach to psychology in which he modeled a progressive concept, his *hierarchy of needs*, still widely referred to today:

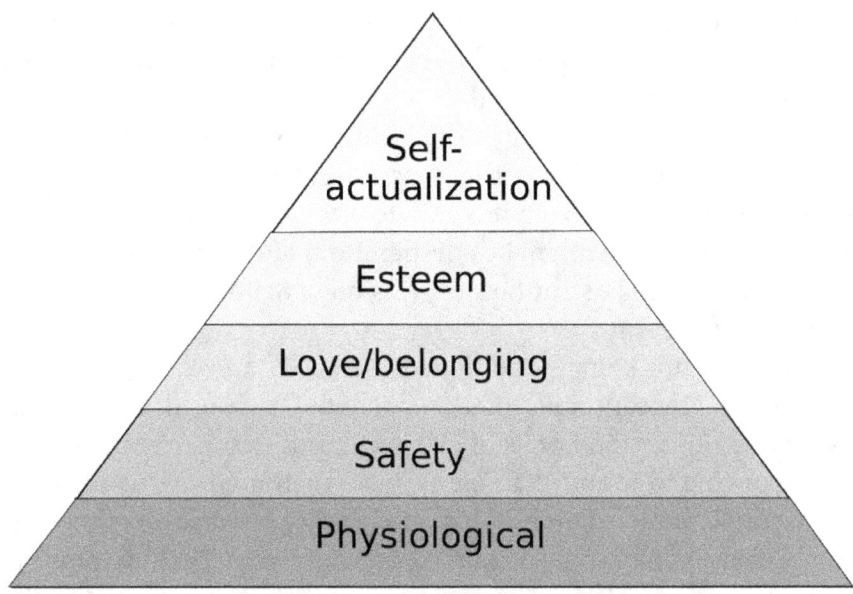
Maslow's Hierarchy of Needs

What Maslow illustrates in his pyramid paradigm is that, until the lower foundational needs are met, most people can do little more than *think* about the ones above it. Until we have our physiological needs of food, water, and air met, he suggests we are not poised to act on attaining anything else, and so on. Because you are reading this here, it is safe to say you live on more than one or two dollars per day, and you likely identify more towards the top of the pyramid when referring to Maslow's model.

Recall the section on the Power of Language: There exist words, phrases, and conversations that confine us into the realm of scarcity, desperation, and dependency. *Need* is one of those words. "Need" is a charged word. It means that something is *essential*. It exudes urgency, evoking absolute necessity and dire circumstances critical of immediate attention. Need engenders stimulation of a primal impulse of impending doom and the intrinsic dependence upon something essential to survive. Consider for a moment walking into a store and hearing "Oh my gosh, I need those shoes!" or "You need to explain why you were late right now!" Where might these expressions land on Maslow's pyramid...or in the context of humanity? Contrast that with a paramedic prying open a car with the jaws of life, while saying,

"You need to do exactly what I say so we can get you out of here." If the subject doesn't comply, not only will their life be in peril, but the rescuer's safety could be as well.

The word "need" is triggering, whether we are conscious of it or not. When we say the words "*I need*" and are not referencing the essentials of food, air, water, it is akin to crying wolf to our psyche; the word charges the space, invites desperation, and becomes a defining shadow that blemishes our best expression of Self—in our eyes and in the eyes of others.

Today we are being conditioned to "need" a great many things, whether we are conscious of this or not. I surveyed some of the best-selling nonfiction books of all time in business, success, and personal growth and found that, on average, each used the word "need" well over one hundred times! This makes sense because all of them are framed in the perspective of transactional thinking. They are prescriptive, advising us to "do this" in order to "get that" as mentioned earlier.

Pervasive today, spun media, advertising, consumption, and materialism—each with their vast array of delivery vehicles—produce more sources of information than ever before. In this environment, the demand to be intentional with language is increased exponentially. "Need" is a charged word. I wonder what Maslow might have called his pyramid today, whether he would have suggested we used the word "need" more judiciously in this different time and era. We may take careful consideration in its use and consider that, with respect to communication, words matter today more than ever.

SUMMARY | ID 4

Something we desire or want is different from something we absolutely need.

The power of words and intentional language in part informs the life we live into. There are very few things in this world that we actually *need*: food, water, air. There exist words, phrases, and conversations that confine us into the realm of scarcity, desperation, and dependency. *Need* is one of those words that triggers such reactions, whether we are conscious of it or not. It is akin to

crying "wolf" to our psyche; the word charges the space, invites desperation, and becomes a defining shadow that blemishes our best expression of Self—in our eyes and in the eyes of others.

CHAPTER 4

Distinctions of Freedom and Imprisonment

ID 5: Real Imprisonment versus Perceived Imprisonment

To be free is not to merely cast off one's chains, but to live in a way that respects and enhances the freedom of others.
~Nelson Mandela

RECALL A STORY OF A MAN who had been in prison for twenty years, his entire adult life, since he was eighteen. That life was all he knew—mealtime, work duty, yard, lights out. It was the same every day, every week, every month for twenty years, a strict schedule dictated by the prison warden. When he was finally paroled, he moved back in with some family members and was made comfortable until he could get back on his feet. He was afforded his own room, and for many days, in the morning when he woke, he got up, dressed, sat at the foot of his bed…and waited . . . and waited . . . staring at the door until a concerned family member knocked and opened it, checking to see if he was all right. He was, of course. You see, every day, every week, every month, every year for twenty years, he had never opened or closed his own door. It was *not up to him*. It took several weeks of being out of prison to recondition his mind that of course he could open his own door. Maybe he forgot—or, perhaps, deep down, he had fear and anxiety around what it meant to open a door on his own volition, embrace his freedom and, along with it, a whole new way of life.

Do *we* do this in our own way sometimes? This story highlights the distinction between *real imprisonment* and *perceived imprisonment*. Understanding the difference between real imprisonment, over which we have no control, and perceived or self-imprisonment, which is within our power to change, is part of accessing Conscious Intelligence.

> **Real Imprisonment**: This is the more obvious of the two. We are all aware of the existence of real physical prisons, penitentiaries that house convicted felons behind iron bars and high walls with barbed wire, hovered over by manned guard towers, every move dictated by a warden and scrutinized by armed corrections officers. This is real, literal imprisonment, where one's actual freedom is taken away and placed in the hands of others.

Another form of real imprisonment is open imprisonment, where a person may not actually be in physical bondage but still lives under the threat of certain demise. Slavery, indentured servitude, and human trafficking are all examples of open imprisonment, where any attempt to escape could result in being hunted down, whipped, tortured, or shot; suffering mental, physical, psychological, or sexual assault; or facing even more unthinkable circumstances than their current one.

> **Perceived Imprisonment** or self-imprisonment can be more pernicious and harder to spot, even though most of us may be more personally familiar with it. Perceived imprisonment exists when the walls that confine us are of *our own* making. We've all done it at one time another: put ourselves in our own prison. See if any of these sound familiar:

My job is miserable, but I need to pay my bills.

Our marriage is not working, but the kids...

I'm stuck, I want to move to a new city, but...

I want to fire this person, but we're so busy right now, I'm not sure I can find someone qualified to replace them.

That person drove a wedge between all of us, and now we all no longer speak to each other.

If I just get to ____, I'll be in a better situation and be happier.

I'm going to prove I'm worthy of their love/pride/ acceptance/approval... and that I'm worthy/deserving/ beautiful/good enough...

Is any of this real? Well, if we are living inside a belief that there is no other choice, or are depriving ourselves of considering another choice, then yes. We are contriving it into a conceptual reality. Who we are being informs the life we live into. Even if the prison bars are not physically real, if we act as though they are, they have the same effect; to what degree is exactly proportionate to how attached we are to our perception.

Could I actually be enslaving myself? Is allowing my fear to second-guess and distrust my essential Self a form of imprisonment? Is my fear having me seek answers from others so that, if I'm wrong, I can blame them and not be accountable? Must I believe others when they say, "You can't," which is really the projection of *their own* fears upon me?

Many of us would rather avoid fear like a rabid dog. We often will even relinquish our own freedom in an attempt to avoid change. Our fear-based struggle to resist confrontation comes at the cost of building prisons around ourselves. In reality, we can't avoid conflict: if we don't address it, it comes to our front door, enters without knocking, moves right in, and makes itself downright comfortable.

By ignoring inner conflict and merely hoping it away, we transform it from *out there* to *in here*, where it lives with us like a virus until we either offload it to others in the form of blame, rage, disproportionate retaliation, and passive aggression, or we bury it deep inside where it poisons us, producing stress, ulcers, fatigue, immune disorders, psychological disease, and depression. When inner conflict is *in here*, it gestates in our psyche, forming fear, resentment, and anxiety. Inner conflict doesn't remain inside the walls of the house for long before it oozes out the front door onto the lawn. With little awareness of our inner conflict, our charming, white picket fence becomes replaced with wrought-iron prison bars and barbed wire.

If this sounds bleak, dark, and depressing, consider *why* we might limit ourselves to such conditions rather than allow for the possibility of life evolving into something inspiring. Do we think that somebody else will facilitate the change and release us from our captivity? Are we waiting for a hero to come and rescue us, or for the warden to come around and say, "My bad, our mistake," and let us out? Are we waiting patiently for the miraculous circumstance called "someday"?

As we refer back to our old, paroled friend sitting at the end of the bed waiting for the door to be opened by someone else—did he forget he was free? Or was his fear preventing him from consciously bearing the weight of responsibility it takes to be free. Did he recognize what being free now meant, after twenty years of real imprisonment, and grow fearful? Was it just more comfortable to remain not in charge? We'll never know, but just considering the question of his circumstance while thinking about our own elevates our consciousness. We are free to choose, limited only by our own self-conceived constraints. When we can acknowledge that the prison bars surrounding us are merely those we have crafted ourselves, we can refrain from setting false limits on our otherwise limitless world.

Confronting why we create circumstances that imprison us is not easy. We create these prisons for very compelling, personal reasons, often not realizing they are merely a choice we've made. Usually we do it to feel safe, to avoid change, or to save ourselves from venturing into the unknown. In other words, *we do it to avoid our deepest fears*—and in the process we deny responsibility to our true, higher Self and the freedom it deserves.

When I see students and clients resisting change, I ask, "Might you be creating limits here in an effort to better control and more easily manage the circumstance?" It is a common misconception that we can better control what is going on in our lives if we create limitations, in the same way that fencing in a herd of sheep helps control them from straying. Life doesn't work that way.

> *It is a myth to believe that, by confining our lives, we can be in better control of what happens.*

Resistance to change is something we are taught, something we learn; it is not natural. The universe undergoes constant change—from the cellular, even sub-atomic level, all the way to the cosmic, cataclysmic level—every moment, every day. Resisting change is impossible, yet we try to do it all the time anyway. We humans have an affinity towards normalcy and perceived stability. Change is uncomfortable and disruptive. It forces us to get out of our everyday regimens, makes us squirm, disturbs our patterns, and places us in new, unchartered waters. We often approach change with fear and trepidation, as if we are encountering a stranger in a dark alley. By creating arbitrary boundaries and rules, we build regimens, habits, and limitations as a means to seek control and safety over our everyday lives. Fear is a very distracting back-seat driver, and when we are inspired by our fear and the need to control, the confining behavior becomes prison bars that surround us and others.

When a daily routine is constraining and closed off, resistant from venturing beyond the immediate surroundings, it is self-imprisonment. Self-imprisonment makes no exception to its surroundings. Its tentacles extend, inflicting collateral damage. Just as with real imprisonment, our families, friends, and coworkers are affected. If a daily routine includes refraining from reaching out and connecting, habitually closing off, rejecting invitations to social events, not checking in or answering check-ins from loved ones, then collateral damage is amidst.

Think about how this plays out in *your* world. Know anybody who is a recluse? Or who has an aversion to applying for a passport to travel? Or who sits on their smart phone for eons, scrolling social media with eyes glazed over, or spends more time gaming than being outside? There are those who subscribe to one specific news channel without ever making the effort to seek comparison with the others. The same holds true when it comes to belief, faith, or life philosophy when the adherence to one precludes consideration of even becoming familiar with the vast array of others—if not necessarily to change what one subscribes to, at least to gain a depth for better understanding, comparison, and perspective.

So, is our life a prison? Do we incarcerate ourselves or allow arbitrary limits to be imposed upon us, others, the world? What if, someday in the future, in some part of our lives, we ultimately come to a realization that all we had to do was walk straight through the prison bars? That day, we discover the bars were figments of our imagination, and we discover our lives, the world, and the universe all follow suit and take on a different shape as a result. What if…we made that decision now?

> *We create the life we live into.*

It may be easy now to think, "Hey, here's a thought! I'm empowered! I can be in control of the prison! I can be the warden who runs the place rather than the inmate. I'll be the boss! This is the lesson, right?" Well…let's play this out. Remember that self-imprisonment is the confined, isolated, fear-driven world our egos create for us in an effort to protect us and let us feel we are in control (how thoughtful!). If we stay in this confined world, we remain in a pattern of predictable outcomes and resist venturing into unchartered territory. Our egos keep us playing small while creating an illusion that we are in control. So, let's say we become the warden—the one who makes sure the prisoner doesn't escape (see where this is going?). As soon as we do that, questions like these appear:

Why does the same type of person keep showing up in my relationships or to fill this position in our organization?

Why can't I attract somebody who fulfills all of my needs and be exactly the way I need them to be to fill the void?

Why is it taking so long for me to get where I need to go, to do what I really want to do?

The answer is the same for all of these: "Hey, it's *your* prison. You run it. Why do you think?" If we are searching for a relationship from inside our own prisons, by definition this means the pool of candidates we are seeking are *fellow inmates*!

So is the objective here to become the warden and boss of the place? No! It actually *doesn't matter* whether we are warden or prisoner. The warden can't leave the place any more than the prisoner can! And don't forget: *you* built the prison in the first place. Both the warden and inmates are participating in this myth called "My Prison."

The prison exists only because *you built it*, so only you can tear it down. Breaking out of our own prison is confronting because we have to battle a part of ourselves that is really dug in. The environment has become comfortable. Even the neighbors and neighborhood have grown accustomed to the state of things. They, too, have become participants in this myth. It is why *breaking free* is a paradigm shift: tearing down our prison disrupts the entire neighborhood. Quitting our job may tick off our boss, our customers, and some employees who enjoyed our indentured servitude. Breaking up with our partner can cause family drama. Leaving the *perceived* safety of our 9-to-5 job to become an entrepreneur, or our apartment to buy a house, or the independence of our daily routine to get a puppy or have children…yes, these disruptive choices are scary and potentially agitating, but breaking free, realizing we are playing small, is *necessary* if we wish to progress. Progress requires courage, conviction, and resolve, and it involves confronting our fear. Until we take responsibility for our own path, we leave it in the hands of others. Until we recognize this responsibility for what it is—the path to freedom—we will remain a slave.

What It Takes to Break Free

> *We imprison ourselves when we remain complacent in the status quo.*
> *We imprison ourselves when we tolerate mistreatment.*
> *We imprison ourselves when our fear of incurring conflict wins out over our drive to push back when the circumstance calls for it.*

WHY? BECAUSE WE CANNOT IGNORE away the requisite friction, resistance, and conflict that, by definition, is required to facilitate growth. We can only stall and prolong progress for a time. By delaying, we delude ourselves into thinking we must tolerate things as they are. In reality, we are only turning the conflict loose inside of us. As if we are possessed, the poisonous, internal struggle tears our insides apart and leaves us isolated and cowering on the floor in our self-contrived prison cell.

Making a Break for It

WE STAND ON A PRECIPICE. Some of us will jump only when the fear behind us becomes greater than the fear in front of us. Until we decide appeasement is more intolerable than facing the source of the fear, we will continue standing there, steeping in our fear. Some of us stand on this precipice for years, losing precious time, our most valuable asset. Will we realize later or sooner…that resisting change and avoiding confrontation amasses a considerable loss of time? Will we choose the terms that bring about change, or will we passively watch things change and wake up while in freefall?

I am reminded of the vivid illustration that can be found in the film *The Fugitive*. Harrison Ford's character, an innocent doctor framed and wrongly convicted of murdering his wife, escapes captivity to take on solving the murder and finding the true culprit. While on the run, he is cornered at the top of a dam by the U.S. Marshal. The Marshal, having snared the fugitive at the edge of a several-hundred-foot precipice, attempts to force the fugitive's surrender.

Ford's character has a life choice to make: either surrender and forever be imprisoned, never again have a chance to prove his innocence and allow the true murderer of his wife to never be brought to justice—or throw himself over the edge, plunge hundreds of feet to an almost certain death…and, if by chance he survives, gain some time to uncover the truth and find justice.

He jumps with the realization at that moment that being wrongly imprisoned for the rest of his life is far worse than risking his own death. That moment of clarity reveals his destined path forward—to prove his innocence, find justice, and restore a thriving life worth living. With all of its consequence, the fear in front of him became less terrifying than the fear behind him. At that point of his realization, jumping became his clear and only choice.

The fugitive's leap is an archetypal leap into the abyss. *The only way out is through.* It is Jonah in the belly of the whale, Alice down the rabbit hole, Harry Potter boarding the train, Luke Skywalker's departure from the Mos Eisley Cantina onto the Millennium Falcon. What's certain is that life is about to change. The leap places us past the point of no return, in full pursuit of the next chapter of our lives. Once the roller coaster starts, we *must* ride it out. We are forced to embrace the decision and make peace with all we leave behind; it is a death of sorts so we may be reborn, like the phoenix into the fire to emerge from the ashes anew. The evolution is a new beginning that takes shape as our next journey. When we lean into our fear, run towards it, and approach it with curiosity, something beautiful happens: We adapt.

> *Change is inevitable. Growth is optional.*
> ~John C. Maxwell

Curiosity Killed the Ego, Not the Cat.

BREAKING FREE MEANS standing up to our fear, confronting it, and engaging it. Breaking free means replacing fear with curiosity, peeking over the ledge, and not retreating back to our cages. Just as lifting a barbell builds muscle and enduring strength over time, when we invite change, we build our character-muscle, cultivating a new way to approach our circumstances. We realize we have choice and power to act, shift, or replace those things that do not serve us. We create a *new normal*, replacing the old part of us that no longer serves us with something new.

Even with all of this courage and curiosity…eventually and inevitably, we *will* run smack into another set of prison bars, and we will realize we have happened upon a larger prison cell. We are faced with a new challenge: to embark upon an even bigger adventure. The difference is that our character muscle recognizes the challenge now as such. We can even count on it and leap with less fear and trepidation.

Playing big and being unstoppable will feel less like a leap off a precipice and more like an eagle taking flight. Freedom is elevation; we cannot elevate consciousness without first breaking free from the confinement of fear, stagnation, and resistance to change. Unencumbered, our spirit is meant to fulfill its highest potential and be freely self-expressed.

SUMMARY | ID 5

Imprisoned – Really? Actually?

Real Imprisonment employs physical prisons, penitentiaries that house convicted felons. It is literal imprisonment, where one's actual freedom is taken away and placed in the hands of others.

Another form of real imprisonment is **open imprisonment**, where a person may not actually be in physical bondage but still lives under the threat of certain demise. Slavery, indentured servitude, and human trafficking are all examples.

Perceived Imprisonment or **self-imprisonment** exists when the walls that confine us are of our own making.

By creating arbitrary boundaries and rules around our fear and resistance to change, we build regimens, habits, and limitations as a means to seek control and safety over our everyday lives.

If we live under the false notion that we have no choice, or if we limit our choice due to fear, ill-perceived control, safety, or predictability, we are most likely self-imprisoned.

The remedy is fierce curiosity.

ID 6: True Freedom versus the Illusion of Freedom

> *Most people do not really want freedom,*
> *because freedom involves responsibility,*
> *and most people are frightened of responsibility.*
> ~Sigmund Freud

WE TEND TO EQUATE FREEDOM with the idea of having no responsibilities or commitments. The exact opposite is actually true. When we find ourselves complaining about the lack of freedom in our lives, we might consider that freedom is not the absence of challenge and responsibility; true freedom actually amasses considerably more of these things. Neither a child dependent on parents nor someone who is literally enslaved is free. The fact that these scenarios exist on significantly different areas of the spectrum has no relevance; the point is that in both scenarios, the person is essentially devoid of responsibility for their own lives and is therefore not truly free. Both examples demand far less day-to-day responsibility than a life of somebody truly free.

> **True Freedom** is abundance of opportunity, not absence of obligation. It means we have the freedom to choose our own lives. True freedom requires considerable responsibility.
>
> **The Illusion of Freedom** is not taking responsibility for ourselves, our choices, or our lives.
>
> *By thwarting responsibility,*
> *we maintain the illusion of freedom*
> *while attempting to offload the accountability to others.*

Why do we typically not recognize what freedom really is? Ironically, our human nature has us trying to have our cake and eat it too: we like to find ways to do less and get more. While it is hard to admit, we are often readily willing to give up freedom to avoid conflict because that is the path of least resistance. We all know that expending effort to overcome the human resistance to change, even if that change means freeing ourselves, is very uncomfortable. Often we'd rather go with the comfort food of appeasement and ambivalence. Taking the reins places us in the driver's seat. As the driver, if we incur resistance or crash in the process of allowing for change, it's on us. Conversely, the *illusion* of freedom falsely allows us to sit back and let someone else drive. That way, if there's a crash, we can blame them. The notion is based on a faulty premise. Once the distinction is illuminated, it is entirely up to us whether we choose true freedom, or whether we elect to bask in the illusion of freedom.

> *Personal power is directly proportionate to*
> *the amount of personal responsibility one takes on.*

Misconceived freedom is born out of the myth that if we don't take responsibility personally for our circumstances, such inaction absolves us from what results. This common misconception attempts to rationalize why, for the same reason, we stay in abusive relationships, don't leave unfulfilling careers, or allow people to walk all over us. True Freedom requires responsibility. Responsibility has no shortcuts; it holds no space for laziness, avoidance, or appeasement. When we blame others for the results we are getting (or not getting), we live inside the illusion that we can thwart our responsibility without it costing anything. In reality, it costs us *everything*. We squander, surrender, or relinquish our freedom either by pawning it off to another or by casting it out into the abyss.

SUMMARY | ID 6

Personal power and freedom are directly proportionate to the amount of responsibility one takes on.

Most people do not really want freedom, because freedom involves responsibility, and most people are frightened of responsibility.

True Freedom is abundance of opportunity, not absence of obligation. It means we have the freedom to choose our own lives. True freedom requires considerable responsibility.

The Illusion of Freedom is not taking responsibility for ourselves, our choices, or our lives. By thwarting responsibility, we maintain the illusion of freedom while attempting to offload the accountability to others.

Personal power is directly proportionate to the amount of personal responsibility one takes on.

ID 7: You Make Me Feel versus I Allow Myself to Feel

Please pay close attention to these following three sentences.

You make me feel worthless / I allow myself to feel worthless around you.

You make me so angry / I allow myself to get so angry when you poke and prod at my patience.

You hurt me deeply when you say those things / I allow myself to believe you when you use those hurtful words.

JUST WORDS AND SEMANTICS, right? Wrong. How we speak and think matters. We inform the world that we live into, even if this occurs without our being conscious of doing so.

You Make Me Feel says: I have no power or responsibility over my own life and feelings. I relinquish it all to you, blame you, and am not accountable. Therefore, I am not free.

I Allow Myself To Feel says: I have power and responsibility over my own life and how I allow you to affect me. I do not give it to you. Therefore, I am free.

When we give our power away to another as in the first version, we delude ourselves into thinking that we are thwarting responsibility by blaming the other. We are playing the role of powerless victim. When we surrender, deny, or yield our choices in a matter, we squander our power and risk basking in the illusion that we are being controlled by someone else. While in the throes of this illusion, when we yield control to another and let them make decisions for us, we get to blame them when we are disempowered and fail. The script in life presents like this: "You told me to do that, so it's not my fault it didn't work out" or "You said (or did) this to me, so it's your fault I am like this now."

Accordingly, when we take responsibility for allowing someone to affect us, we own the permissions we grant them to affect us the way they do. "Allowing myself to feel…" illuminates my option to dis-allow being affected by another, an option not present in "you make me feel." This is what lets us own our power and not allow it to be usurped away from us.

Choosing to disallow ourselves to feel or be affected by someone's behaviors or actions, doesn't mean we don't feel. It means we own how we allow things to make us feel; we do not give or blame away that allowance to another. This distinction introduces us into something I like to call personal sovereignty, visited in the next distinction…

SUMMARY | ID 7

Control is all in our perception.

There exists much personal power in language. Our careful choices in words and in how we speak very much determine our locus of control in our lives. When you say: "You make me feel," that conveys this message: I have no power or responsibility over my own life and feelings. I relinquish it all to you, blame you, and am not accountable. Therefore, I am not free. On the other hand, when you say: "I Allow Myself To Feel," it says that I have power and responsibility over my own life and how I allow you to affect me. I do not give that power to you. Therefore, I am free.

ID 8: Boundaries versus Walls

We welcome change and openness;
for we believe that freedom and security go together,
that the advance of human liberty
can only strengthen the cause of world peace....
Tear down this wall!
 ~Speech by US President Reagan[4] to the former
 Soviet Union and its leader, Mikhail Gorbachev

A VERY POWERFUL DISTINCTION EXISTS between boundaries and walls. Like many of the Invisible Distinctions, just placing the two words side by side engages our minds, perhaps in a way not considered until now.

Boundaries delineate specific areas within shared spaces that are meant to be respected and appreciated by all who interact and collaborate within such spaces. Boundaries serve as a necessary means of maintaining our personal sovereignty, values, and expression while interacting with others. Accordingly, others enjoy reciprocation, as they are afforded the same personal sovereignty in return.[3] Boundaries are the Goldilocks for social interaction and order: too much structure is confining and can start resembling a wall, and too little can leave us exposed, excessively vulnerable, and prove to be hazardous.

Walls, by contrast, are rigid barriers. While circumstances may very well require such an extreme remedy, walls otherwise risk shutting people out indiscriminately. They also shut us in, confining and isolating us, diminishing the means for us to interact with, and relate to, others. Whether physical or psychological, walls are typically erected as a reaction to an affliction such as trespass, violation, fear, or perceived threat.

When separation or isolation is the objective, walls are a viable option. Our home has walls to keep out the elements and to provide privacy and protection, as do prisons, zoos, dams, and quarantine facilities. While occasionally walls may prove necessary, they imprison us and just beg to be leapt, circumvented, burrowed through, tunneled under, or knocked down. We humans are not meant to be isolated. Our human spirit is meant to be freely expressed and collaborative.

Walls can dramatically limit perspective. They limit the expression, connection, and flow of fresh ideas necessary to promote diversity, inclusion, creativity, and acceptance. When human civilizations are conditioned over generations to root down into a tradition that results in the building of walls, a culture of fear and isolation results. This culture instills the divisiveness, antisocial behavior, and stagnation that often ultimately lead to conflict.

Boundaries, on the other hand, establish what access is and is not permissible. They set limits we respect with regard to others, and that others must respect around us. As a result, safety, comfort, and ease in common space can be cultivated.

When we talk about sovereignty for a country, we talk about the fact that it has rights to exist and not be conquered by another. The country can thrive, govern itself, decide its own laws, and exercise free will over itself…as long as the act of doing so doesn't infringe on or violate its neighbors' sovereignty. The same concept applies when considering boundaries and walls with regard to personal sovereignty as an individual person. Personal sovereignty means exercising our boundaries in an effort to govern ourselves and to lawfully inhabit our own personal space.

Establishing Boundaries While Remaining Boundless

WE ARE ALL AWARE that some boundaries have explicit lines that are written into actual law, such as not taking material goods that belong to somebody else. From the perspective of Conscious Intelligence, do we have a moral obligation to make our own boundaries clear—to telegraph them to others in a specific way? When it comes to personal boundaries, there are many circumstances—cultural, religious, personal preference, and otherwise—that can make it very difficult to know where someone's boundaries are.

Leaving the determination of our boundaries to others is unreliable and needlessly risks violation of our personal sovereignty.

So many unnecessary incidents occur innocently when one party either is not clear about another's boundaries or assumes that the other party's boundaries are the same as their own. (I am speaking here of completely harmless and innocent acts, not of acts that are malicious or that breach boundaries that should be understood by thoughtful people.) Do we have some sort of moral obligation to project boundaries in order to head off any sort of embroilment, just as *an ounce of prevention is worth a pound of cure*? Of course! Letting boundaries be clearly known can be helpful whether someone *does* or *does not* have malice or misguided intentions. Telegraphing boundaries can expose these intentions early on. It can act as an early warning system that can give notice and attention to a misstep about to happen, can confirm with more certainty any potential mal-intentions, and can initiate action earlier on, before the circumstance progresses or escalates.

When we drive a car, it is not required to use the turn indicators—but why wouldn't we? It helps us get where we need to go, eliminates the mystery, and allows others to help us and plan their own paths accordingly. Setting our own boundaries, indicating them, and adhering to them also allows others to enjoy the serenity of their own boundaries and to feel more secure in their clarity of ours.

Why depend on others' interpretations (or misinterpretations) of boundaries? Why open ourselves up to ambiguity and the increased risk that others will, by default, decide our boundaries for us? Personal sovereignty has the best possibility of persevering when boundaries are effectively established.

Allowing others to determine our boundaries increases the chance of an undesirable or unexpected incident, whether intended or unintended. Communicating our boundaries is one way of owning our own lives and helping ourselves and others prevent a completely unintentional incident.

Accountability to Boundaries

*Don't let others change who you are
to become what they need.* ~Unknown

When we allow morally conflicting wants and needs of others to be placed above our own, we risk encroachment upon our personal sovereignty.

By marginalizing our own value, we become increasingly vulnerable to harm and prone to feeling used, depleted, and undervalued. Allowing ourselves to be marginalized also increases the risk of becoming complicit in the event that our personal sovereignty is encroached.

If we do not take responsibility and make clear our personal boundaries, we increase the likelihood that others will not have clarity about our boundaries either. The most innocent, well-intentioned people can find themselves unintentionally stepping on a landmine because the boundary simply is not clear to them. Suddenly, they are amidst a volatile situation they genuinely didn't expect or intend to trigger. This, too, falls in the realm of personal sovereignty.

Now, we cannot ignore the fact that there are cases where people are not so well-intentioned. Make no mistake, dysfunctional and misguided people are out there, just as there are bad drivers peppering the freeways. (From my experience, it would seem most of them live in Los Angeles.) Even the establishment of clear boundaries does not inoculate us from getting into a fender-bender or worse. No matter how clear, boundaries can and will be trespassed. When clarity is established around boundaries, and encroachment occurs, it carves out a clear path to accountability. It becomes immediately clear who has overstepped. Clear boundaries leave little room for claiming one didn't know better and allows trespasses to be more readily identified and addressed.

SUMMARY | ID 8

Personal Sovereignty is best maintained when we clearly define and establish our boundaries, stand by them, and allow everyone around us to know them.

We are all aware that some boundaries have explicit lines that are written into actual law, such as not taking material goods that belong to somebody else or touching someone inappropriately. Do we have a moral obligation to make our own boundaries clear—to communicate and telegraph them to others? When it comes to personal boundaries, there are many circumstances—cultural, religious, personal preference, and otherwise—that can make it very difficult to know where someone's boundaries are. Leaving the determination of our boundaries to others is unreliable and needlessly risks violation of our personal sovereignty. Cultivating clear and consistent boundaries publicly and prominently leaves very little guesswork to others, makes it glaringly apparent when they have been violated, and establishes our personal sovereignty.

CHAPTER 5

Distinctions of Personal Power

Until we discover that we are responsible for our own life, we will give that power to others.
Until we become the author of our own beliefs, we will be subject to the beliefs of others.   ~Gene Oliver

ID 9: Selfishness

OFTEN, WE HEAR THE WORD "SELFISH" used to describe a person who is self-absorbed and thinks only of themselves. For example: "That boy refuses to share any of the toys with the other children; he is so selfish." The word has developed a negative connotation, mostly because it gets confused with the more appropriate term "self-serving." In the context of the Invisible Distinctions, "selfish," in its naked essence, is neutral. Its spectrum ranges from *self-serving* to *self-preserving*.

During my service with the fire department, responding to emergencies commonly meant we ended up in dangerous environments, be it a roadway, the ocean, on or below a cliff, or in swift water. The first rule for any first responder when arriving on scene, before anything else, is to secure scene safety; i.e., make sure we are as safe as possible before doing anything else. We do this for a very important reason, one I learned the hard way while I was a cadet in my Ocean Rescue Response training academy.

The incident occurred during a swift-water rescue test involving a treacherous rock formation named "The Giggling Crack." The brisk, cold morning fog and ocean swell laid backdrop to the exercise. The

Crack could be described as an open blowhole. Its formation is a sheer cliff carved out of rock. Extending outward at its base, it becomes a flat table rock where it meets the ocean, with a huge crack that opens outward from the cliff, forming a V shape filled with jagged rocks and ocean water. This V-shaped crack pools ocean water and creates three simultaneous inflow/outflow currents: a fill/drain current, a heavy rip current, and a washing-machine current, which in concert all form a perfect storm that marries pounding sea with sheer cliff. Each swell constantly washes in from the Pacific Ocean, fills the V until it overflows, plows against the cliff seawall, and, like a volcano, overflows, sending water spilling over the flat rock, sweeping everything in its path along with it back into the crack and onward out to sea. It is very dangerous, and increasingly so during more sizable swells...such as the ones Mother Nature gifted us that morning.

WANT TO CHECK "THE CRACK" OUT?
https://youtu.be/II_lmmDMylM

For the test, it was up to us to jump in with our rescue tubes (the red floatation rescue devices every surf lifesaver carries), navigate the explosive currents, engage the subjects, and swim them out via the open sea to an adjacent shore. As a note, the academy still does this same training exercise all these years later, but now cadets get to wear helmets. How times have changed.

Just prior to the exercise, the chief instructor asked, "If an impending wave is going to smash you and the patient into the rocks, what do you do?" He scanned us, squinty eyes glaring from his salt-of-the-sea, sun-weathered face. Nobody raised a hand because, frankly, the guy scared the shit out of us. Eventually his eyes fixated on *me*; he gestured, demanding my response.

I said, nervously, "We should place ourselves between the injured subject and the rocks to prevent further injury to the subject, optimizing our chances of saving them." I figured that was pretty obvious, sort of a no-brainer.

The chief replied, "Ohhhh, I see. So to protect the subject from impact, take the impact yourself because it is your job and you are the rescuer?"

I nodded affirmatively.

He asked the rest of the academy to raise their hands if in agreement.

Pretty much everyone did.

"Awww, you cute little heroes," he said. "For that answer, you receive a group FAIL."

The correct answer is: We take the subject and place him between the rocks and us. We use him as a bumper—or, if the situation dictates, a broken-bleeding-body buffer—to prevent ourselves from injury or from impacting the rocks. The chief lashed at us, "If you get injured, there are now two patients and NO rescuers, and you, Mr. Valiant Hero—" pointing at me, "—along with our precious actual patient, will become fish food. The patient has found his way into deep trouble. Without us, he's in certain peril. So, it is imperative that we preserve above all else our own well-being so that we can all get out, even if the patient is worse off for it!"

And then, in addition to our doing the exercise for a few hours and the group fail, he threw in a bonus—a three-mile, round-trip consisting of a swim up the beautiful California coastline in the brisk 52-degree water and a dry three-mile land run back, barefoot, in our Speedos, so we could air-dry in the 55-degree breezy, early morning sunrise. I think I finally stopped shivering from that test about an hour ago!

Seriously, though, this was one of the most powerful, caring lessons a teacher could impart to his students, regardless of the chief's gruff manner. After all, the point of the exercise was to illuminate the most effective way to minimize risk to ourselves and have everyone out of peril as swiftly as possible. As counterintuitive as it may initially appear, this advice makes perfect sense. When we fly on an airplane, for example, before we even leave the gate, we receive a safety briefing that states, "In the unlikely case of cabin depressurization, oxygen masks will drop down. Please affix one onto your nose and mouth first before assisting others."

Positioning ourselves to act from a place of strength while elevating and assisting others is, in part, a selfish act. It is an act of self-preservation that sits in stark contrast to being self-serving.

We can't help anyone if we ourselves are in peril. We cannot elevate ourselves or others while we are chained to an anchor and drowning.

This is true while caring for our families or maintaining a business. By contrast, if we seek ascension at the expense of another—if we seek to exploit with the intent to gain, causing another to be deprived—we are being self-serving. We are no different from the kid that is hogging all the toys.

> ## SUMMARY | ID 9
>
> ### Selfishness with respect to Conscious Intelligence.
>
> There exists a distinction between selfish and self-serving. In the Conscious Intelligence perspective, the kid who refuses to share any of their toys with the other children is not being "selfish," they are being "self-serving." When we fly on an airplane, for example, before we even leave the gate, we receive a safety briefing that states, "In the unlikely case of cabin depressurization, oxygen masks will drop down. Please affix one onto your nose and mouth first before assisting others."
>
> Positioning ourselves to act from a place of strength while elevating and assisting others is, in part, a selfish act. It is an act of self-preservation that sits in stark contrast to being self-serving. We can't help anyone if we ourselves are in peril. We cannot elevate ourselves or others while we are chained to an anchor and drowning.
>
> By contrast, if we seek ascension at the expense of another—if we seek to exploit with the intent to gain, causing another to be deprived—we are being self-serving. We are no different from the kid who is hogging all the toys.

ID 10: Shades of Pain

SEVERAL TIMES IN THE COMING CHAPTERS there will be clusters of elements falling under one distinction called "Shades of ___." This arises when a group of elements are all inter-related. A distinction need not be merely between two things. Multiple shades of concepts can become conflated. By euphemistically employing a *prism to distinguish the multiple colors*, we can illuminate their distinction with respect to each other.

Discomfort versus Pain

DISCOMFORT—WHETHER PHYSICAL, MENTAL, OR EMOTIONAL—is something we all experience. As we adjust our lives to meet the dynamic changes that our environment undergoes, discomfort is but one component propagating adaptation. We burn the midnight oil, endure lack of sleep, and carry crippling loads of work in our efforts to excel in school and work, learn a new trade, or execute our entrepreneurial vision. More primal than that, mothers-to-be bear children, adolescents endure the aches associated with rapid growth, and we place ourselves on restrictive diets to lose weight, share heartbreaking news with loved ones, and heal from medical procedures. We endure this discomfort and, in doing so, we gain and are better for it. Discomfort is a part of our natural existence.

As an athlete, I am all too familiar with discomfort from having endured years of rigorous training and conditioning as a means to prepare for and meet my competitive goals. The body is resilient and has adapted as a means for survival for millennia. When we strategically place constructive stresses on it physically, mentally, psychologically...it adapts. This is called a "conditioning effect." We do an arm curl, and the body's systemic feedback says, "Well, isn't this stressful! How can I alleviate this?"—and then answers by stimulating growth in the bicep muscle and sending more blood and nutrients. After a while, when an arm curl happens again in the future, the systemic feedback says, "Much better!"

Or, we run ten kilometers and, if you are like me, you pretty much feel like we are going to throw up and die (I am fonder of the water).

But after a time and with repetition, the heart adapts and strengthens to pump more blood to the legs, the lungs adapt to oxygenate that blood, the leg muscles adapt to better support the weight necessary. We *adapt* as a means for our body to create balance and stasis so that when we run that ten kilometers again, the body says, "Ahh, much better!" (Even though my head says, "*Oh come on!!! Not again!*")

But what of *pain*, as opposed to discomfort? The distinction is akin to our degree of tolerance to injury versus irritation. What this means is that we all endure different degrees of *discomfort* due to irritation. This is not the same as enduring pain due to injury, physical or otherwise. Enduring discomfort depends on our own individual tolerances along with what we are willing to trade in exchange for our drive for achievement. This is *subjective*. We may be willing to tolerate irritation as mere discomfort if the trade-off seems worthy to us—and the challenge can test our abilities to endure a discomfort if what can result is our reaping the rewards. We may, in other words, justify our work towards adaptation so that we can reach a new, improved, enhanced state. Perhaps I continue my 10K runs, and in doing so justify to myself, the discomfort I must endure in order to be committed and ready to survive that 10K fundraising run for breast cancer coming up in a few weeks.

Working through pain, on the other hand, as if it were only discomfort, can further injure us no matter how high our tolerance or how strong our drive. This is *objective*. We all have endured pain when injured, but we also discovered *continuing the activity* does not serve us. We best take measures to stop the activity and treat the injury. When we don't, the universe usually steps in and does it for us. It is often better to do it on *our* terms.

When we are injured and continue to stress the body, we do not heal, recover, adapt. The body gets further torn up; the immune system does not build—it depletes. The wound grows and expands, the afflicted area tears and becomes more irritated. From the historically primal perspective, this leaves us vulnerable, weak, and incapacitated; we fall easy prey to a predator. If we are accessing Conscious Intelligence, we are looking at the much, much broader message here that holds 100% true—this is a universal life lesson about our holistic wellness, not just about a physical injury.

> *What results when we push through actual pain is that we amplify the damage to ourselves, not reduce it.*

When we push through certain kinds of pain, whether physical injury or otherwise, adaptation and evolution cease to move in an affirming direction. Our efforts instead become self-defeating, causing increasingly serious injury. No degree of tolerance or bravado will change this, nor will it bring about healing.

Our willingness to be bold and endure discomfort in the face of resistance invites growth. Inviting pain willfully is not growth but something else entirely. To recognize when discomfort shifts to pain is to understand that once such a threshold has been crossed, no growth will result in its furtherance. Pushing ourselves to those lines, expanding them, and at times discovering we stepped over them is to find the distinction between discomfort and pain.

Pain | Suffering | Struggling

> *Although the world is full of suffering, it is also full of the overcoming of it.* ~Helen Keller

NORMALLY, PAIN AND SUFFERING are a natural process and necessary part of our human circumstance. Incidentally, it is also our human nature to evolve, adapt, and heal—as long as we don't disrupt this natural process. While much research exists on the subjects of pain, suffering, and convalescence, and while we experience a broad spectrum of types of pain, our purpose here is very specific: to identify our individual relationship to pain, suffering, and struggling, and to distinguish the contributing source.

> **Pain** is the physiological and/or psychological response to a harmful stimulus. It is the acute sensation of discomfort our bodies and/or our minds experience as a result of injury.

Suffering is the result of enduring pain over a prolonged period of time. It distracts, limits, and/or prevents our ability to otherwise enjoy life.

Struggling is what we do in an effort to free ourselves from the chains of oppressive suffering. The dictionary describes it as proceeding with difficulty or with great exertion; employing strenuous effort in the face of challenge or opposition.

The most important decision we make is whether we believe we live in a friendly or hostile universe. ~Albert Einstein

When we endure prolonged pain, whether physical or emotional, we have few choices with regard to suffering. We can focus on rehabilitation, choosing to approach it constructively, own it, become enrolled in facilitating our emergence from the condition. Or, we can settle in and get downright comfortable, wear our suffering as if it were a badge of pride, and let it define us.

If we find ourselves choosing the latter, consider something else is at play. Consider we are using the suffering as a means to get something (likely from others) or to resist giving something (perhaps our efforts in otherwise requisite commitments). If this is what we are doing, we can be quite confident that we are fabricating the ongoing struggle as a means to perpetuate the stuck-*ness*. That struggle is not from the affliction at hand, but likely something else. Identifying and acknowledging the source of the suffering and manufactured struggle will define whether we are actually trying to eradicate it or manufacturing excuses for its continuation.

There is the light that illuminates and the light that burns. What is to give light must endure burning.
~Viktor Frankl

When authentic, we can see struggle as a means to an end: a "best way out is through" perspective. In such circumstances, struggling is requisite to help move us through and past suffering. On the other hand, if we continue giving ourselves license with impunity to sink into the role of perpetual struggling and stuck-*ness*, something else is at play. We can consider, whatever the source is, however uncomfortable, we are getting something out of its continuance. By our participation, we are being inauthentic to ourselves and to those around us.

When our struggle is affirmative, compelling us to grow, learn, and evolve, it grinds us past our impediments, just like the sand pebble that agitates the oyster to create the pearl. Conversely, when our struggling keeps us from addressing our deeper, real issues, fear-based excuses will replace any real progress.

When we *dwell* in suffering, all of the struggling in the world will not contribute to progress; we will progress no further along than a hamster on its proverbial wheel.

Marinating in the stagnant version of struggle breaks us down from the inside, taking the form of anguish, anxiety, frustration, exhaustion, shame, and loss of hope. Distinguishing which perspective of struggling we are operating from is important in identifying the source of the struggle and determining whether we are dwelling in victimization or poising ourselves to elevate through the circumstance. The most powerful test in determining which version is at play is to ask, "What am I getting out of its continuation?" No matter which of the versions we are sourcing, make no mistake, we are getting something out of its continuation. Will our path be that of suffering or of triumph?

The Wound That Won't Heal

THE VAST MAJORITY OF THE TIME, our body's ability to recover is remarkable, but seldom is it easy or a path of least resistance. When we consider that recovery can require a highly disciplined, often challenging, and sometimes painful regimen of therapy, we can shut down or check out. If we replay the pain-causing incident in our heads, we can become re-traumatized and fraught with fear. We might become resigned, quit, keep medicating, and even subconsciously resist progress. We might even hide in the complacency of remaining injured. When this happens, the physical wound becomes a psychological or psychosomatic wound, an excuse to avoid the thing that pretends to be the wound: *facing our fear.*

Our wound can ultimately become a pretext for us to be unaccountable for our recovery. It can become a justification to blame the wound for why we are not progressing from this injury as well as in other areas of our lives.

Actively deciding to resolve our suffering is not about denying that we suffer. Rather, it is about coming to terms with our suffering without lying down and bathing in it—by wading through it to the other side. So much suffering exists in this world. So, too, do we witness the resilient who choose not to allow their enduring pain to define them or prescribe the kind of day they are going to have.

Oh, those infamous six words: "Maybe it will just go away." Or these six-and-a-half: "It's as good as it gets." Or, we just decide we don't want to put our time or effort into changing it. When resistance to letting go of suffering disrupts healing, we can be fairly certain that something else is at play. This dwelling in suffering is not a victimless crime, either; it generates an environment of suffering that impacts the world and people around us. It short-circuits other areas of our lives, sabotaging us by leaving imbalance, un-wellness, and lack of accountability in its wake. Eventually it defines us by becoming the way the world shows up to us, as well as how we show up to the world. We may even discover the reason this current wound is not healing is because we are still clenched onto a previous injury just like it. Until we address the wound and make an active decision to resolve our suffering, it will become our new baseline, our new status quo, our new normal.

> *The powerful distinction is that we can choose how we show up in any given circumstance and elevate above it, rather than dwell in it.*

Empathic Sufferers

SOME PEOPLE HIDE from their own issues by taking on the suffering of another. Do you know someone like this? Empathic sufferers hide from their own internal fear by facing another's struggles instead. When this is at play, our antennae best go up; we are standing witness to a suffering soul with a yet to be addressed affliction.

Empathic sufferers often are extremely nurturing by nature. They are known to do prolific things in the world for others, but they can also commandeer the circumstance, usurping focus back onto them, perhaps without meaning to or being aware of it. Tending to another becomes a way to skirt responsibility for their own afflictions. Displaying compassionate solidarity for another can make it easier to cloak oneself behind the distraction that another's suffering provides. In an effort to hide amid another's pain to avoid their own, empathic sufferers are afflicted by an unrelenting dark wound that won't heal until it is brought out into the light. They need patients to mask or hide from their own suffering.

While their generous care can be profoundly beneficial to the other person, such care from an empathic sufferer is rooted in a malady of their own from within. Harsh as this sounds, due to their copious amounts of generosity, their empathy is sourced in something they are desperately trying to hide. As long as the empathic sufferer is trying to fill the hole inside themselves with situations from outside (such as caring for others), the affliction will persist. Holding space for them with our own empathy and care is as important as maintaining our own energetic boundaries so as not to get drawn down by the darker shadow. Knowing they are suffering deep inside is to provide them with an opportunity to let in the light and give them an opportunity to exhale. Until the inauthenticity is brought out into the light and addressed, the dark shadow of their affliction will carry on.

SUMMARY | ID 10

Pain is our body communicating to us that something is injurious.

Discomfort—whether physical, mental, or emotional—is something we all experience. As we adjust our lives to meet the dynamic changes that our environment undergoes, discomfort is but one component propagating adaptation.

But what of *pain*, as opposed to discomfort? The distinction is akin to our degree of tolerance to injury versus irritation. This is not the same as enduring pain due to injury, physical or otherwise. We may be willing to tolerate irritation as mere discomfort if the trade-off seems worthy to us—and the challenge can test our abilities to endure a discomfort if what can result is our reaping the rewards. But this is quite different from enduring pain when injured, where we inevitably will discover *continuing the activity* does not serve us.

ID 11: Adapt versus Accept

*Examine your greatest strength,
and therein lies your greatest weakness.* ~Unknown

Our basic, innate ability to adapt has secured our existence on this earth for millennia. Incidentally, our human strength of adaptation can also be one of our most profound weaknesses.

Remember the idea we mentioned previously, that the longer something strange persists, the more normal it becomes? When a distinction is not initially made, the conflation becomes a blind spot in our programming. Consequentially, we adapt.

It is in our nature to resist change. We just don't like it; it's uncomfortable. Change disrupts our habitual patterns, jars us free of our regimens, and displaces us out of our comfort zone. Such disruption often makes us feel we are out of control. The truth is, we never were truly *in* control because life is constantly changing and evolving; we have merely created a normalcy around it to make us feel as though life is static. Often this works for a while...until it doesn't.

When we accept conditions that are not serving us, our world will eventually adapt around them until they become the new normal. At this point, a significant consequence results: we tend not to even see these conditions anymore. They become invisible to us. And when we no longer see the conditions that don't serve us, we no longer endeavor to eradicate them. Instead, we live with them without even being aware that they are there.

The longer we operate with limited choice (because we don't even see the conditions that we've adapted to), the more challenging it is to recondition our programming to restore our optimal state. Just as the longer we remain sedentary and allow our muscles to atrophy, the more challenging it is to snap our bodies back into shape.

I had an experience in my life that illustrates this. Like many competitive swimmers, I have back muscles that tend to be overly developed with respect to the opposing or *antagonistic* muscles in front that are normally meant to counterbalance them. Because of this, I once experienced a muscle spasm where the muscle locked down and contracted so hard that it ripped my back and spine out of alignment. The sounds that emerged from my mouth were ones I had never heard a human make, and I immediately dropped to the ground in intense pain. I had brought on this condition because I hadn't built up enough of the opposing muscles to protect my back, which would have prevented this problem. The great strength of my back muscles became a great weakness. When I finally made it to my doctor several days later, she saw my spine contorted 45 degrees and literally shed tears (which was both comforting and a bit discomforting).

When injuries are not treated, something interesting happens. Our bodies are amazing in their ability to adapt and adjust in an attempt to alleviate tension and discomfort. Our primordial evolutionary programming has always done this as a means to survive. And so, with an untreated injury, the body begins the process of adapting as best it can to the new positioning of the spine, muscles, etc. Our brain also pitches in, doing what it can to further dissociate and distract us from the pain. With our entire system working to adapt, acute pain eventually turns into chronic discomfort; the pain may or may not go away completely, but it becomes less acute.

Finally, one day, we visit the doctor. She identifies the sourcing of the muscle spasm and gets to work on restoring the spine to its more appropriate, intended position. What happens next is quite eye-opening: as the muscle is coerced back to its intended position, the pain and trauma skyrockets again—in my case, which I barely recall, I nearly passed out. Why? Because the muscles, ligaments, tendons, and nerves have already *adapted* to their newly contorted positions. So when they are contorted back to where they belong, they experience the trauma all over again.

Adaptation is a powerful gift that developed from our evolutionary survival, and it is both our strength and our weakness. Not taking account of misalignments in our lives bears the risk of their soon becoming invisible; a contorted, twisted, new normal. When we allow them to linger and do nothing, hoping they will just dissipate, we are accepting a permanent shift from where things are otherwise intended. Doing nothing is *actually* doing something.

When adaptation is used to ignore an injurious malady, we become complicit in avoiding the hard work necessary for proper recovery. This is a prime example of our exploiting our strength in an effort to avoid …recovery?? That makes little sense, but when we recognize that sometimes our well-being requires a dose of transitory discomfort, we can welcome change and allow our innate strength of adaptation to bring about prolific resilience the way it's meant to.

SUMMARY | ID 11

Adapting to accept things or accepting the task of adapting to things, that is the question.

Our basic, innate ability to adapt has secured our existence on this earth for millennia. Incidentally, our human strength of adaptation can also be one of our most profound weaknesses. It is in our nature to resist change. We just don't like it; it's uncomfortable.

Change disrupts our habitual patterns, jars us free of our regimens, and displaces us out of our comfort zone.

When we accept conditions that are not serving us, our circumstance eventually adapts around them until they become the new normal. At this point, a significant consequence results: we tend not to even see these conditions anymore. They become invisible to us.

Not taking account of misalignments in our lives bears the risk of their soon becoming invisible—a contorted, twisted, new normal. A choice to do nothing is actually doing something.

When adaptation is used to ignore an injurious malady, we become complicit in avoiding the hard work necessary for proper recovery. When we recognize that sometimes our well-being requires a dose of transitory discomfort, we can welcome change and allow our innate strength of adaptation to bring about prolific resilience the way it's meant to.

ID 12: Accept versus Condone

Speaking of accepting...

Accept is to endure and give admittance or approval to, even if there is disagreement; to tolerate. This distinction refers to "accept" as it relates to behavior and tolerance, not its close relative, *acceptance*, as it relates to the final stage of the grieving process. The kind of accept we are addressing in this distinction is exemplified in the *Serenity Prayer*:

> *Grant me the courage to change the things I can,*
> *the patience to accept the things I cannot change,*
> *and the wisdom so that I may know the difference.*

Condone is to deliberately overlook, ignore, disregard, or pardon without protest or censure.

WE ARE LIKELY GOVERNED by the inherent belief that we all have the right to our processes and beliefs as long as they don't encroach upon those of others. The U.S. Constitution describes them as our *Inalienable Rights*, but this idea is pervasive, expressed in the First Commandment of the Bible and in the Golden Rule, among other places. They all remind us *to do unto others; to not throw stones in glass houses; to judge not, that you be not judged*, it is *the pot calling the kettle black*, etc., to name a few.[1]

To live powerfully means to accept these principles, to accept others for their differences and transgressions, but we are left with a plaguing challenge. Among us there are those who (how do I say this affectionately?) we sometimes just want to strangle. Oh yes, such individuals have a certain way of doing things and treating people that is abrasive, antisocial, or, worse, detrimental, crazy-making, falling just short of harming anyone. Their way is just... not how we are aligned or wired.

So, *must we accept them?*

If our path is committed to elevating consciousness, then as fellow members of the human race, *yes*. We may love this other person; we may not...or, heck, we may just plain not like them, the choices they make, the opinions they have, or the conduct they display in certain areas of their lives, even to an extreme. They could be a work colleague, a subscriber of an idea that is counter to our viewpoint, a family member who marches to the beat of their own drum, or the proverbial black sheep.

Regardless, when we still choose to *accept* them for everything they are and for everything they are not and strive to understand them, we access Conscious Intelligence. We may reject most everything they stand for; we may not condone their behavioral choices. But if we reject *them* straight out (rather than disagree with some of their choices), we are judging them. If we judge them, we deem ourselves better than they are by bestowing such a righteous authority upon ourselves. There exists a perspective where we all are still humans, where no one is more human than another or in possession of more human-*ness* than another.

All the same, this *does not* require our *condoning* their conduct or behavior. We can acknowledge them *without* subscribing to their beliefs, habits, or choices. When we do this, we can elevate perspective in our own personal viewpoints while remaining nonjudgmental. We can give another the right to their processes, while at the same time retain our power and personal sovereignty—as well as a bit more of our sanity.

SUMMARY | ID 12

Can accepting someone sometimes mean saying "no"?

Accept is to endure and give admittance or approval to, even if there is disagreement.

Condone is to deliberately overlook, ignore, disregard, or pardon without protest or censure. To live powerfully means to accept these principles, to accept others for their differences and transgressions. Yet that choice leaves us with a plaguing challenge.

Can we accept people into our life while we disagree with them? If our path is committed to elevating consciousness, we must.

All the same, this does not require our condoning their conduct or behavior. We can acknowledge them without subscribing to their beliefs, habits, or choices. We can give another the right to their processes, while at the same time we retain our power and personal sovereignty—as well as a bit more of our sanity.

ID 13: Giving Up versus Giving In

THIS DISTINCTION WAS CHALLENGING for me to learn because I'm a lifelong athlete, and to me, "giving up" and "giving in" both sound a lot like *quitting*. Nobody, especially a driven person, aspires to bear any resemblance to being a quitter.

> **Giving Up** can cut two ways: It can demonstrate a lack of conviction and integrity, as in failing to complete an endeavor after committing to it, or it can demonstrate the maintaining of our personal integrity when involving the release or liberation of something, someone, or ourselves—that either does not serve, never has served, or no longer serves us.
>
> **Giving In** is releasing our *attachment* to the way we think things need to go. For example, choosing to let go of our attachment to being right is *giving in*.

Let's look at these more closely. *Giving up* is indeed quitting, but quitting is a two-edged sword, which is why we have a distinction to make. On one hand, failing to complete an endeavor after committing to it demonstrates a lack of conviction and integrity—if not to another, at least to those who hold their *own* integrity sacred.

Giving Up

CUTTING THE OTHER WAY, *giving up* something that has no inherent value, or somebody whom we allow to control us, is quite different. The former corrodes our integrity while the latter illustrates giving up something *without losing anything*. Quitting smoking, drinking, drugs, or other vices, or giving up a role we play, like being taken advantage of, abused, or exploited, stands in stark contrast. When we shed the crippling burden of codependence in exchange for gaining back our personal integrity, we can view giving up in an entirely different light. This is the type of giving up of something that has never and will never serve us. Alcohol, nicotine, the misuse and abuse of drugs, and the allowance of others to walk all over us are toxic and disempowering. We will never wake up one day to discover suddenly that such things elevate us or inspire growth. So, walking away, giving up, and quitting can, in this light, be prolific.

But…sometimes it's not that cut and dried. Compare what was just mentioned to circumstances we morally feel we *cannot* walk away from—or, even if we can, we are compelled not to. Walking away from a person or a situation because the circumstance is unresolvable, toxic, or disempowering at the time introduces a different dynamic altogether. People can change, circumstances can change, and, most importantly, *we can change*. Add to this a dynamic that the person is, for example, a family member, spouse, child, or other loved one, and giving up may violate a deeper, personal moral code that forbids us to consider abandoning such a person. Perhaps walking away places us in direct conflict with our conscience, vows, integrity, or faith; as a result, we struggle in a conundrum. This feeling of moral obligation and principle sits in opposition and weighs on us: "I cannot abandon this person. I cannot give up on this family member, friend, relationship, job, project, partner."

These conflicting principles complicate the dynamics and throw us off balance. A crisis of conscience and even morality emerges, seeded both in feeling an obligation to protect the other as well as in the promise to uphold ideals within ourselves. The conundrum pits our basic principles of self-preservation, honor, and code of living in direct conflict with the relationship presently dwelling in a toxic environment. In such conflicting circumstances, remaining in the question while being patient and allowing the broader universal dynamics to play out, can very well reveal the answer in time.

> *Being in control*
> *is learning how to let go*
> *of the things we cannot control.*

Giving In

GIVING IN is releasing our attachment to the way we think things need to go in order for the circumstance to resolve. Giving in is powerfully choosing to let go of our need to be right and have things go our way. Giving in does not mean caving or succumbing; it means *choosing powerfully* not to meet a person in toxic waters again and again if this is where they insist on swimming. Walking away doesn't have to mean leaving, just as taking a stand for love can sometimes mean saying no. Rather than descending into the toxic waters to join our fellow human, we can instead choose to drop a ladder and invite them out and hold a space for them in the sunlight when they do.

Giving in can also mean *choosing powerfully* not to continue in a situation not serving us. Borrowing from an adage all successful entrepreneurs know well: Don't cling to a bad position just because much time and money was invested establishing it. A common misstep is to stick with a project that isn't working just because considerable funds, energy, and labor have been consumed on it for months or years. In business, this is known as *throwing good money after bad*—or continuing to pour resources into something just because significant resources have already been poured into it. Meanwhile, while precious time and money have been squandered in a single-minded focus, others have completed and launched next-gen projects, leap-frogging *this* one into obscurity.

Redoubling our efforts in such a case seldom gets us to our destination. Rather, it often only accelerates us more quickly into a brick wall of antiquated oblivion. From time to time, we are better off acknowledging that the ship has sailed (or sunk), and that chasing it down or salvaging it is more costly than building a new one. Sometimes the powerful choice is to fold the bad hand and deal some new cards. Sometimes it is getting up from the game entirely and finding a new one. If you think I am still just talking about the business venture mentioned previously and not a universal principle, please reconsider.

Giving in can also mean pivoting. It is not giving *up* on the destination; it is acknowledging that the current path isn't getting us there, and perhaps it is time to alter course. Giving in may feel as if we've *lost the battle*—and perhaps we have, but in owning this reality, we can powerfully recalibrate to create circumstances that will *win the war*.

SUMMARY | ID 13

Identifying whether or not releasing something truly serves us.

Giving up and giving in both sound a lot like *quitting*; but are they?

Giving Up can cut two ways:
1. It can demonstrate a lack of conviction and integrity, as in failing to complete an endeavor after committing to it, or it can demonstrate the maintaining of our personal integrity when involving the release or liberation of something, someone, or ourselves—that either does not serve, never has served, or no longer serves us.
2. Giving up something that has no inherent value, or somebody whom we allow to control us, is quite different. The former corrodes our integrity while the latter illustrates giving up something *without losing anything*. Quitting smoking, drinking, drugs, or other vices, or giving up a role we play, like being taken advantage of, abused, or exploited, stand in stark contrast.

Giving In is releasing our *attachment* to the way we think things need to go. For example, choosing to let go of our attachment to being right is *giving in*. Giving in does not mean caving or succumbing; it means *choosing powerfully* not to meet a person in toxic waters again and again if this is where they insist on swimming.

ID 14: Shades of Consent

Compromise | Negotiation | Sacrifice | Being Compromised | Appeasement

> *Ahhh compromise . . . the art of slicing a cake in such a way that each child believes they have received the biggest piece.* ~Unknown

JUST AS THERE EXISTS THE CONCEPT OF INALIENABLE RIGHTS, there also exist ideals that emanate from elevated consciousness simply not subject to compromise: *Our values. Our principles. Our integrity*. This distinction brings attention to the different ways we approach circumstances in life when discord, disputes, and friction arise. It has much to do with what we are willing to compromise, what is produced as a result, what that compromise costs, and whom it benefits. When we read the distinctions in context one after another, we can begin to extract the powerful subtleties.

Let's begin with *compromise* and *negotiation*. While both seek a resolution that everyone agrees upon, each proceeds in a markedly different way.

Compromise is an agreement approached from a perspective where making concessions for the benefit of all outweighs parsing gains and losses for each individual side. The distinction is in the *approach*, whereby everyone is committed to *pulling in the same direction* to find resolution for the benefit of all. The shared vision is commonly long-sighted, tonally reflecting the added effort of investing in a long-term relationship.

Negotiation is a process where, distinctively, each party is pulling in opposite directions. This doesn't mean the parties are not mutually trying to create resolution or open to making concessions. *They are*, or they wouldn't be negotiating. In a negotiation, however, both parties parse gains and losses by employing tactics and strategies with the purpose of giving up as little as possible for as much gain as possible. Each side tries to hold onto its gains at the expense of the other side relinquishing theirs—resulting in a commensurate loss. The focus is often short-sighted, where emphasis on completing the transaction is the objective, placing little or no value, effort, or interest in cultivating a long-term relationship.

Continuing with the other distinctions in this grouping:

Sacrifice is when what we give up costs us dearly or leaves us depleted while another benefits.

Being Compromised is what happens to one side when the other side establishes a tactical advantage, is emboldened by overstepping its boundaries, or takes from the first side, leaving it depleted.

Appeasement is when the one being compromised is aware or made aware that this is happening and is still willing to participate. Due to the complicity of the willing party, more extreme cases of appeasement risk fostering and perpetuating an environment of entitlement to the other party.

Compromise embraces the notion that when all parties come together for the greater good, they achieve more, even if there is some short-term dispensation. It is about keeping focused on the long game, the "whole" being viewed as having more value than the "sum of the parts." Compromise happens when the focus moves beyond the challenge at hand and becomes more about establishing an environment for continued betterment for all, not only now but well into the foreseeable future. It could be said that with compromise there exists a social return on investment in addition to merely the divvying up of material things. What's interesting is that as the relationship builds over time, so does consensus, interdependence, and intimacy. As a result, the effort required to maintain an environment that invites compromise typically decreases as the confluence of like-mindedness increases. Compromise emanating from elevated consciousness inspires consensus and cultivates sacred space where trust, dignity, and self-respect exist for the benefit of all.

SUMMARY | ID 14

The nuances of conflict resolution.

Just as there exists the concept of inalienable rights, there also exist ideals that emanate from elevated consciousness simply not subject to compromise: *Our values. Our principles. Our integrity*.

Compromise is an agreement approached from a perspective where making concessions for the benefit of all outweighs parsing gains and losses for each individual side. The distinction is in the *approach*, whereby everyone is committed to *pulling in the same direction* to find resolution for the benefit of all. The shared vision is commonly long-sighted, tonally reflecting the added effort of investing in a long-term relationship.

Negotiation is a process where, distinctively, each party is pulling in opposite directions. This doesn't mean the parties are not mutually trying to create resolution or open to making concessions. *They are*, or they wouldn't be negotiating. In a negotiation, however, both parties parse gains and losses by employing tactics and strategies with the purpose of giving up as little as possible for as much gain as possible.

Sacrifice is when what we give up costs us dearly or leaves us depleted while another benefits.

Being Compromised is what happens to one side when the other side establishes a tactical advantage, is emboldened by overstepping its boundaries, or takes from the first side, leaving it depleted.

Appeasement occurs when the one being compromised is aware or made aware that this is happening and is still willing to participate.

ID 15: Culpability

*I know you didn't do it on purpose,
but you didn't do enough
to make sure it didn't happen by accident.*

THE DISTINCTION BETWEEN *not on purpose* and *by accident* stands on the noble virtues of compassion, understanding, and forgiveness. This distinction was a sleeper for me, then one day struck me like a bolt of lightning. The story of how that happened involved a fellow Aikido practitioner, Andy, a gregarious, well-intended guy about twenty years my senior and, at the time, blackbelt-ranked notably higher than I.

In Aikido, we practice techniques in partners, switching around so that, eventually, everyone trains with everyone else. Naturally, this meant that I would get partnered with Andy from time to time. In a mixed-level class, it is common that one practitioner will outrank the other. When this happens, it is the duty of the higher-ranking practitioner to determine the limitations of the lower-ranked partner and practice at the level commensurate to their ability. Both are to practice with temperance, but it is beholden on the practitioner with more experience to find and not step over this line. Despite Andy's friendly nature, my training with him regularly resulted in injury. What always followed the mishap was Andy's consolation, expressed through compelling sincerity and concern: "Ohhh, are you all right? Oh, shoot, that's *gotta* hurt. So sorry!"

Every time this happened, my inner critic stepped in, kicking me while I was down, insisting that it was *my* fault because Andy was a second-degree black belt; if not for my inexperience, my voice told me, this would not have happened. The reason I was injured was probably because *I*, and not Andy, had screwed up.

This was my prevailing, harsh inner-voice—even though, when the tables were turned and *I* outranked somebody, I viewed this solemn duty of protecting well-being as sacred. But when it came to me and Andy, I somehow thought it was *my* responsibility. How inequitable our inner critics can be!

Despite my being convinced of his regret every time for these incidents having occurred, this same scenario just kept on happening.

Over time, despite my nature to forgive, a growing resentment brewed inside of me. (Hey! It friggin' hurt!!!) Something just wasn't right.

This is typical of when something happens *not on purpose* as opposed to *by accident*: The incident is followed by a sincere, genuine apology and an appeal for forgiveness—which is customary to give—and we carry on. But often, something in us knows it is not okay, and resentment grows. It wasn't until years later, as I experienced this broken record repeating in other areas of my life, that this valuable distinction was illuminated.

> **Not on purpose** means unintentional. It means you didn't anticipate it or plan for it.
>
> **By accident** means there was no clear fault; the circumstances, as presented, provided no reasonable way to avoid it happening.

Just because we don't intend something to happen doesn't mean it wasn't our fault. The circumstance, while not intentional, was a result of not being *intentional enough*. It resulted as a deficit in investing the requisite time or foresight to ensure it *didn't* happen.

It is completely understandable and conceivable that inadvertent, one-off mistakes that cause injury happen on occasion when practicing martial arts. If it is a sincere accident, no matter how well-intentioned and nice the person is, we take into account how and why it happened, become vigilant, and redouble our effort to ensure that it doesn't happen again. But when adequate precaution and responsibility are not addressed and the same situation keeps occurring, after a while, it becomes inexcusable. The subtle distinction that hides in plain sight from the person seeking forgiveness is their lack of responsibility for holding up their end of the deal.

Seeing this distinction for what it is reconciles our inner conflict when our forgiving nature contradicts our boundaries. It restores our sanity by liberating us from feeling the injury is our fault.

SUMMARY | ID 15

Oops, I did it again!

This distinction was originally called: "I know you didn't do it on purpose, but you didn't do enough to make sure it didn't happen by accident." *The distinction between* not on purpose *and* by accident *stands on the noble virtues of compassion, understanding, and forgiveness.*

Not on purpose means unintentional. It means you didn't anticipate it or plan for it.

By accident means there was no clear fault; the circumstances, as presented, provided no reasonable way to avoid it happening. Just because we don't intend something to happen doesn't mean it wasn't our fault. Be conscious when a circumstance, while not intentional, results from not being *intentional enough*.

CHAPTER 6

Distinctions of Personal Sovereignty

ID 16: Responsibility | Accountability | Blame

We cannot control the circumstances the universe serves up. What we can control is our attitude, conduct, and response to the circumstance. ~Tony Dungy

Responsibility is our duty to take a given action or nonaction (not taking any action at all is considered a form of action and can make one complicit, especially when inaction results in harmful consequences to another or to oneself.)

Accountability is the ownership of any ramifications that result from the taking of that given action or inaction.

Blame is assigned after the fact, when it is too late to *be* responsible...so, instead, someone is *held* responsible.

THE PURPOSE OF MAKING THIS DISTINCTION is to provide context for each of these things in relationship to the others. We commonly witness the thwarting of responsibility, seeing it passed along to another in an effort to avoid embarrassment or punishment. We witness people avoiding responsibility like Ebola, either by pretending the situation does not exist or tossing it to another as if playing hot potato. Often, the tool used to do this is blame.

We each have responsibility for the things that happen in our lives. Like all chores in life, if we don't take on the task and pull our own weight, we are ultimately just placing that responsibility on another's shoulders. This is a law of physics: the law of conservation. Stuff doesn't just vanish into the ether. If we don't wash the dishes in the sink, they begin to pile up. We run out of clean dishes and the space to prepare and eat future meals. Next, the dirty dishes begin to stink, ants and other bugs arrive on the scene, and the place becomes a pig sty, then a toxic hazard, and is eventually condemned . . . until someone comes along and shoulders the task to clean it all up.

This is an example of responsibility. But, you may ask, how can we be responsible when someone else is to blame? Let's look at this through the lens of elevated consciousness. Elevated consciousness thrives in the gaining of perspective above the circumstance, not in merely assigning blame or judging within the circumstance. Punitive actions have their place in courts of law, principals' offices, and HR departments; they are not to be ignored, but they are transactional. They focus only on one element within the circumstance—bringing the perpetrator to justice. When we elevate above the circumstance, there exists a space for resolution where all parties, both afflicted and accountable, bear responsibility.

An elevated perspective does not judge the circumstance in terms of right and wrong, good or bad, as such. Conscious Intelligence introduces a perspective where the circumstance just is. It is completely possible to *own up* to a circumstance while possessing no design or control over it. The elevation of consciousness involves changing our relationship to our circumstances, including painful ones, by changing our perspective about them. Changing our perspective does not mean ignoring or pretending circumstances away; it involves choosing how we allow them to affect us.

In changing our relationship to a circumstance, we can disallow it from having power over us. We can elevate above the circumstance—beyond the realm of blame and victimization, for example. Elevated perspective reminds us that we cannot always control the circumstances we find ourselves in, but we are ultimately responsible for ourselves and our conduct within them. We risk dwelling in the realm of victimization until we own our circumstances, especially the ones we have no design in. The perspective doesn't conflate what happens on the outside with what defines us on the inside; it is an understanding that what happens to us has little or nothing to do with what defines us, *unless we allow it to*. We are defined by what we do and by the responsibility we take while conducting ourselves. When we take responsibility in this manner, we bestow ownership of our circumstances upon ourselves and to nobody else. Others may do the same, but it is not up to us to make that determination or insist on them to do so.

> *The best way out, is through.* ~Robert Frost

When we choose to step over, deny, dwell, or blame others in an attempt to quell painful circumstances, we relinquish our personal sovereignty and become both unaccountable and irresponsible. Some go further by seeking remedies as a means to shoulder the intense, unrequited emotions. Engaging in further measures to artificially numb, fog, or medicate in an attempt to run away, deny, or bury our head is called *escapism*. Clearly, upon our return to reality, either physically, mentally, and/or psychotropically, we discover that the circumstance is right where we left it—still requiring our addressing.

> *You cannot change the circumstances, the seasons, or the wind, but you can change yourself.* ~Jim Rohn

"Sure," you may say, "it's all fun and games until someone loses an eye." Let's say someone does (lose an eye). A child in a classroom loses an eye because another child decided it was fun to toss sharp pencils around the classroom. After blame is assigned, someone is identified as responsible, and they are punished and held accountable. It is, of course, important to identify the source of what went wrong so it can be resolved and prevented from happening again.

What is the Invisible Distinction here? Let's unpack it.

All of the settlement money, surgery, occupational therapy, detention for the culprit, public restitution, etc.—even outlawing pencils—will not regain the eyesight of the one who lost the eye. What does an elevated perspective look like? It identifies the inflictions and accountability to be had in the entirety of the circumstance, by all involved. The calamity affected *all* parties; in the bigger picture, each was injured. The child whose eye was harmed in the circumstance must move past any victimization, frustration, or blaming for their new condition if they wish to shed the infliction. While the child is innocent, they are permitted to feel all of these things. While they are not accountable for what happened to them, they must take accountability for this new normal. The child must account for their new set of conditions if they wish to elevate above the circumstance and shed the suffering that resulted when the infliction occurred. Only the resilience of the child can act as the fuel that elevates them. Moving into elevated consciousness involves taking the responsibility for how things are now, forgiving the culprit, and, if need be, forgiving oneself. It means letting go of any resentment and finding peace within. Without this, there is no chance for the true healing to begin or for suffering to end.

What of the child who threw the pencil? They are accountable for what happened. But there's more. What of their suffering? Unless they are a sociopath, there is likely deep guilt, anguish, internal strife, and suffering too—or, if they meant to inflict harm, some sort of serious, psychological issue. The child is faced with the solemn duty of self-resolution and self-forgiveness either way, and that's not easy. This child, too, must forgive themselves, repent, and find inner peace again.

There's more…Conscious Intelligence in this circumstance expands to include several more parties. The parents, the teacher, the principal. What of their pain in feeling they failed to protect the children? For them as well, the struggle to find inner peace and inner forgiveness is a challenging path they must endure in order to find resolution and shed the weight of inner suffering.

The only way out is through.

So, we come full circle, and again I pose the question: How can we be responsible even if another is held completely to blame? To blame is to find fault. Blaming and finding fault has punitive results for certain; at best, it punishes the wrongdoer. On a level of dispensing justice, this may prove necessary. But blame and finding fault contribute *nothing* towards remedying the injuries or transforming the circumstances of the afflicted (*all* who are afflicted).

Most forms of punishment don't teach responsibility but rather dispense shame and summon one to serve penance. Blame does little to resolve the underlying cause of a circumstance, cultivate forgiveness, or inspire resiliency. Until all parties—trespassers and those trespassed upon—own responsibility for their part, elevation above the circumstance cannot be attained.

SUMMARY | ID 16

An ounce of culpability, a pound of accountability.

We commonly witness the thwarting of responsibility, seeing it passed along to another in an effort to avoid embarrassment or punishment. We witness people avoiding responsibility either by pretending the situation does not exist or tossing it to another as if playing hot potato. Often, the tool used to do this is blame. We each have responsibility for the things that happen in our lives. Like all chores in life, if we don't take on the task, we are ultimately just placing that responsibility onto another's shoulders. When we choose to step over, deny, dwell, or blame others in an attempt to avoid circumstances, we relinquish our personal sovereignty, become unaccountable, irresponsible, and disempowered. Conscious Intelligence introduces a perspective where the circumstance just is. It is completely possible to *own up* to a circumstance while possessing no design or control over its occurrence. Changing our relationship to our circumstances by changing our perspective about them paves the way to a new option: choosing how we allow the circumstances to affect us.

ID 17: Justice | Revenge | Mercy

We can have no influence over those for whom we have underlying contempt. ~Martin Luther King Jr.

Justice and Revenge

In an ancient story of Japan, a great Samurai warrior is summoned by his overlord to deliver justice to the murderer of the overlord's wife(as by the codes of law at the time and culture). The revered Samurai soon tracks down the culprit and has him cornered. The warrior draws his sword and is moments away from dispensing justice when the murderer, in the pure terror of his impending fate, spits in the Samurai's face. The Samurai sheaths his sword and walks away.

Why did he do that? The story is a lesson about the hazards of clinging to our anger and how a warrior's code forbids him to act out of dishonorable self-interest if he wishes to walk an elevated path. The act made the warrior angry. The killing of his adversary would have become an act of personal revenge driven by his ego, rather than an act of justice dispensed without prejudice.

This story makes the distinction between *justice* and *revenge* in the context of one's personal commitment to an elevated code of conduct.

Revenge is sourced from an emotionally reactive order and stands in dire contrast to *justice*. Left unresolved, injustices can ferment internally and corrode us from the inside. They can evoke strong, desirous emotions and hamper one's ability to bridle their anger. Some allow themselves to be triggered to act out, foregoing any restraint that could allow reason and rationale to prevail.

The yearning for revenge evolves from the same place addiction does. Just as another cigarette, drink, or piece of chocolate only temporarily satisfies our void within, so too do solutions that involve revenge. Revenge does little to address the real cause or underlying ailment. In reality, nothing located outside us can fill a void sourced and manifested internally. Such a void can be eradicated only from within.

We cannot control what the universe doles out to us, but we can control how we conduct ourselves when it does. We realize that revenge is a toxic, misguided, and false form of justice motivated by emotions left unchecked: anger, hatred, and fear. It can serve only as short-lived gratification and move us further from any semblance of balance, harmony, and civility.

Mercy

> *Mercy is what you give people who don't deserve it.*
> *~Bryan Stevenson*

BRYAN STEVENSON, a professor of law at New York University Law School, an author, and the executive director of the Equal Justice Initiative, has done extensive work with death row inmates, both those who are guilty and those who later have been found to be innocent. He describes how the places where we are truly freed from the clutches of the wounds inflicted upon us are located deep within ourselves, and how we can free ourselves only from within.

> *Human beings are more than just a crime they commit. There is strength, a power even, in understanding brokenness, because embracing our brokenness creates a need and desire for mercy, and perhaps a corresponding need to show mercy. We begin to recognize the humanity that resides in each of us.*

Elevating our consciousness is not as much about pointing out the flaws in others as it is about disallowing those flaws to live, grow, and metastasize within ourselves. Holding onto hate, anger, and pain does precisely that. The clinging onto these toxins poisons us from within; the poison oozes out into other areas of our lives where it serves neither ourselves nor others.

What about people who have committed truly heinous acts, whether they have been convicted, held accountable, atoned (or not); whether they are serving a life sentence or perhaps are no longer even alive? How do we reconcile such trespass?

On some levels, we don't. We can't. We needn't.

The distinction between accept versus condone holds up in these extremes as well. It's called *mercy*. One of the most powerful dimensions we humans are gifted with is our unique capacity for compassion and empathy—to walk in another's shoes and to feel another's pain.

To recognize both our and others' humanity, even of those who have committed trespasses, is to find mercy. Approaching these and other irreconcilable circumstances with this level of humanity is to recognize a fundamental component of elevated consciousness.

SUMMARY | ID 17

We are all human even when struck by the shadows of inhumanity.

Revenge stands in dire contrast to justice. The yearning for revenge evolves from the same place addiction does. Just as another drink, hit, or piece of chocolate only temporarily satisfies the void within ourselves, so, too, do solutions that involve revenge. Left unresolved, injustices can ferment internally and corrode us from the inside, much like our drinking poison yet expecting the other person to die. Revenge does little to address the real cause. We can have no influence over those for whom we have underlying contempt. We are truly freed from the clutches of the wounds inflicted upon us when we free ourselves from allowing those people to negatively infect us. We demonstrate our resilience in our striving to understand brokenness, because embracing our brokenness creates a desire to show mercy. When we do this, we begin to recognize the humanity that resides in each of us.

ID 18: Anger versus Resentment

> **Anger** is an outward emotional expression about inner feelings of disappointment, frustration, or conflict. It is a natural and powerful emotion.

Anger is also the second of the five steps of the grieving process: *denial, anger, bargaining, depression, and acceptance.* The interplay of the grieving process with respect to some of the distinctions has a powerful role and will be illuminated periodically. For now, it is important to make clear that the grieving process doesn't happen only after someone dies. A form of grieving results during every significant change in our lives, such as quitting a job, moving away, or even dieting. As the term indicates, these steps are a *process*, meaning that we move through them. We advance until we reach the other side. Likewise, anger is also a process. Undisrupted, it runs its course and plays its part as a natural, human process.

Anger helps us communicate to others that boundaries have been crossed or that we are struggling with a perceived injustice. When dispensed in sensible doses, anger is tolerable and considered reasonable to those around us when the source is understood and justified, such as when one is grieving.

We are accountable for our anger. Blaming another for our anger demonstrates a lack of ownership and accountability, just as yelling at seeds to make them grow demonstrates a lack of proper crop-cultivating skills. Blaming others for our anger causes the irritant to persist. All the while we remain stuck, looking onto a barren landscape that is neither productive nor fertile. While we can't always consciously avoid circumstances that result in the expression of anger, what we *can* do is distinguish whether it is serving us as it passes through or serving some deeper affliction and persisting.

It is healthy to express inner hurt by exhaling our pain and disappointment. Anger allows us to discharge the build-up of pressure and emotion and relieve the burden weighing heavily upon our chests—as can a good cry, screaming into a pillow, or, my favorite, a good workout. Mindful practices like yoga, meditation, and breath work teach us to calm our minds, get out in front before the pressure builds, and help us mitigate anger when it risks lingering and becoming a source of chronic suffering.

Anger becomes a deeper affliction when it remains unresolved, turns into blame and vilification, and is projected towards others. Anger ceases to serve us when projected or mixed with deeper psychological ailments, especially when entangled with abusive behavior. It also does not serve us when repressed. Compounded over time, unexpressed anger can boil over, resulting in projection and passive-aggressive behavior, and can degrade into resentment.

> *Holding onto anger is like drinking poison*
> *and expecting the other person to die.* ~Unknown

> **Resentment** stems from an enduring attachment to anger. It is toxic and corrodes the insides of those who cling to it. A central philosophy commonly attributed to Buddhism is the tenet that attachment breeds suffering; resentment, as a form of attachment, is a glaring example of this. Over time, resentment festers into a cancerous cluster that metastasizes and grows, commandeering the internal weather within us. Before long, it takes control of our conduct and weaves itself into the fabric of who we are being.

The objective here is two-fold: to make distinctions around the sourcing and expression of anger so that we can gain perspective, and to identify when anger crosses into areas where it is misunderstood or misconceived. Observing the affirmative sides of anger while understanding the source of resentment is a powerful navigational tool of elevating consciousness. When we cling to anger, it devolves into resentment. Like any other persistent injury, its corrosive properties begin to morph and shape us—who we are being and how we occur to others and show up in the world. As conscious observers, we can gain perspective by identifying circumstances where we get stuck, catch ourselves when we are off the beam, marinating in dark negativity, and, in doing so, effectively navigate back onto the beam and into the light.

SUMMARY | ID 18

Shout, shout, let it all out...

Anger is a natural, outward emotional expression about inner feelings of disappointment, frustration, or conflict. Anger becomes a deeper affliction when it remains unresolved, turns into blame and vilification, and is projected toward others. Anger ceases to serve us when projected or mixed with deeper psychological ailments, especially when entangled with abusive behavior. It also does not serve us when repressed. Compounded over time, unexpressed anger can boil over, resulting in projection and passive-aggressive behavior, and can degrade into resentment. Resentment stems from an enduring attachment to anger. It is toxic and corrodes the insides of those who cling to it. Before long, it takes control of our conduct and weaves itself into the fabric of who we are being.

ID 19: Disappointment

THERE EXISTS A DISTINCTION between *having* disappointment and *being* a disappointment, between disappointing someone and being a disappointment to someone. Do you hear the difference? With this distinction, just saying it out loud makes it clear. Yet it is not uncommon to witness this distinction being collapsed on a regular basis. The repercussions can be devastating, especially to an unsuspecting, impressionable youth.

A stark example happened while I was coaching Junior Lifeguards, a program that prepares kids to train, try out, and become ocean lifeguards. The junior lifeguard program is much more than merely physical training and lifesaving drills; it emphasizes leadership development, teamwork, and self-esteem. The cadets memorize a saying that constitutes the backbone of the program, "*IT takes four Cs*: Integrity, Teamwork, Community, Commitment, Courage, Caring."

This particular morning, we were doing drills called *ins and outs* on the beach. This particular drill includes a progression of runs in the soft sand up the coastline, transitioning to swim sprints through the surf out around a buoy and back in...and then repeating the whole sequence several times.

One of the smaller kids, Kyle, was not as physically developed yet as most of the other kids, and he would struggle a bit on the physical drills, often finishing among the slower kids. However, on practical and written tests, first aid drills, and academic-related activities, he always posted among the highest marks.

One morning, he became especially frustrated at falling behind the bigger kids in the physical drills. Out of frustration and anguish, he appeared to trip one of them on the run (unconfirmed), and then, moments later, he cut the buoy swim by ducking under the water halfway out, taking a U-turn underwater, and blending in at the finish among the returning kids in the lead. I saw this but said nothing—initially. Instead, the normal fanfare and high fives went around among the first kids out of the water, Kyle among them this time. The others were surprised and not necessarily buying the legitimacy of his stellar performance.

Later, when the kids were on break, I pulled Kyle aside and congratulated him for such a fast swim to see what he would say. He was quiet—and thankfully, as kids do so well, he acted conspicuously guilty. I maintained a neutral facial expression, hoping he'd confess on his own without my prompting. He didn't. With mock curiosity, I inquired about how he was able to make such a precipitous improvement, posting such a fast time. Looking down at the ground, unwavering, he mumbled, "I dunno," completely avoiding any direct eye contact.

Finally, I professed, "Ya know, Kyle, out of all the kids, you are the last one I'd expect would choose to cut the course to falsely come in ahead of your teammates. I admit I am disappointed."

He looked away, teared up, and said, "I'm sorry I'm such a disappointment." As he stood there, his frustration and guilt visibly turned into a watershed of upset. He had obviously had a long build-up of feelings of inadequacy about his performances in the physical events…and, likely, also about other activities in his life.

After a time of letting him exhale and purge this feeling, I replied, "Kyle, I said that I am disappointed, not that *you* are a disappointment. There is a huge difference. Do you hear the difference?"

He looked up at me, noticeably processing.

I continued, "You made a *disappointing choice* in cheating the course, then another one by being untruthful to me about it. Those choices don't mean that *you* are a disappointment. Indeed, what a person does consistently in their life defines who they are. A couple of poorly chosen mistakes do not define that human being as a mistake. The person you ultimately cheated is yourself, and for that, I was disappointed because that conduct does not reflect your true character—at least the person I see you being committed to each day. Is it? If you learned this today, we both can consider this day and this circumstance a success. Do you hear the difference?"

He looked up, drying his eyes, and in his own time replied, "Yes, sir."

"Now, Kyle," I continued, "you know there's something left to do here, right?"

Kyle nodded. He went to join his compatriots with purpose in his walk. He confessed and apologized to his fellow teammates, acknowledging that his conduct prevented the other members of his team from getting their deserved credit for their achievement, and for that, he was sorry.

The kids were so heartening and receptive. They knew he struggled in the physical events; they were out there and witnessed it. They knew Kyle, and they sensed his frustration. In this moment, one could see and feel a shift in the group from anger at the injustice to empathy and forgiveness. They gave him pats on the back and were done with it. I heard one kid say to him, tongue in cheek, "Help me with the first-aid practicals, Doctor Kyle, and we'll call it even."

And, to close out the story, Kyle had a growth spurt later that year, and returned the following summer. He chalked up several wins in the physical training exercises and became a team captain. When he turned eighteen, he qualified for and graduated from the academy, and went on to excel as a stellar addition to our Ocean Rescue Response Team.

It torments me to know that some children (and adults) conflate this distinction, *having disappointment versus being a disappointment*, never understanding the difference. They grow up actually believing the latter. Kyle made me so proud; he couldn't be further from being a disappointment. It is my belief that making the distinction with him that one day likely changed his trajectory and how he viewed stumbles and losses in his life—not as brick walls, but as springboards.

SUMMARY | ID 19

What a bummer, or is it just me?

There exists a distinction between *having* disappointment and *being* a disappointment, between disappointing someone and being a disappointment to someone. The former is a transitory mishap; the latter can cripple and derail the entire trajectory of one's life who believes this about themselves.

There exists a distinction between *experiencing* disappointment and *being* a disappointment, between disappointing someone and being a disappointment to someone. People who suffer disappointment experience a transitory mishap. To *be* a disappointment to someone can cripple and derail the entire trajectory of the life of someone who believes this is who they are.

ID 20: Shades of Shame

Shame | Guilt | Humiliation | Embarrassment | Regret | Remorse | Sorry

> *Let he who is without sin cast the first stone.*
> *~King James Bible*

FEW AFFLICTIONS ARE KNOWN to be more debilitating than shame. Shame can be insidiously debilitating, and it afflicts all of us in one way or other. Understanding the distinctions around shame and its siblings can move us into a more elevated perspective. It can facilitate a deeper understanding of what afflicts our ability to live more consciously. It can forge a path out of the dark, downward spiral of shame and lead us upward, through the thick fog, back into the light.

Shame takes many forms and can weave its way into our daily lives without our even being aware. It's contracted through our upbringing, instilled by our culture, learned from our peers, teachers, family, or the media, and ingested in countless other ways throughout our lives. See if any of these sounds familiar:

> We don't talk about *that*.
> I don't deserve to be…happy, successful, loved…
> Something is wrong with me that I don't want others to find out.
> Maybe they were right about me, about my unworthiness, my problem, my deficiency.
> I am inadequate.
> I'm so stupid; I never should have made that mistake.
> I don't want anyone to know how little money I make.
> I should have accomplished more by my age.
> I should be more desired/thinner/adored/stronger.
> I don't know how to talk to people, I'm not good at being social, so I don't ever go out.
> My friends are so much more accomplished and have more success than I do.

My life is so boring and mundane compared to everyone else.

I don't want anyone to see me in a bathing suit.

The distinctions of shame and its siblings naturally divide into contrasting pairs. Each pair has one sibling representing a growth opportunity where elevation can be thought of as an upward spiral, and one representing its sibling's dark shadow that plunges us into a devolving, self-consuming, downward spiral. Recognizing the distinction between these pairs literally dictates whether we live every day forging a path of empowerment and connection or one of despair and isolation.

SHADES & SPIRALS OF SHAME

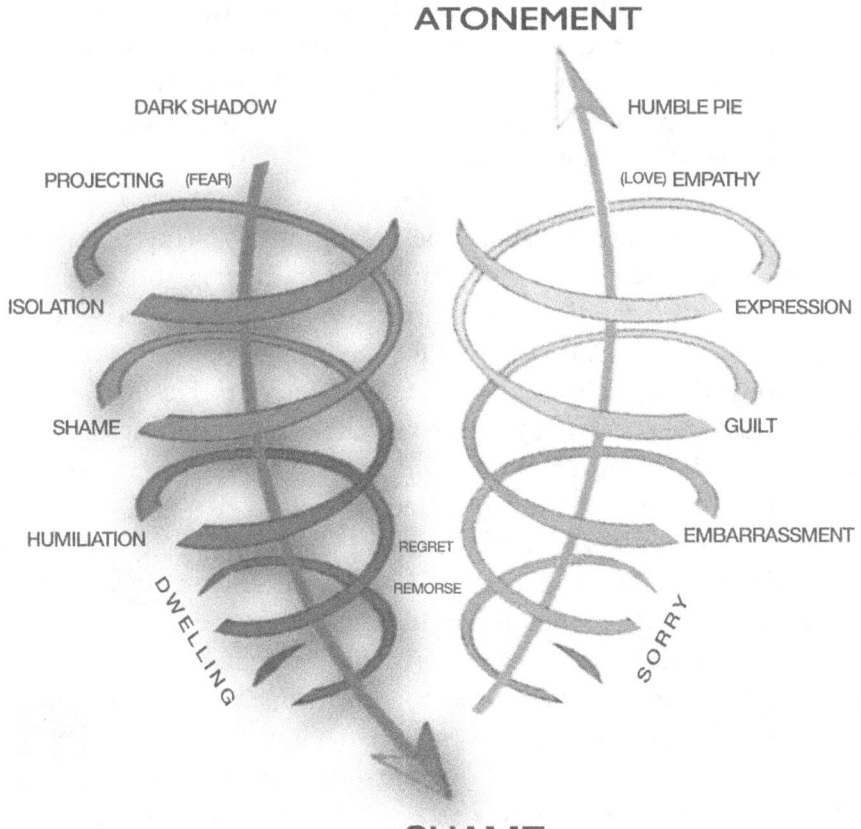

Let's look at each of these pairings more closely, keeping in mind that the first one in the pairing is the one that offers the opportunity to elevate, while the second confines us and leads us to descend into the darkness of shame.

Guilt versus Shame

Guilt shows up in our self-talk as "I *did something* bad/wrong/stupid." The act, despite how egregious, nor whether it was actually bad/wrong/stupid, doesn't really matter. What matters is that the act is perceived as something we *did (or neglected to do)*.

Shame shows up in our self-talk as "I *am* bad/wrong/stupid." It is the intensely painful feeling that we are unworthy of love and belonging. We internalize this into our psyche as a way of being, and therefore incorporate the perception into our identity: this is *who I am* versus merely *something I did*.

BOTH GUILT AND SHAME share the feeling of deserving blame or a sense of inadequacy for having committed an offense. It is important to note that this is true whether the offense was real or perceived.

Guilt, in this pairing, provides for the growth opportunity to spiral us upward, as it allows us to stand outside ourselves to gain perspective. In this *space*, we can observe that we messed things up while also recognizing that *we, and the messed up thing, are not one and same*. In reality, they are not conflated.

Shame, on the other hand, is the dark shadow. It is rooted in our fear of disconnection, isolation, and perceived unworthiness. Unlike the space for growth that guilt provides, shame provides none. Rather, it is emboldened by the belief, "*I am alone.*" Secrecy, silence, isolation, and judgment provide fuel for shame to metastasize—and, in these conditions, it will. For these reasons, shame is commonly *a dirty little secret, an unmentionable,* or a *"we just don't talk about that."* Shame embeds in our identity. It acts as a catalyst to cultivate depression, addiction, eating disorders, bullying, hate crimes, and violence. It causes self-loathing and stress, which contribute to a whole host of physiological afflictions such as exhaustion, sleep disorders, high blood pressure, accelerated aging, cardiovascular disease, stroke, and other stress-induced disorders.

The remedy: Shame cannot survive empathy; it cannot survive our exhaling to someone who holds the space for us, warts and all, to express our vulnerability as a path to atonement. Exhaling to another means someone who supports us—not despite our vulnerability but because of it. It can be a beloved friend, a professional individual, a group or an organization, or a member of the clergy. It is why support groups, therapy, and programs such as Alcoholics Anonymous are successful. They provide an audience of support and safety for us to exhale to another who has earned trust and confidence in our sharing. This remedy illuminates the distinction between the *wound* and *us*, that we are not the wound, that it is separate and not a part of our overall identity. Once we distinguish that we are not defined by our circumstances, we can move into acknowledging the mishap. We can apologize, make amends, forgive ourselves, and move out of the dark shadows back into the light.

Embarrassment versus Humiliation

THE DISTINCTION BETWEEN these two depends upon how we process the circumstance. Both embarrassment and humiliation begin the same way—with an *oops* or a foible of some kind. How we process the foible determines which sibling will appear. Will it be an upward spiral or downward one?

For both of these, the jaunt begins when we do something, or are attributed with doing something, that we most commonly perceive as stupid, bad, or wrong. Whether this action actually *is* any of these is not relevant; what matters is that we perceive it as such. (Note: Clearly, the word "stupid" is harsh and judgmental. I employ it here intentionally to help illustrate the distinction.)

When we do something we perceive as stupid, both embarrassment and humiliation conjure the same initial response: our own inner critic, or an outside critic, launches an attempt to shame us for it. But what happens next is where the distinction is made.

The distinction between embarrassment and humiliation comes from whether we know better than to allow "that stupid thing we did" to define us, or whether we allow ourselves to be defined by launched assaults of shaming by others. When we allow the projection of shame from another to land, humiliation results. When we disallow a shame assault to land, the result is embarrassment. How we choose to allow an assault to land determines whether we spiral downward, bathing in shame and humiliation, or spiral upward with a dose of humble pie, digesting the character-building nutrients of guilt and embarrassment.

> In **embarrassment**, we are present of mind to *know better* than to take the foible to mean that *it is us*. It is *not* us, nor is it indicative of *who we are*. By not conflating *it with us*, this upward spiral is akin to the other upward spiral, guilt. We *did* something perceived as stupid, as opposed to shame, which translates to we *are* stupid.

> In **humiliation**, however, we allow ourselves to be convinced by others that we *are* stupid. We allow the shaming to land a blow, and therefore become humiliated.

Humiliation is akin to shame: we make it about ourselves, we feel alone and isolated, and we do not make the distinction between *the act of doing* versus *a way of being*. As a result, we spiral downward, piling on more layers of shame and feeling more deeply isolated, until we withdraw completely.

Embarrassment is akin to guilt: When we own the fact that we may have done something stupid but *realize* the act doesn't mean we *are* stupid; we successfully make the distinction between *the act of doing* versus *a way of being*. Whether an attempt to humiliate and shame is sourced from another's cruel intention or our own inner critic, we avoid the mistake of defining ourselves by the act. As a result, we avoid the dark shadows and downward spiral. Instead, by stepping into the light, we own up to the mistake, then account and atone for it. The resultant by-product is guilt or embarrassment. We allow the weight of the circumstance to dissipate, setting us free to ascend back into the sunlight. Without a doubt, these humble pie ingredients can be tough to choke down, but they are short-lived and leave only a temporary bruise rather than a permanent scar.

We have the ability to take a prolific dose of embarrassment on the chin without wearing it there permanently as humiliation. We can make a mistake without being defined by it or permitting another to convince us otherwise. By assessing our mistakes and extracting the lessons, we elevate above our circumstances rather than dwell within them.

Compassion, Even When We Feel Most Vulnerable

HERE IS A POWERFUL and important realization: Another's attempt to shame us is more reflective of *them* than it is of *us*. Being shamed by another is projection where the shame is not ours, but actually sourced deep within the one shaming. Further, such shame often metastasizes into the likes of bullying, violence, abuse, and addiction. Commonly, the shame was introduced to the shamer at some earlier point in *their* life. If we are not careful, the affliction can proliferate like a contagion. When someone chooses to shame another, it is a convenient way to allow their inner shame to rear its ugly head in toxic, passive-aggressive, and inappropriate ways.

When we recognize that another's need to launch an assault is a projection of their deep-seated shame and not our own, we become better equipped to weather the blows. By instinctively knowing that our mistakes don't define us, we grow keenly aware when someone else attempts to convince us otherwise. Most powerful yet, we can open up and feel the other's pain without allowing its transfer. We can open up yet remain vulnerable. Even at a peak moment of embarrassment, we can still have the capacity to offer compassion and empathy to another's shame when we recognize its true source.

When we can stand in a storm of shaming and remain compassionate, we become powerful beacons of strength. Rather than being the ship in the storm that crashes onto the rocks, we become the lighthouse that illuminates the path, offering opportunity for other ships to navigate and course correct.

Regret and Remorse | The Stepchildren

> **Regret** is typically a crisis of conscience about something that, as a result of a choice we made, didn't go well. We can regret a situation that arises either as a consequence of our behavior or passively as a missed opportunity. For example: He regretted not expressing his love for her before his deployment, resulting in her marrying his best friend instead.

WHILE REGRET CAN RESULT from a miscalculated action we took, it can also be the product of inaction that brought harm to others. For example: The boy regretted having been too frightened to jump into the swift river to save the neighbor's pet. Whether or not he forgives himself will determine if this moves down the spiral or up.

If a path to self-forgiveness and atonement is not taken, dwelling in regret can devolve into remorse.

> **Remorse** occurs as a result of dwelling in regret for a prolonged period. Rather than the passing stomachache, it becomes the chronic ulcer. Remorse can come from the persistence of unresolved guilt that degrades into an affliction and ultimately metastasizes into shame.

Shifting the Downward Spiral Upward | Sorry

THERE IS A DISTINCTION between *being sorry* and saying *"I'm sorry."* Shame thrives in deep, dark, unexpressed pits of isolation. We may be sorry for something, but until the trespass is outwardly expressed and addressed, it cannot escape the black hole of shame where it corrodes our insides and manifests itself in toxic ways.

Saying "I'm sorry" to damaged parties when we've hurt them initiates a shift from the dark shadows of shame, upward. It also demonstrates accountability and moves us out of the depths of isolation by giving others an opportunity to offer compassion, empathy, and, if needed, forgiveness. This is atonement. An apology is the proverbial olive branch that we offer not only to others, but also to ourselves to quiet our inner critic. It is releasing the ordeal from the depths of our innards out into the light—ouch—which means we are exposed and can be seen eating our humble pie. While it is never easy, saying "I'm sorry" is profoundly powerful. Creating the space for the purging of grief clears the space of lingering negativity. It allows the witnessing of our vulnerability and our openness to inviting the wronged party to exhale their grief and frustration. *Humility* is a powerful character trait worthy of investment. It is a strong indicator that we are accessing Conscious Intelligence.

SUMMARY | ID 20

Dirty little secrets.

Shame has many forms and can weave its way into our daily lives without our even being aware. The distinctions of shame are divided into contrasting pairs. Each pair has one sibling representing a growth opportunity that provides us a prolific dose of humble pie, and one representing its dark shadow that plunges us into a devolving, self-consuming, downward spiral. Recognizing the distinction between these pairs dictates whether we live every day forging a path of empowerment and connection or one of despair and isolation.

Guilt shows up in our self-talk as "I *did something* bad/wrong/stupid." We acknowledge it as such and realize it does not define who we are.

Shame shows up in our self-talk as "I *am* bad/wrong/stupid." It is the intensely painful feeling that we are unworthy of love and belonging. We internalize this as a way of being and identity: this is *who I am* versus merely *something I did*. Shame emboldens the belief that *"I am alone."* Secrecy, silence, isolation, and judgment provide fuel for shame to metastasize—and, in these conditions, it will. For these reasons, shame is commonly a *dirty little secret, an unmentionable, or a "we just don't talk about that."* The remedy for shame is empathy, shining light on the dark shadow that it is, communicating it, making amends, if required, apologizing—atonement.

Shame cannot survive our exhaling to someone who holds the space for us, warts and all, to express our vulnerability as a path to atonement and outer and inner forgiveness.

Other contrasting pairs respectively:
Dark Shadow: Shame, Humiliation, Dwelling
Humble Pie: Guilt, Embarrassment, Atonement (apologizing)

ID 21: Shades of Dwelling

Dwelling in the Past versus Building on the Past

*Do not dwell in the past
lest we become consumed by it.*

Dwelling in the past is resistance to letting go of circumstances from the past, resulting in the juxtaposing of those circumstances into the present. What results is a clouding and contamination of the lens in the present. Dwelling is a form of attachment. It injects and conflates the present with an unresolved stigma from the past.

Do not forget the past lest we repeat it.
~Unknown, possibly Edmund Burke

Building on the past is extracting the lessons learned from the past so they can contribute affirmatively in the present. When the lessons of the past consciously contribute to the elevation of perspective in the present, they provide great insight and serve us powerfully.

BUILDING ON THE PAST gives us 20/20 hindsight. It calls us to be wise and vigilant of past mistakes by employing our experience and perspective. It compels us to learn from past circumstances, mishandlings, and injustices. Consider such examples as the Holocaust, genocide, slavery, and the Crusades, as well as the fiscal recklessness that caused the 2008 financial meltdown in the US and internationally.

When we become familiarized with signs and recognize patterns from the past, we can avoid repeating costly mistakes and become better for them. That way, when these signs materialize in the present, we are reminded to be vigilant and to proceed cautiously. We use the insights learned from loss, failure, and tragedy to avoid peril again, and as a result, we secure a better outcome.

In contrast, *dwelling in the* past has us holding onto something that isn't serving us. Such things present as corrupted files in the database of our memory. Dwelling can be the opposite of exhaling. It is an insistence that we keep our hooks in. It is the insistence of clinging and attaching, not letting go of wounding circumstances, artifacts, events that long since have proven to be toxic.

When we dwell, a present circumstance triggers a negative memory yet resolved from our past, giving the impression the same thing is happening all over again—and, to a large extent, it is. When we allow a current circumstance to ignite a memory that is saddled with fear, pain, anger, victimization, or shame, we re-live that memory as though it were happening in the moment. When this occurs, we do not distinguish between the present circumstance and the memory from the past, and we react to the current circumstance as we did in the past, with the same feelings of powerlessness and naïveté that we did back then.

Dwelling happens when past events remain traumatic and unresolved—and because this is the case, those who suffered those effects are destined to suffer a similar fate...again! The trauma will continue to travel with the afflicted throughout their life until it is properly resolved, filed appropriately in the past, and no longer juxtaposed into the present.

How do we move past this? By stripping the past circumstance down to a neutral set of facts. The facts can be decoupled from the trauma itself and from the meaning we attached to it. Like a corrupted computer file, we can pull our memory out, locate the corrupted file, make corrections, and swap it back in as a neutral, unstigmatized file. By identifying what we made the circumstance mean, and by acknowledging how we allowed ourselves to be stigmatized by it, objective perspective can be achieved. We can release the stigmatized memory, now properly in context, and return it back into the past. From there, we become present; we re-establish an unburdened, uncorrupted, fresh approach to our present circumstances.

You may recognize some of the names we call this *stuff*: we call it baggage, skeletons in the closet, or self-fulfilling prophesies. All of these represent versions of the injurious stories we haven't yet cleaned up or transformed. It is the ex-spouse who cheats on us and breaks our heart or the ex-business partner who embezzles money from the corporate coffers, leading our fear-fueled egos to tell us we can never trust anyone in any partnership ever again!

We know we are dwelling when we're attached to a certain way of being or thinking. The program continues playing on repeat, we keep finding ourselves in the same quagmires, the same relationships, experiencing the same consternation and pandemonium. Here's what this might sound like:

> Here he goes again.
> This is going to suck.
> She keeps dragging this on.
> This is always the part when it gets difficult.
> Watch out, I've seen this before, it's coming…
> I can't, I have never been able to do that.
> He never listens, will never understand.
> She is so unappreciative.
> He makes things so difficult.
> She is so selfish.

The powerful distinction between *dwelling in* and *building on* is one of different altitudes. *Do not forget the past lest we repeat it* poises us at a thirty-thousand-foot perch, providing perspective and objectivity from above the circumstance. This frees us to remain present in the circumstance. Conversely, the destructive and disempowering version—*do not dwell in the past lest we become consumed by it*—keeps us anchored in the swamps of fear-induced trauma perpetuated from our past. This keeps us revisiting the emotionally charged, muddied waters that we siphoned from a traumatic event from our past.

Still Dwelling? Consider You're Getting Something Out of It

It is challenging to extract oneself from this karmic merry-go-round that dwelling and attachment perpetuate, but here's how we do it: We ask ourselves, "What am I getting out of this?" Our ego voice will say, "Nothing, that's ridiculous," in its own defense. We can, of course, stop the inquiry here, choose to remain inauthentic and continue to self-delude, but we will keep getting what we are getting. Yep, it is that definition of insanity thing: Doing the same thing over and over and expecting different results. Until we acknowledge our resistance, until we are accountable, and until we overcome the resistance to change, we remain blind to the presence of an alternative.

Keeping at the question while insisting there is another way to approach our circumstance will bring perspective. Soldiering forward will quiet the ego voice and allow our essential *Self* to be heard. We discover there is something we are getting out of our dwelling... typically the thing on which we expend the most energy, convincing ourselves it can't possibly be. Acknowledging the predicament is never easy because it is rooted in fear, specifically in our fear of change.

What seems grim initially is, until we face our resistance to what change will bring, we will fear the results we actually want. What will the consequences be for facilitating the change? What will it cost to overcome the resistance? Is this change *really* serving us? These are the stakes. Once we illuminate the thing we are attached to, we expose the fear from which we are required to detach ourselves. Monsters look a lot less scary when standing in broad daylight. We can unveil the sheet from over the monster's head. When we do, we discover it is just the ego sporting a really poor excuse of a costume as it trembles in its own shadow. Releasing our attachment allows the flow of change to break the restrictive chains that confine us to our dwelling. Where we once off-loaded blame, this restores our accountability in the circumstance. It is like: *Ding. The captain has now switched off the "fasten seat belt sign," and you are free to move about your life again.*

Likely extracted from Buddhist philosophy, this insightful quote is an elegant philosophical response to the distinction between *dwelling in* and *building on* the past:

> *In the present, we are our essential Self.*
> *The secret of health for both mind and body is not to mourn the past or anticipate or worry about troubles in the future but to live in the present moment.*

Dwelling versus Grieving

It's okay to look back, just don't stare. ~Doris Roberts

GRIEVING IS A NATURAL and essential part of our human experience. It diverts us onto new paths and facilitates our growth and expansion. Recall, grieving is said to happen in phases, commonly known as the five stages of grieving, which together make up the grieving process: denial, anger, bargaining, depression, acceptance. Recall my recent reference just earlier—the grieving process is commonly attributed to the circumstances around somebody dying, but the multitude of other reasons for grieving extend far beyond the passing of a life. We also experience the five stages of grief in times of drastic change, such as losing or changing jobs, breaking up with a significant other, sending a child to college, walking away from a relationship or habit that doesn't serve us, or even changing our diet. These are circumstances involving change that represent the death of persistent, old ways of being.

Dwelling occurs when we get stuck in our grieving process for too long. It can initiate in any or all of the five stages of grieving. If not addressed, dwelling risks sending us on the downward spiral into, *yep*, here we are again—shame, isolation, and self-imprisonment.

SUMMARY | ID 21

It's okay to look back, just don't stare.

Dwelling in the past is resistance to letting go of circumstances from the past, resulting in the juxtaposing of those circumstances into the present. What results is a clouding and contamination of the lens in the present. Dwelling is a form of attachment. It injects and conflates the present with an unresolved stigma from the past.

Do not dwell in the past lest we become consumed by it.

Building on the past is extracting the lessons learned from the past so they can contribute affirmatively in the present. When the lessons of the past consciously contribute to the elevation of perspective in the present, they provide great insight and serve us powerfully.

Do not forget the past lest we repeat it.

ID 22: Victim/Survivor versus Prevail

> *No one saves us but ourselves.*
> *No one can and no one may.*
> *We ourselves must walk the path* ~Buddha

WHEN ADVERSITY HITS, it seems reasonable at the end of the day that, given a choice, we all would prefer to be crowned survivors and not victims, *but...*

...have you considered that being a survivor still carries with it *victimization*? That *survivor* and *victim* exist as two sides of the same coin? As psychologist Antonio R. Damasio explains it, the condition of survival is born out of the condition of victimhood in the same way that a cure cannot exist without an illness, a solution cannot exist without an equation, and an action has an equal and opposite reaction. For all of these, without the former, the latter cannot exist.

The distinction does not concern itself with where we land on the spectrum of victim/survivor—or even that, once formerly a victim, one proves strong enough to survive.

What is critical is our belief that we must reside on this spectrum *at all*. The belief that survival is the endgame is *itself flawed* because it still has us residing on the spectrum that includes victimization. Survival still carries with it victimization, just as the cure still carries with it the illness—the "tails" side of the coin carries with it the "heads" side. They are inseparable by their very nature.

Prevail | A State of Being, Not A Condition

> *Why merely crawl over the finish line*
> *when we can cross it a champion?*

THE IDEA OF PREVAILING does not refer to prevailing over another or over a trespass, disease, or ailment; it refers to prevailing over the entire circumstance. While surviving is a means of getting over victimization, *prevailing* is a means of getting over the circumstances entirely.

We've all heard the expression "get over it!" This is precisely the point of prevailing, but not in the simple way it's usually meant.

Prevailing is about recognizing that the circumstances need not have any bearing on our internal weather—and, in reality, they *don't*, unless we allow them to. In prevailing, we recognize that *we get to choose* the perspective from which we perceive the circumstances.

> *Ships don't sink because of the water around them;*
> *ships sink because of the water that gets into them.*
> ~Unknown

When we are presented with trying circumstances—a trauma, a disease, a passing weather front—it is not uncommon to experience a misperception and think that the disease *is* us or the trauma *is* us, *as if we and it are one and same*. We collapse the distinction between what we *are* and what is *happening around us or to us*. When we do this, when we conduct ourselves based on this misperception, we perceive we have no choice but to participate inside of it.

The true reality is that the weather front *is not us*. The disease *is not us*. It does not define us; it has nothing to do with us. We and it, on this particular day, just happen to be encountering each other. We may very well be required to hunker down, circumnavigate, perhaps even brace for impact. Sometimes the storm does us in; sometimes the disease does us in. But does it, did it, define us, our circumstances, or our conduct with respect to the trajectory of our lives?

We prevail when we elevate above the circumstances. How is that possible? Well, *prevailing* is *realizing that the something that has adversely affected us, is not us*. In reality, it is *extrinsic*. This distinction is whether we perceive what is happening *to us* as *defining* us, or whether we see it for what it really is—something happening *around* us, *affecting* us. The distinction has to do completely with our perspective and how we choose to be defined by what happened—or in the case of prevail, *not defined* by what happened.

So, prevailing requires we understand that the squall is not commanding the helm of our ship; it is not driving unless we allow it to (or are operating under the pretense that it is). We are merely incidental benefactors of the storm's path, a ship in a storm, and not the storm itself. How we conduct ourselves during the squall ultimately defines us. It determines whether we wash up in pieces on a beach or soundly berth back at our port of call.

By distinction, prevailing eliminates the inappropriate measuring tools we commonly use to keep score. Transactional methods of measure do not exist in the *prevail* realm; it is not measured in haves and have nots, gaining at the expense of another losing, nor the victim and survivor scenario. Rather, it is absent such a binary lens and, as such, remains a state of inner weather untouched by outside conditions.

Prevail | Over Another versus Over Circumstances

If we feel we have prevailed over another,
we simply aren't playing big enough.

FROM AN ELEVATED PERSPECTIVE, prevailing over another is a low order or state because it doesn't account for the empowerment of all parties or really any of the parties at all.

Now, we engage in competition all the time as it is baked into our fundamental, cultural framework—winning a client, a sale, a contract over another firm, a judgment at a trial; receiving an award or acknowledgment from an accredited body. In our cultural tradition, these are examples of how we thrive in our lives. We also love defeating a rival in sport, in a fun bet, at a trivia challenge. There's a reason for this. Symbolic rituals of fighting to win have been in the human tradition for millennia. Back in less civilized times, the Romans used the Colosseum to pit gladiators against each other, *literally* personifying a symbolic ritual by contriving a fight to the death with another in order to feed the people's archetypal urge to prevail over those who threaten conquering them. Such endorphin festivals provided a cathartic rush and stood to represent humankind prevailing over the challenges they faced in their everyday lives.

We still do the same thing today, albeit with significantly reduced casualties, in sports, games, and other challenges where we feed our archetypical yearning for empowerment. Hundreds of millions of us play or watch live sports, or participate in virtual, interactive gaming, to experience the feeling of metaphorically prevailing over the antagonistic forces in our own lives. Prevailing requires us to challenge our inner human spirit to prevail over our fear, our ego, and any other demons of resistance. We create symbolic life acts as a way to practice and sharpen our skills in the event that real life tests present themselves. These symbolic rituals assimilate the annihilation of an opponent to gratify our most primal yearnings to experience victory and prevail. They are assimilations, symbolic in nature, to make us victorious in a feel-good kind of way.

> *Not so fast, though. There exists another level—one that crosses into the realm of prevail with respect to Conscious Intelligence.*

When a lapse in distinction occurs between these symbolic rituals and real life, we are fast to witness the corrosion of human decency. Today, the line is obscuring, getting blurred and harder for some to distinguish. It isn't really *prevailing* when one party celebrates the demoralization, peril, or literal annihilation of another party. When this line is crossed, we instead witness our humanity taking a dive. From an elevated perspective, when this happens, all parties lose.

Prevail | When Harm Is Intentional versus Arbitrary

WHAT IF SOMEONE intentionally inflicts harm upon us? Is the realm of prevailing still available to us? Well, when a hurricane rolls through and its debris strikes us, did the storm do this personally and *intentionally* to us, or did the storm, in its passing, *arbitrarily* inflict collateral damage to us while we were caught in its path?

The elevated perspective of prevailing observes the circumstance like this: Even if someone intentionally inflicts harm upon us, we are merely the beneficiary of that person's condition. While injurious, even intentional, their dysfunction of acting out inappropriately at our expense is still arbitrary to us...unless we internalize the wound and make it mean more. From the elevated perspective of prevailing, the external storm—whether literal or figurative—needs not have any impact on our internal weather *unless we allow it to.*

Let's be clear: is this suggesting that we can't be hurt, that we are immune to experiencing the infliction of injury? *Absolutely not!* We completely experience the effects of transgression and trespass, whether caused by others, injury, disease, a business deal, nature, infidelity, or anything else. Just like any other time we are wounded, it is important to take proper and necessary steps to heal. It is what we make the injury *mean* beyond this that dictates whether we allow it to persist.

Whether the trespass was caused intentionally or arbitrarily, it is not something we deserve either way, yet we incur the collateral damage from a condition sourced outside of ourselves. The circumstance from an elevated perspective is neutral; we are merely arbitrary benefactors of the storm's path. Is the trespass some sort of appropriately deserved retribution? No! The disruption of our well-being is due to that condition, not our own. Is the culprit undergoing some misguided, toxic, internal storm leading to inappropriate choices in their conduct at our expense? Yes! We can choose to be victimized by the circumstance or we can choose to prevail over it. What we choose determines whether we are a victim, a survivor, or one that removes ourselves from that paradigm entirely to be one who *prevails*. Finding and facilitating our grace in such an environment is what it means to elevate consciousness.

Here's another level to consider: Elevating above the circumstance means being accountable for the mess even when we weren't the cause of it, just as we clean up the debris in our backyard after that hurricane rolls through because the hurricane isn't coming back to clean it up. We must do it if we wish for our yard to be restored to its orderly standard. Otherwise, the destruction sits unaddressed; it disrupts the flow of our lives, we carry around with us blame, resentment, disappointment, and the resulting chaos eventually becomes our new standard, our new normal.

What of the Trespasser?

PREVAILING, BY DEFINITION, leaves all parties better off without making anyone worse off. The instrument of measure extends to include *all* parties—even the *trespasser*. Whether that is a person, disease, or anything else, we take on being accountable *even if the other is the culprit and held to blame*. How? There exists a wound, condition, cause within the trespasser that enabled such a trespass. Until this condition is cured, confronted, addressed fully from our standpoint, we will carry it *within us* as well, *and* it can become highly contagious!

Prevailing is the illuminative way of viewing the circumstance. This distinction takes a perspective that is elevated above the circumstances. It doesn't mean forgoing the punitive process when the trespasser is a person. Remember that the punitive process is transactional: trespass/punishment, right/wrong, good/bad, victim/perpetrator. From such perspective, we have *choice* in maintaining our internal weather and how things will go moving forward. On the transactional level we seek justice, but on an *essential Self* level, we seek *absolution*. That is, we absolve ourselves and all parties from the circumstances entirely by our not remaining plagued by them.

Once we release ourselves from the victim/survivor paradigm, we can restore our ability to prevail over the entire circumstance and get over it rather than wasting time in the space of surviving victimization. Elevating above the circumstance, rather than remaining entwined within it, has us inhabit the space where prevail lives.

Remember the kid whose eye got poked out? Prevailing requires them to ultimately forgive the pencil thrower, to forgive themselves and not dwell, to find a way through their struggles, and to find absolution. They are challenged to let go of all resentment and blame so they can thrive in their life despite their newfound circumstances. Having an elevated perspective does not mean others do, nor is it our place to judge them if they don't. We are accountable for *our* elevation of consciousness and for *holding the space* for others to do so, without attachment or judgment. If we become attached to, or insistent on, the accountability of others, we move out of the realm of prevail and back to the victim/survivor paradigm.

The condition of prevailing does not carry the weight of victimization and, as such, does not require survival. Elevating above the circumstance rather than becoming entangled in it allows us to prevail. Prevailing at its highest expression elevates us above the circumstance, not merely over a trespass. The state of prevailing is a choice, a perspective, a way of being, and a frame of mind. It defines us.

Sacred Spaces

> *As iron sharpens iron, so one man sharpens another.*
> *~Proverbs 27:17*

WITHIN THE ECOLOGY of prevailing exists *sacred space*, a conceptual place where we can train and strengthen our ability to prevail. Powerful examples of these spaces exist all over the place. When we walk into a church, a courtroom, a library, an ancient burial cave…we are drawn to conduct ourselves differently. We feel different, we lower our voice, dress a certain way, whisper, act with humility. Why? Many are nothing more than four walls, a floor, and a ceiling, or a place located in nature. So, what makes them sacred? *We do.*

How do *we* create sacred space? Esteemed either by community or personal sentiment in the spirit of tradition, it is created with focused intention and purpose. It is reserved and restricted for only that purpose. It need not even be a physical space. It could be the presence of a best friend, lover, spouse, or confidant; breaking bread with family at the dinner table; the observance of gratitude; a place of reflection; a space in which to invite the Divine; or even a sports arena where people or teams compete.

The Olympics are a powerful example of sacred space. They personify the trials, challenges, and adversity of the human spirit reaching its highest expression of potential. The inspiring energy is felt by all as we witness man and woman pushing themselves and each other beyond the limit of what is considered possible. Such feats highlight the true spirit of competition and of prevailing, and they embody the hero's journey. When we walk into an empty, quiet arena, church, or sacred space where sacred acts have taken place, we feel something, a presence, a humility, a sense that something much bigger than ourselves is at play. We feel this same sensation when we close our eyes, hear our breath, quiet our mind, and journey inward in meditation.

Our brains process our experiences in sacred spaces as visceral exercises the same way we tackle feats in real life. In this example, the athlete becomes the hero personified in the ritual of competition, sharpening and being sharpened by a worthy adversary, experiencing the elation of being a champion and the agony of being defeated, both of which provide powerful life lessons. The trials, rituals, and practices, in this and all sacred spaces, create a passage inward where we can focus our attention, set aside the noise of daily life, be intentional, elevate the human spirit, accomplish feats never seen, break through barriers, and inspire others to do the same. What permeates is a mirror of life, a connection to our essential Self. Sacred space illuminates our strengths to negotiate real-life challenges and adversities and, as well, our ability to prevail and to recognize our gifts.

SUMMARY | ID 22

Why merely crawl over the finish line when you can cross it a champion?

When adversity hits, it seems reasonable at the end of the day that, given a choice, we all would prefer to be crowned survivors and not victims. *But* have you considered that being a survivor still carries with it *victimization*? That *survivor* and *victim* exist as two sides of the same coin? The distinction does not concern itself with where we land on the spectrum of victim/survivor—or even that, once formerly a victim, one proves strong enough to survive.

What is critical is our belief that we must reside on this spectrum *at all*. Survival still carries with it victimization, just as the cure still carries with it the illness.

The idea of prevailing does not refer to prevailing over another or over a trespass, disease, or ailment; it refers to prevailing over the *entire circumstance*. While surviving is a means of getting over victimization, *prevailing* is a means of getting over the circumstances entirely. When the circumstance as a whole no longer plagues us, our mind, our focus, we move forward, adapt, adjust, and are no longer saddled with the ordeal. We have to powerfully choose this perspective.

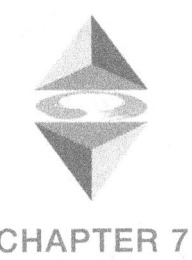

CHAPTER 7

Distinctions of Advancement, Productivity, and Leadership

Don't mistake my willingness to be vulnerable for weakness.
~Unknown, but spoken by many
great visionary thought leaders

ID 23: Problem versus Challenge

ONE OTHERWISE NORMAL MORNING while at my first corporate job, I arrive at our offices straight from the airport after two major pitch meetings for clients in San Francisco. I am greeted by my receptionist who is wearing an atypical, alarmed look on her face. Before I even reach her desk, she erupts with alarming news, her trembling voice betraying her anxiety. The president of our largest corporate client is on the phone, he does not sound happy, and he is looking for me. Cognizant of the fact that this executive's staff typically arranges his meetings and that he *never* picks up the phone to initiate a call, I clarify, "*He* called?...*He* is on the phone...right now?" The receptionist nods, as the look on my face writhes to resemble hers.

I soon discover that a key decision had been made by our production department, contrary to the client's wishes and without my knowledge or authorization. As if I arrived to the scene of a tsunami, I call a meeting with our department head, Robert. To this day, he remains the best boss and mentor I have ever had. Emotionally charged, tension tightening my face muscles, my anger still glaringly apparent, I enter his office and blurt, "We have a problem!" I begin to download the fiasco...and get about three words in to my saga before I am interrupted.

Robert calmly utters one word, but I can't make it out...because I am in full rant. So I pause, still flustered, and offer back to him—

"Pardon?"

"*Challenge*," he states in a level, peaceful voice that folds into my rant. He waits for me to settle a bit, then adds, "We have a *challenge*, not a problem."

Silence reigns as he is completely still, eyes staring at me, his face matching his content, pleasant smile. His hands are folded on the desk in front of him. I have his whole attention. He leans in with anticipation, intent on listening to what I have to say. He knows me, understands my passion and dedication to the job and our clients, and understands there must be real gravity to the situation because I would not approach him in such a manner unless... oh, hell, I was freaking out!

With a quiet confidence, he gestures for me to continue.

The echo of his word reaches the back of my head, and my face that had mirrored the receptionist's now starts to relax, reflecting his instead. The tense air I tracked into the room dissipates and is restored with oxygen once again. One word completely re-*set* me. I proceed, this time describing the *challenge* we face due to the misstep.

In a relatively short time, we devise a plan to collaborate with the production staff to address the issue at hand and create a very compelling and generous solution to make good with our cherished client. When I call the client back to propose the solution, I proceed with the same demeanor, tone, and cadence my boss demonstrated, greeting him on the phone with full accountability for the issue.

The client's charged voice and tone transforms from agitated to calm, *matching mine* as he engages with me to work out the plan, dispose of the remaining toxic debris, and iron out the remaining details. When we hang up the phone, the client is pleased with the strategy we proposed. Not only was the bomb dismantled, but also—by engaging the client, letting him vent, maintaining a level demeanor, and creating an environment where we both rolled up our sleeves and worked together—our relationship elevated to a new level. That day I walked out of the offices a changed man, not only having resolved a major calamity, but also, from that time forward and to this day, I have all but eliminated the word *problem* from my vocabulary. And I don't miss that word at all.

Why does just changing a word change everything? The word *problem* is plagued with a huge dose of toxic radiation. It is a charged word; people can be observed having a visceral response, recoiling into their chairs when someone marches into a boardroom, classroom, family room, spewing the words "We have a problem." Commonly, we physically, mentally, and psychologically adopt a posture as if to brace ourselves for impact when we are faced with problems.

In a parallel scenario, when someone enters a boardroom and launches the words "We have a challenge," people lean *in*; they lean forward. *Challenge* is actually quite an affirmative word. We are wired for challenges; we get lit up because challenge transforms a brick wall into a springboard. A challenge is something that incites the resilient nature inside of us.

We are energized by challenges, while depleted by problems. Problems connote perpetuity; even if we resolve them, their nature has them remain permanently embedded in our psyche like a latent virus. It is no different than the victim/survivor, problem/solution, disease/cure paradigm we just discussed. Challenges live in the same realm as prevail.

The realm where *problems* exist is a realm that programs others to conduct themselves in a similar, reactive fashion. For example: while among a group of friends, one whispers, "Sally is bringing her kid today. They have some sort of *problem*—some condition or such, so act casual and try not to look like you know." It doesn't really matter what the "condition" is; it could be that Sally's child is super intelligent, somewhat eccentric, or just an introvert and nervous around strangers. When people start treating the child differently, they create a circumstance of "something's wrong" that just becomes amplified. Tell the child they have these conditions, and the child believes it too. Despite the fact that there really isn't anything *wrong*, the entire environment surrounding the child and the circumstance is created around *something's wrong*. So, everyone begins to conduct themselves as if this were true. The adults conduct themselves around the child as if the child has a problem, the child believes they have a problem evidenced by the way people are acting, and contrived out of the "something's wrong" label, the environment is created. All becomes a contrived problem rather than a transitory challenge.

Words matter. While the distinction may appear literally semantic here, it really isn't. When we label something a "problem," we offer down a verdict on it; we decide and infer a permanence about the condition. To label something a problem is to mask choice in the matter and infer permanence. Such labels have the power to influence a person's path in life by plaguing them with an affliction they think defines *who they are* rather than *something transitory*, especially if they are a youth or otherwise impressionable.

With *challenges*, we possess the opportunity to prevail. Given a challenge in life, we respond with purpose; we become creative and strategic. We are inspired and, in turn, recruit, engage, and inspire others. Challenges are neutral and give us the opportunity to elevate above the circumstance rather than forever be inflicted by it.

SUMMARY | ID 23

Game over or game on?

Problem: We are energized by challenges, while depleted by problems. Problems connote perpetuity; even if we resolve them, their nature has them remain permanently embedded in our psyche like a latent virus. It is no different from the victim/survivor, problem/solution, disease/cure paradigm we just discussed. Challenges, on the other hand, live in the same realm as prevail.

Why does just changing a word change everything? The word *problem* is plagued with a huge dose of toxic radiation. It is a charged word; people can be observed having a visceral response, recoiling into their chairs when someone marches into a boardroom, classroom, family room, spewing the words "We have a problem."

Challenge: However, when one launches the words "We have a challenge," people lean *in*; they lean forward. *Challenge* is actually quite an affirmative word. We are wired for challenges; we get lit up because challenge transforms a brick wall into a springboard. A challenge is something that incites the resilient nature inside of us. Consider your usage of each of these words in everyday circumstances. Virtually eliminating the word "problem" from one's vocabulary can be life-altering.

ID 24: Shades of Fear

Fear | Danger | Courage | Bravery

> *We have nothing to fear but fear itself.*
> *~Franklin Delano Roosevelt*

> *Do one thing every day that scares you.*
> *~Eleanor Roosevelt*

Fear versus Danger

FEAR. IS IT REAL? Most would say, of course it is…but if you were asked to point at something material and label it fear, could you? Chances are you can't, because fear doesn't exist in the physical world. Rather, it is conceptual—a notion invented in our heads or a feeling we have, typically enhanced by chemicals our brain releases into our body as a result. What transforms the notion of fear into something real is our mind. We manifest the effects of fear from thought into the physical world. Fear doesn't exist, but our expression of fear makes it so.

Danger, on the other hand, is real and *does* exist. It poses a real risk and exposure to harm, injury, and loss.

Why is this distinction important? Think about it—imagine how unstoppable life would be absent fear. Fear is the main culprit of our getting in our own way. Consider that our mind dictates our behavior, whether it is driven and operated by fear, love, or anything else. When our mind successfully convinces us that what it fears is real, we believe it and behave as such. Our fear causes us to make choices that affect our physical reality all the time. As a result, fear manifested into behavior (expressions of fear) has real consequences.

A dangerous situation can invoke fearful thoughts, but a mere fearful thought alone can't itself make something dangerous, unless the person lets that thought manifest into a dangerous situation. Fear itself is not dangerous, but a person acting out of fear can be.

Let's bring in courage and bravery, and then we can pull all these elements together and make some powerful distinctions.

Courage versus Bravery

THERE ARE TWO MAIN ELEMENTS to the distinction between courage and bravery. The first is whether there is a presence or absence of *fear*. The second is whether the person perceiving something as courageous or brave is the person *doing* the act or one *witnessing* the act.

> **Courage** is attributed to one engaging in an extraordinary feat despite the presence of fear. Courage is driven by a cause that makes the perceived risk worth it. An individual fueled by courage perceives that they are small in the face of the feat before them. In essence, one is attributed as being courageous when, absent certainty of their capability, they make a willful choice *anyway* to engage in the feat, regardless of the consequences.

> **Bravery** is attributed to one demonstrating the ability to confront pain, danger, or intimidation *without* experiencing fear. It is an observed strength in character that allows a person—whether more or lesser powerful, properly equipped or not—to negotiate a crisis *without fear*. Bravery is not a conscious quality of the actor; it is something that just comes naturally to them. This designation is a quality bestowed onto the actor from outside observers.

An example can be drawn and illustrated from another first responder story: On this particular day while we are patrolling, a southern hemisphere storm is swirling, kicking up some sizable surf, and resulting in large rip currents at our Southern California beaches. My team and I respond to an emergency that includes reports of large waves pounding the jetty, one of several cobbled boulder breakwaters that jut out from the shore, creating extremely hazardous conditions. Despite our regular patrols and issuing warnings to those opting to dwell along the coastal regions, some choose to stroll onto the rock jetties anyway. Incidentally, a series of large storm waves had just swept several of these dwellers into the water where a rip current then sucked them out into the rough, churning sea.

We arrive on scene to observe five people floundering offshore in the rough waves. This includes a good Samaritan who, witnessing the distress from a safe distance, dove in, initiating an effort to help. He has one person in his grasp when we arrive, albeit now he is personally struggling and in peril. We jump in, more properly equipped and, after a time, successfully retrieve everyone. We apply necessary lifesaving protocol and transport everyone via boat back to shore. We transfer the injured into the waiting paramedic truck, towel off, and write up the report. Moments later, we are dispatched to another, similar emergency call further north.

Let's break out the distinctions from this scenario. In this summary, fear, danger, courage, and bravery all are illustrated. The storm and resulting sizable surf and rip currents present *real*, physical *danger*. The group of onlookers that chose not to jump in to help, refrained out of *fear* for their own lives. It can be debated whether the good Samaritan was simply *brave*, acting without any compunction, or whether the circumstance required him to conjure up *courage* to respond. Regardless, the group of witnesses (which had now grown larger, including local news media) praised him for his *bravery*.

> *Courage* involves the presence of fear, while bravery does not.
>
> *Courage* is always gripped by cause, be it in the form of love, passion, concern, devotion, or compassion.
> *Bravery* maintains its very essence without requiring a cause.
>
> *Courage* is a result of mindfulness. It is one's decision to fight despite frightful consequences.
>
> *Bravery* is an inherent characteristic. It doesn't involve much thinking at all. It is second nature for those who have it.
>
> *Courage* is a means. Its end would be the cause that drives it.

Bravery is a characteristic that is, in itself, a means and an end all at once.

Why does this distinction matter? Conscious Intelligence draws distinctions about the sourcing of action and determines whether it is coming from authenticity or from something else—quite often fear. These terms illuminate shades of fear in an effort to understand it, process it, and gain perspective around the elements that afflict us the most. Perspective can assist us in guiding our conduct. By observing the shades of fear, we can transform trepidation into inspiration, dampen or eliminate its crippling influence, and initiate a deeper conversation within ourselves to gain clarity, situational awareness, and courage. We can gain perspective about our motivations, actions, and conduct in an effort to elevate our consciousness.

SUMMARY | ID 24

Nothing to fear but fear itself, but danger is another story.

Remember the distinction between physical reality and conceptual reality?

Fear doesn't exist in the physical world. What transforms the notion of fear into something real is our mind. *Danger,* on the other hand, is real and *does* exist. It poses a real risk and exposure to harm, injury, and loss. A dangerous situation can invoke fearful thoughts, but a mere fearful thought alone can't itself make something dangerous, unless the person lets that thought manifest into a dangerous situation. Fear itself is not dangerous, but a person acting out of fear can be.

ID 25: Proactive | Reactive | Responsive

> *Between stimulus and response, there is a space.*
> *In that space is our power to choose our response.*
> ~*Viktor Frankl*

HAVE YOU EVER BEEN on the receiving end of a professional tennis player's 120-mph serve? It is humbling. Most people can't move fast enough to even react, much less respond. By the time they see where the ball is going—or even take a step or raise their racket—the ball has already whizzed past and hit the back fence. For a professional who has trained for years, though, it's different; their eyes and body recognize a broader set of conditions, not just that of the ball. Pros describe the ball as appearing to slow down. By processing their opponent's body and foot position, toss of the ball, entire body movement, wind-up, and many other components, they are able to process the event far quicker, project how the ball will behave, and anticipate where it will go. As pros learn to recognize the entirety of the progression—components commonly not visible to average people—they gain the ability to coordinate their visual processing with a command over their eyes, muscles, reflexes, and body position. Their cognitive processes are honed to respond optimally, without reaction-time delays. Remember, while just getting to the ball is a feat for you and me, they are way ahead, already determining where they wish to redirect it. Their task is not merely to react to the served ball; they are tasked to respond to it.

This distinction applies to all sports, of course, but also, more critically, to life. In the space between a stimulus and a response, we have access to a broad spectrum of choices. As they become visible and we gain mastery over optimizing these choices, our abilities to respond elevate just like those of the tennis pros just mentioned.

Do you recall my mentioning earlier that *Distinctions are not definitions?*

This distinction illustrates clearly how the Invisible Distinctions are not the same as definitions:

> **Reaction** (Dictionary definition): A response to a stimulus. An action performed or a feeling experienced in response to a situation or event.
>
> **Response** (Dictionary definition): A reaction to something. Something constituting a reply.

As you can see, the dictionary definitions are conflated; the words are used to define each other, therefore making no distinction at all between them.

Now, let's look at the powerful distinction between being reactive and being responsive applying The Conscious Intelligence Paradigm.

> **Reaction** (CI Distinction): A reflexive action; something that happens absent the presence of thought. To be reactive means that, following a stimulus, we act without any additional input to alter the outcome.
>
> **Response** (CI Distinction): An intentional engagement of thought whereby a stimulus is processed to gain perspective so it can be *actively guided* to an outcome. It is a presence of mind where the ability for a stimulus to be processed exists before a response is elicited.

There exists a space between a circumstance and our relationship to it. When we can approach the circumstance equipped with our power to choose, we can better control our responses and better direct our conduct. Responsiveness is possible when being present allows us to lean into a circumstance with the understanding that we are *not* the circumstance. Then, even if the circumstance is entirely unforeseen, we can approach it better situated to negotiate it with a level head, poise, and grace.

Let's now introduce another dimension: the notion of being *proactive*. We tend to think of proactive as meaning *taking initiative*, but it's more than that. It also means being "response-*able*"—literally, having the ability, willingness, and aptitude to *respond*. The word *proactive* is not new. Its modern meaning was made popular by Austrian existential neuropsychiatrist Viktor Frankl, who is quoted at the beginning of this distinction. He used the word to describe a person who takes responsibility for their own life rather than passively awaiting cues from others.

> *There is nothing either good or bad*
> *but thinking makes it so.* ~William Shakespeare

Proactive people are responsive and not reactive. Proactivity, like responsiveness, advocates that we have choice in the matter. Proactive people have the ability to choose their response grounded in their values; they do not place blame on circumstances, conditions, or other people for their conduct. They *own* their behavior, as it is theirs and theirs alone.

The contribution of the brain processing thought following a stimulus is what alters, affects, and intentionally guides an outcome. Such active participation is not automatic; it is a conscious choice to be accountable based on one's inner driving principles. Absent conscious intention, one's passive reaction can leave them susceptible to the mechanisms that lead to affliction and victimization.

The way we choose to conduct ourselves under certain conditions is a function of our decisions, not of the conditions themselves. It is key to make a distinction between the circumstance itself and our relationship to it.

As humans, we assign meaning to things. This is no different when it comes to a stimulus and our response to it. Sometimes it may seem as though there is only one possible response for a given stimulus. Here's a silly but pointed example: Chocolate. Let's say, when you see chocolate you get happy. Of course, we know that there are countless different ways someone might respond to seeing chocolate based on any number of unique sets of preferences, experiences, and disciplines. Maybe they don't like chocolate, maybe they are allergic, maybe it reminds them of dieting, lack of control, and shame; maybe they are tired of people constantly assuming that *everyone* loves chocolate or that they can be bribed by it. Whatever the case, the chocolate itself, the stimulus, is a neutral thing. The *meaning* we assign to the chocolate is what determines how we feel about it. Once we have a feeling, the brain then interprets this feeling and assigns a meaning to *that*. What results is what elicits an emotional response: delight, anger, sadness, ecstasy, or anything else.

Let's parse this down a bit more. When faced with a stimulus, our brain engages to process it, searching our memories for familiar instances when we experienced a similar stimulus. The brain does this to add context and assign meaning so that it can determine what to do next. This happens in a split second and is not entirely done consciously. What our brains *decide* in this moment makes all the difference because it sets into motion a physiological response. It sets into motion *the way we feel*. For example, let's say when we see the chocolate, we feel a tingling in our belly and our mouth begins to salivate, our knees buckle, and we lose any track of thought or ability to speak (or is that just me?).

It's important to note that feelings and sensations are initially neutral—they just *are* until our brain assigns meaning to them. As such, feelings and sensations are not the initial drivers of our action or conduct. What can and often does happen next, however, is key. Our brains do yet another level of interpretation by *assigning meaning to the feelings and sensations*, shifting them from an objective sensation to a subjective one. One might say it is at this point that we formulate our narrative about our feelings or sensations. The subjective-*ness* is why people sometimes laugh at funerals or cry at weddings. There is no such thing as a *correct* emotion. There are, however, circumstances that can be best served from our having *command over* our emotions.

The array of emotions that result from a subjective emotional narrative depends on an individual's experiences and conditioning; they can vary along the entire emotional spectrum. In other words, it is not until our heads get involved and assign meaning to a feeling that an actionable, charged emotion takes shape.[1]

Emotions are the products of our thoughts that are generated about a given stimulus. Without thoughts, emotions could not arise, and while emotions are results of our thoughts, *they do not have to be drivers of our actions*! If we choose to allow them to be drivers, we risk charging the circumstance with tension, especially when those drivers are unresolved fears conjured up from our past. In essence, we add our own soundtrack. When we *react*, we do so out of these reflexive emotions and unsettled memories. In this trajectory, we drastically reduce the likeliness we will chart a path to an optimal resolution.

This powerful distinction can now become illuminated: While we cannot control our feelings, we *can* gain mastery over our thoughts that drive them. By achieving this, we identify and address the unresolved triggers anchored to the past feelings attached to them. Further, we gain perspective over our thoughts and memories and can then shift our attitude towards them. What results is that we gain discipline over our emotions so that we can direct our actions to optimally desired outcomes.

> *The key opportunity to being responsive versus reactive lies in the space between where our feelings are initially generated into thought, and where their formulations from thought are converted into action.*

We circle back to Viktor Frankl: Between a stimulus and a response, there exists the power of choice. Our emotions can be decoupled from our feelings and need not dictate our behavior or conduct. Once we reestablish a neutral charge to our thoughts and memories, we can commandeer our choices around them. We can either passively allow them to drive our reactions, or we can actively direct them to elicit an intentional response.

The notion of utilizing the space where we have choice and direct our minds to respond accordingly is not unfamiliar to those who exercise profoundly extreme levels of restraint. We describe some as possessing "nerves of steel"...which leads us to *stoicism*.

Stoicism

> *If you can keep your head while all around you are losing theirs and blaming you...*
> ~Rudyard Kipling

Stoicism is the ability to keep control of our emotions and maintain composure in a challenging environment.

Distinctions of Advancement, Productivity, and Leadership | 155

MOST OF US ARE AWARE that it is critical to keep emotions in check during emergencies such as a traffic accident, a natural disaster, a terrorist attack, a mugging, or a market crash. The people advantaged to help are the ones who stay calm and disallow their emotions to guide their actions. Just as valuable is our ability to subordinate our emotions in everyday events, such as listening to a slick sales pitch or political stump speech, getting blindsided by an unforeseen event at work or a friend's misspoken words, facing social injustice, or delivering a difficult eulogy. Left unchecked, these stimuli can inundate us with feelings that can elicit a watershed of emotions and charged responses. They can disrupt our flow, throw us off balance, and prevent us from effectively discharging the task we have set out to do.

By no means does this discipline intend to diminish the value and importance of our emotions; actually, it is more the contrary. The discipline is all about learning to gain mastery over them while in a circumstance best served by doing so. When we are faced with circumstances that require a measured and balanced response, our power of choice and ability to control the degree to which emotions influence us is what it means to employ Conscious Intelligence.

By remaining level-headed, stable, and focused in a charged environment, we gain the ability to mitigate our emotions. We can think more clearly, conduct ourselves with grace, and not misstep and regret our actions later.

> *You're either a part of the solution, or part of the problem.*
> *~Eldridge Cleaver*
> *(...and my mother. If you say it as much*
> *as she did, you get to own it too)*

Imagine witnessing a car accident. Heaven forbid, someone is trapped in their car, head bleeding, there's smoke...and this is just what you can observe from your vantage point. Now imagine these two scenarios.

Scenario 1: The medics arrive. The rescue responder shrieks at the sight of the blood and, moments later, starts crying and says, "Oh my gosh, you are bleeding really badly! Oh, heaven help us, please don't die!" Notably upset, sad, and scared, the responder is paralyzed with anguish, disoriented about what lifesaving skills to implement, and can't see straight through all their tears. Imagine you were the person in that car. That driver would probably be in a panic, thinking, "That's it, I'm going to die!"

(Note: This example is obviously for comparative purposes only, as it would be unlikely that an actively employed first responder would react this way. In reality, the rigorous hours of training would not typify this. After all, the professional's title is first *responder*, not first *reactor*.)

Scenario 2: The medic arrives. The rescue responder observes and processes the scene, maintaining a compassionate, confident, and relaxed facial expression and approaches the person in the car. With an unwavering voice, they say calmly and clearly, "My name is Blair. I'm here to help you. What is your name?" After the subject responds, "Kelly," the responder says, "Kelly, listen to my voice and look into my eyes. Breaaaathe. I'm placing a compress on your head, can you help me by holding it in place?" They take a deep breath together, and then the responder continues, "We're going to make sure everything is okay and get you out of here. Now, the smoke you see around you is *sodium azide*, the propellant from your airbag that deployed; the car is *not* on fire." (Or, perhaps it *is*, and they will need to use the jaws of life to free the person in the car. But pointing out this information may not serve either of them at that moment.) The first responder is already prepared with a protocol to respond based on the order of immediacy that the situation presents. After the medic completes the protocol, they say, "Let's get you out of here to safety; you're going to be just fine."

Now, in the first scenario, it is obvious the *reactor* cares very deeply about the person in the car, but their emotions and visceral reactions are *not* helping the situation. Their reaction is counter-productive, actually making the circumstance worse and more dangerous.

In the second scenario, the *responder* cares equally, is just as compassionate and empathetic, but also understands that in order to serve the circumstance optimally, they must decouple their emotions and keep them in check. They know that the best way to care for this patient is to do their job, calm the patient, stop the bleeding, cut them free, treat the injuries, and get them transported to the hospital. Any emotional outbreak that diverts the responder from this mission is an impediment that can place all involved in peril. When the responder does their job without distraction from their emotions, they have the ability to focus and respond optimally, appropriately, and powerfully. While their caring and compassion is not in any way discarded, they have tempered these feelings so that they do not impede in the discharging of duties. This is a form of stoicism, as well as an example of being *responsive* versus *reactive*.

Everyday life is really not much different. We all have the ability to respond rather than react to life's everyday crises, dramas, or provocations. Reactivity amplifies and complicates rather than deescalates and simplifies a circumstance. We are either part of the solution or we are part of the problem, and frequently, the emotions and subsequent behaviors emanating from them can play a significant role in which scenario plays out.

SUMMARY | ID 25

Grace under pressure; an ounce of prevention is worth a pound of cure.

There exists a space between a circumstance and our relationship to it, as there exists a space between stimulus and response. In that space is our power to choose. When we can approach a circumstance equipped with our power to choose, we can better navigate to the best possible outcome. We cannot always control our circumstances, but we can control how we conduct ourselves within our circumstances.

The distinction between reacting and responding is profound: Reacting occurs without any additional input to alter an impulsive, reflexive action. Responding is an intentional engagement of thought whereby a stimulus is processed to gain perspective so it can be *actively guided* to an outcome that, by its very nature, is more intentional.

ID 26: The Distinction of Time and the Myth of Someday

If you want something done, ask a busy person to do it.
~Benjamin Franklin

"I don't have enough time... If I only had more time in the day...."

SOUND FAMILIAR? Consider that the one uttering these words is confining themselves to be a slave to time. Every one of us has twenty-four hours in a day, don't we? No more, no less. Think this is not enough? We might consider looking at people like Bill Gates, Elon Musk, Tim Cook, Oprah Winfrey, or Mark Zuckerberg; these people are likely much busier than most, even taking into account the staffs that they manage in an effort to sustain the workload. How do they do it? Are the twenty-four hours in a day really not enough, or are *we* just complicit in using the concept of time as an excuse to play small?

A plethora of resources and *how-tos* are available to help us organize our lives and manage our time efficiently. This is *not* one of those—not in the traditional sense anyway. As with everything else in the realm of Conscious Intelligence, this distinction is not transactional, not a "*How to do this to get that*" instruction manual. It is not a path; it is a *light*.

This distinction is about our relationship to time in the context of *not having enough of it*. Exceptional times can be trying and are not what the distinction is about, although an understanding of this distinction can mitigate some of the pressures during such challenging times.

This distinction is about the way we think about time. It is how we delude ourselves into believing we don't have enough of it, when in fact we do. For most of us, there is plenty of time, and it helps if we stop wasting it by complaining we have none. The myth of not having enough time often presents as a cloaked excuse to cave into our fears. It clouds our perception, permits us to keep playing small, convinces us that we can best control our environment by keeping things static and predictable. What better excuse to not play big than to convince ourselves that we just don't have a choice, that we *juuuust* don't have enough time?

We are not slaves to time. We need not hope that someday in the future someone will open up an imaginary cage door, free us, and set the earth's rotation onto a thirty-six-hour day cycle rather than a twenty-four. We need not wait for someone to direct us over yonder, wherein lies salvation in the form of life synchronized with time's highest and best use. It is already freely available to us.

The only reality that our self-imposed prison bars possess is that which we create. The deeper our resistance to *change*, the thicker the prison bars.

The Myth of Someday

So I ask: Which quote relates to you more?

> *Life is what happens while you're busy making other plans.* ~John Lennon

OR

> *Life is a journey, not a destination.* ~Emerson

THE LAW OF PHYSICS predicates that we cannot be two places at once. When our head is literally fixated in the future, we are missing life here and now, in the present. The present is where the living of life happens. Preoccupying our head in the throes of *someday* is to live in scarcity—be it of time, of the stuff we don't have now, or the stuff we hope to have in the future. The same applies for dwelling in the past, longing in regret, or basking in the belief that past results dictate future ones. It is to squander our otherwise abundant time where the experience of the life we are living into is happening. Think about it: If the goal in life is to reach the finish line, dying would logically be the ultimate goal…as said earlier, likely not a great application of transactional thinking. That's just not the way it works here.

Now, this does not mean we don't make goals and plans for our future. It means we consider the consequences of being so preoccupied with what life *will be* when we achieve those goals that we miss out on the *here and now*. The present is the *only* place where the means to do so reside. It is no coincidence that some of the ways we get present is through the practices of meditation, yoga, mindfulness, or prayer. These disciplines acknowledge the noise and distracting thoughts we have all the time that divert our attention from the present. They are all primarily focused on guiding us back to the present, to our breath, to the here and now. If not now, when?

What does being present have to do with the myth of someday or of being a slave to time? Being present in and of itself does not solve our time management challenges or handily provide us with more time in the day. It does, however, help us identify what constitutes the authentic and essential stuff that matters in our life. It helps prevent us from fixating on the scarcity of time and squandering it in the throes of someday. It provides for clarity by providing space to recognize and set our priorities. When our priorities are clear, we are poised to eliminate the stuff that doesn't serve us—time-consuming things—and, in that context, we see how being present plays an essential role in accessing Conscious Intelligence.

SUMMARY | ID 26

Squandering our time by complaining we don't have enough of it.

The law of physics predicates that we cannot be two places at once. When our head is literally fixated in the future, we are missing life here and now, in the present. The present is where the living of life happens. Preoccupying our head in the throes of *someday* is to live in scarcity. To be fully present here and now is the only access we have to living in gratitude and abundance.

This is a bold statement, but it is a universal truth. This does not mean we don't make goals and plans for our future or have a reverence for our past. It means we consider the consequences of being so preoccupied with how life used to be—or what life *will be* when we achieve those goals—that we miss out on the *here and now*.

ID 27: Opinion versus Misconception

> *Everyone is entitled to his own opinion,
> but not to his own facts.*   ~Daniel Patrick Moynihan

ELEVATING CONSCIOUSNESS requires more than just becoming aware or having awareness. Consciousness is the state of being awake and present.

Few situations exist more certain to fuel a contentious, roaring fire of rhetoric than confusing the distinction between opinion and misconception.

> An **opinion** is a preference for, or judgment of, something. For example: my favorite color is cobalt blue. This is an opinion. It may be unique to me or shared across a general population, but it *cannot* be verified outside the fact that I believe it. With an opinion, there is not a factual right or wrong.

> A **misconception** is something that can be disproven by existing facts or research. Misconceptions are not opinions; there is a factual rightness or wrongness that is being accidentally or intentionally ignored.

There exists a common misconception that an opinion cannot be wrong. Someone merely declaring "this is my opinion" following a rant devoid of rationale, does not immunize their words from being 100% rubbish. When one's opinion can be challenged by factual research, it's not an opinion; it's a misconception.

Still, some go even further when that same someone cries foul, suggesting they are being attacked for their beliefs; they may even reach for the victim card claiming they are being attacked... Whoa, whoa, time out! Let's review the play.

Imagine a world where people have bought into the misconception that an opinion can never be wrong and that the bar to prove something as true is simply "because I said so" or "because it is my opinion." One claiming that the world is flat is more accurately an example of a misconception. Despite the absurdity of such a reach,

Distinctions of Advancement, Productivity, and Leadership | 163

people employ these tactics all the time and inflict tremendous carnage as a result.

Three questions help make the distinction regarding opinion and misconception:

1. Is it really an opinion, i.e., is it really not possible to verify outside the person who believes it?
2. If it is an opinion, how informed is it, and why does the person hold it?
3. If facts are presented, are they reflective of the entire truth?

Let's look at the first question: Is it really an opinion, meaning something that cannot be verified by facts? The challenge comes from people whose opinions are actually misconceptions. If one thinks climate change is a myth, that person is expressing something that is factually incorrect. This is a misconception, not an opinion. The fact that one may truly believe such a notion does not change the fact that it is factually wrong; nor does it shift this misconception into the realm of a valid opinion. Even if many others share this misconception, as is often the case, it still does not give it even one more ounce of validity.

Some people are of the "opinion" that the Holocaust did not occur. Such a notion means absolutely nothing in reality because it has no value outside the holders' own misconception. Abundant testimony, scientific and historical data support the contrary to this, full stop.

The scientific community attests to the fact that sometimes initial data can be inaccurate or unclear, discovered to be tainted, or subject to the evolution of technological instruments. There was a time when the world was believed to be flat, that the universe revolved around the earth, or that bleeding someone to near death was the remedy to certain diseases. One's informed opinion can be a placeholder for the advent of further discovery, but—and this is a big but—there still remains a distinction between having considered all the existing facts versus not considering the facts at all. There is also a difference between a belief versus the facts a person just doesn't know, hasn't considered, or has flat-out ignored.

> *Even the devil can cite scripture for his purpose.*
> *~William Shakespeare*

This leads to the second question: If it is an opinion, is it informed? And, why has one come to believe it? The context of this question requires employing an elevated perspective—it is not an opinion if the information or facts available are completely ignored, partially ignored, or devoid of any value or merit; it is instead a misconception. One example of this could be calling on someone for their expert opinion. In real estate this could be to value a property. An appraiser is hired to elicit their *expert opinion* on the valuation based on many factors like comparisons with other property in the area, current market conditions, land value, improvements made, such as the addition of a pool, and the overall condition of the subject property, to name a few. If these observable facts are notably ignored when the opinion is presented, the opinion lacks merit. Even worse is one's intentional parsing and/or use of select pieces of information, while omitting and ignoring other pieces, with the intent to guide others to a predestined viewpoint (as is popular in politics). When unscrupulous people are involved, it is not uncommon that we discover statistics to be unscrupulous in much the same way.

The third question refers to facts versus truth: Simply presenting a handful of facts does not necessarily illustrate the truth. Facts can be incomplete, not placed in proper context, or creatively arranged to paint an entirely different picture from the truth, and the mere citing of facts doesn't necessarily mean anything without context. It also doesn't exonerate someone claiming that there is "nothing I stated that wasn't fact" to sidestep the truth. Context, completeness, and comprehensiveness matters.

So, when we consider either our own or someone else's claim to opinion versus misconception, we can consider these questions: Is the notion really something that cannot be factually verified outside the holder's belief? If it is an opinion, how informed is it, and why does the person hold it? Finally, if facts are presented, are they reflecting the absolute and complete truth?

Honorable Mention: The Truly Gifted Confabulators

THERE EXISTS A TALENTED ELITE, truly gifted folk who state opinions as if pure fact. They typically omit the words "in my opinion" to anything they say. More concerning is that these folks are so self-absorbed that they appear to have little awareness that other perspectives even exist—or, heaven forbid, have any validity. They effectively and convincingly state something as a fact even if it's just an opinion—or, worse, a misconception. Only the most sophisticated, developed ear can root them out. These are *confabulators*.

A confabulation is a lie or misconception told honestly. Calling foul-ball to gifted confabulators can often offend them, but just because someone is offended does not make them right, nor any less wrong. A bit later, we will advance up The Conscious Intelligence Paradigm to illuminate the distinction between Right versus Righteousness, a place where gifted confabulators, among others, love to hide.

> **SUMMARY | ID 27**
>
> **Everyone is entitled to their own opinion, but not their own facts.**
>
> With an opinion, there is not a factual right or wrong. An opinion may be unique or shared across a general population, but it *cannot* be verified outside the fact that one believes it. A **misconception** is something that can be disproven by existing facts or research. Misconceptions are not opinions; there is a factual rightness or wrongness that is being accidentally or intentionally ignored. There exists a common misconception that an opinion cannot be wrong. Someone merely declaring, "This is my opinion," when that opinion can be challenged by factual research, is not an opinion; it's a misconception.

ID 28: Distinctions of Respect | Disrespected versus Offended

Respect isn't something owed; it is something one earns.

With All Due Respect

THE DISTINCTION OF RESPECT comes from different perceptions about how respect is doled out, who's entitled to it, and when. We commonly witness lapses in this distinction by people holding (or perceived to be holding) authority and leadership positions. Ah, yes, there's nothing quite like the dance of the mighty who expect and think they are entitled to respect. Power is threatened, feathers get ruffled, and commonly the retaliation ranges from employees getting reprimanded to an all-out playground-style brawl. When one becomes offended, it is all but certain that ego is driving because *only the ego can be offended*. The key determination of the distinction is how we process stimuli such as criticism. How we process stimuli influences how we ultimately respond (or react).

The perspective we gain from making this distinction does not in the least inoculate us from the harshness of criticism. Keeping one's ego in check has nothing to do with whether the insinuation is valid or not; nor does it mean that another's insinuation won't sting. Sometimes others get it wrong; sometimes we get it wrong. We are all allowed to feel; we are all human. Regardless, there exists a distinction.

When making the distinction, we can consider two different perspectives. The first perspective develops when the sting originates out of our attachment to things such as our pride, stature, prestige, etc. Born out of the stimulus-response paradigm, the ego is primed to say, "I'm offended," resulting in emotions and actions we associate with being offended—the desire to avenge or our feeling hurt, sadness, anger, fear, and shame.

The second more elevated, perspective recognizes stimuli such as criticism in one of two significantly more powerful ways.

1. Criticism that can be sourced as feedback generated from another who *trusts us enough* to be freely self-expressed around and to us. If the other doesn't feel comfortable or trust that we can *receive* this feedback, they will refrain from saying anything or will talk behind our backs. People open up when they feel safe and when they perceive that what they wish to say will be heard without judgment, condemnation, or retaliation. They exhale when trust has been established to do so and when we invite them to do so.

2. Criticism that can be identified as the other's ego projecting its damaged pride, stature, or prestige onto us. When we identify the context as a projection of the other's ego, we can respond with curiosity, perspective, and empathy rather than being drawn in where we risk being offended ourselves. Because the ego is devoid of the tools necessary to walk a path of elevated consciousness, it gets *offended* as a defensive reaction to fear. If we fail to recognize the other's ego-sourcing and allow *our* ego to be drawn in, then ego is driving. It engages, we react, fail to rise above the circumstance, and become entangled as a result...and then we get *offended*.

The Reverse Angle

LET'S BRIEFLY OBSERVE this from the reverse angle, that is, when someone *earns* our respect. There are two ways this can go:

First, if what we respect are the other's ego-driven values—say, materialism, vanity, or elitism—then our respect speaks to and feeds *our* ego and draws us further away from the expression of our essential *Self*. This type of respect leads us to disempowerment. It keeps us basking at the ego-level and lacks the fertile ground for us to elevate.

The second is the converse: If what we respect aligns with another's elevated value system, then our respect emanates from our essential *Self* and not from ego, resulting in elevation of all parties.

Authentic power springs from our empowerment of others, from being accountable, and from living value-driven principles. Possessing this breed of power proves worthy of earning respect because it provides a fertile path for inspiring others to do the same. True power is sourced from our holding the space for others to be freely self-expressed. Seeking to understand another's humanity and offering that person freedom, dignity, and sacred space for their own self-expression is to elevate humanity—and along with it, ourselves.

In Summary

WE STARTED OUR JOURNEY through the Base Distinctions observing the power of words, communication, and miscommunication. We traced the path of how our words can propagate into our actions, and how our actions can define who we are and how we occur out in the world.

We observed how we imprison ourselves, limiting our ability to have personal sovereignty, freedom, and self-expression.

We gained perspective on how fear can devolve us into a reactive state, and how addressing it changes the game. Conscious Intelligence is all about illumination and is fueled by the elevation of consciousness. It replaces mere reaction with agile responsiveness, guiding us to conduct ourselves with grace to facilitate an optimal outcome. We discovered that respect and leadership is earned and that their true power is sourced in the empowerment of others.

We are now primed to investigate the Central Distinctions…

SUMMARY | ID 28

Respect isn't something owed; it is something earned.

The distinction of respect comes from different perceptions about how respect is doled out, who's entitled to it and when. When people hold (or are perceived to hold) authority and leadership positions, it is important to observe what powers placed them there. If authority is through force, intimidation, privilege, and/or fear-based threats, this can be a very low form of power when it is wielded with very little winning of consensus. This can be evidenced by the sentiments of those being controlled reveling in the prospective hopes of this person losing the power. On the other hand, if authority and respect is gained from a consensus through inspiration, accomplishments, and achievements—deeds that elevate the consensus of people who freely relinquish and entrust the authority—respect is earned. This is the most powerful form of leadership.

THE CENTRAL DISTINCTIONS

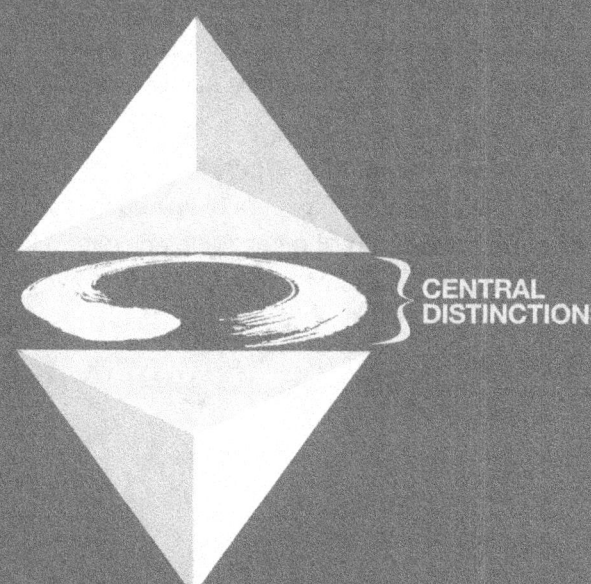

LOVE
Essence & Expression

CENTRAL DISTINCTIONS

Introduction to the Central Distinctions

What's love got to do with it?
~Tina Turner, written by
Terry Britten and Graham Lyle

WHAT DOES *LOVE* have to do with Conscious Intelligence? Isn't the subject of love really more appropriately discussed in the context of relationships, communication, personal growth, and development? If we approach this question from a universal perspective and consider humanity, connection, meaning, and consciousness, we realize that career, productivity, accomplishments, along with relationships, communication, and personal growth, are merely a subset of the *entirety* of our life. Loving our life, our surroundings, what we do, who we are, what we are creating and living into has *everything* to do with the elements of our life where we occupy space and invest time. Love has *everything* to do with that! It has everything to do with our connection with family, friends, our colleagues, community, organizations, and customers. It inhabits our environment, our motivations, our vision. These are all essential at a personal level, a public level, an organizational level, and universal level because in the broader scheme, *they are not separate.*

Conscious Intelligence spans a far broader scope than our trade, career, or vocation. No successful corporation's mission statement these days reads: "Work harder, make money, rinse, repeat." The most successful, illuminated thought leaders, disruptors, and business executives today attest to the notion that their success is informed by much broader sets of criteria than merely a business model, a handful of vocational skills, hard-working employees, and the bottom line.

They also understand and prioritize work-life balance, social responsibility, purpose, people, authentic leadership, and the value of time versus money. We can always make more money, but "all your money won't another minute buy" (heartfelt and powerful lyrics from the song "Dust in the Wind" by Kansas).

Is the elevation of consciousness merely a facet of the elements just mentioned—business, productivity, growth, etc.—or does it also contain the illumination of ideas that shape the quality, connectivity, and meaning in our life? The answer certainly becomes clear with deeper consideration that *we can't have one without the other.*

> *Love. Where does it come from?*
> *Who lit this flame in us?*
> *No war can put it out, conquer it.*
> *I was a prisoner. You set me free.*   ~Terrence Malick

Everything that we humans consciously do can be sourced from two categories: that which comes from love and that which comes from an absence of love…most typically, fear.

Only from an authentic source can love be expressed and received. How we experience love is no different. If the source is rooted from inauthenticity, the expression will only feign being from love. While entire volumes of books, professions, movements, religions, and the like are dedicated to defining the meaning of love, Conscious Intelligence *makes distinctions* that pertain to whether something is *sourced from love or sourced from something else.* The meaning of love itself is a determination for each of us to make and discover through our own unique paths and experiences.

In illuminating the distinctions around love, and gaining perspective over where we collapse, confuse, conflate, or mistake love for other things, we become better equipped to identify what may or may not be authentically coming from a place of love, and we can become more conscious as a result.

Love's Two Realms

CONSIDER THAT LOVE EXISTS in two simultaneous realms. The first is the realm where love just is. This is-*ness* of love is absolute; it has no opposites, and it is either present or absent in a circumstance. The second realm is love's expressions, a verb, the infinite ways love is expressed by us out into the world. In other words, there is (L)ove (with a capital "L") as an absolute, a formless presence that is beyond dimension, and there are the infinite expressions of (l)ove (with a lower case "l"), the realm where love is actualized out into the world by us, through us.

The is-*ness* of Love is formless, but the infinite expressions of love propagated by us, that flow out of us, manifest that formlessness into form. We create love's form through our expression of it out into the world. We can draw an analogy to light: Light does not create meaning. We humans create meaning in what light illuminates. Light in its own nature just *is*; it is formless. Our brain processes what the light makes visible, combs our memory to recognize the object. Our brain makes the best sense it can out of the object, and then formulates and assigns a meaning to what is illuminated in front of us.

Continuing with this analogy, we are like projectors. A projector is a conduit that transforms light into a movie. By flowing light though a piece of story medium (like celluloid or film), a moving, dynamic anthology blossoms. Love in its absolute form flows through us in much the same way. As the uniquely formulated story within each of us is projected out into the world, so does love in its unique, expressive forms—project out from us onto the screen that is our life.

The Conscious Intelligence of Love:
What It Is, and What It Isn't.

THINK OF THE CONSCIOUS INTELLIGENCE PARADIGM using the image of a flowing river. CI focuses (upstream) on whether something is sourced from love or sourced from something else. Contrast this to our *experience* of love. Experience happens (downstream) after its expression has already been conveyed. We can see that the *way we experience love* is altogether different. We all express and receive love in wholly unique and individual ways.

We can think *source*, not *expression*. CI does not concern itself with interpreting or translating loving gestures or behaviors (again, these are experiences *downstream*). By definition, these are loving gestures already expressed (a rose, is a rose, is a rose). Such gestures are subjective, unique experiences that require no distinction at all. Further, what *inhibits* the experience of love most commonly involves barriers rooted in either love's miscommunication from the giver, or in the missing of love's communication by the receiver…or any combination of the two. We can also include love not experienced despite its being present. All of these examples embody love's *expression*, not its *source*.

> *Love not expressed*
> *is like a wrapped gift that remains unopened.*

If you are interested in learning more about the ways we *experience* love, I highly recommend any of the books or work done by Gary Chapman around what he calls "*The Five Love Languages.*" He offers a terrific look at identifying the five different ways that we as humans uniquely express and receive love. While experiencing love is profoundly important, Conscious Intelligence focuses upstream in love's *sourcing*.

We are now primed to take a closer look at some of the most common distinctions surrounding love and how their dynamics appear and play out in our daily lives. This is where we determine whether something is *coming from love* or *coming from something else*; every one of these distinctions centers around that.

CHAPTER 8

The Anchors of Love

WHAT I REFER TO as the anchors of love are distinctions about states of being we often experience around the subject of love. An "anchor" can commonly do one of two things: ground us, seat us, and hold us in place...or, in the eventuality that we are out of our depth, an anchor can become a burden, weigh us down, and pull us under.

Remember, Conscious Intelligence does not stray into the realm of judging things as good or bad, right or wrong. Rather, we are making the distinction about things that are attributed and mis-attributed to love. Judgment is something we subsequently place on those things separately. Conscious Intelligence illuminates the distinction between whether something is coming from love or from something else, so that we can gain perspective around what shows up (or doesn't show up) as a result.

ID 29: Love versus Lust/Infatuation

LUST AND INFATUATION are passionate expressions of love that arouse romantic sentiments. Both trigger intense feelings and often happen while a relationship is still novel, unfolding, and evolving. Because lust is more simply an emotional, physical, sexual impulse, it risks also drawing out darker shadow byproducts such as jealousy, insecurity, and obsession. Incidentally, the feelings of lust and infatuation correlate to the same areas of our brains that engender passion, impulsiveness, and cravings.

We all know that romantic love is often instrumental in the initiation of new relationships, but it can be fleeting unless it progresses into greater and deeper substance. When it focuses on pleasure and self-gratification, it can appeal to that end, to a more primal part of our brain. We often affectionately attribute this to the "honeymoon" phase of a relationship.

A couple undergoing the infancy phase of a relationship, passionately in love, typically knows little more than the enticing and appetizing surface qualities each admired initially. Yet, romantic passion ebbs and flows. Over time, it can peel away to expose what truly dwells deep within the heart. It is beyond the honeymoon phase that a couple will eventually encounter more salient tests of their love and discover whether indeed their union has the strength to endure.

Using an analogy, lust and infatuation are like shiny pieces of fruit satisfying a momentous craving and ephemeral hunger, while the presence of authentic love is based in deeper connection; it's the tree that bears abundant fruit season after season. Such a tree has a matured root system that develops permanence over time by enduring severe weather systems, droughts, fires, or insect infestations. In the same way, those in an enduring relationship look upon stress, disagreements, strains, fallings out, or trauma and are not easily shaken.

Science has studied how lust and infatuation can evolve into deeper, enduring connection. Studies dating back more than a century make the distinction when it comes to the attraction and selection of a mate. What one might find fascinating is that these studies include notable names such as Charles Darwin. While Darwin's work is more popularly recognized as a discussion of natural selection, which is a more primal evolutionary process, his lesser attributed studies also include observing love, romance, attraction, and factors affecting the active selection of a mate.[3]

Lust involves the release of brain chemicals, namely dopamine, along with the sensory input from any of our five senses. Together, these induce longing, distraction, and focused attention. Neural networks then become established, acting to progressively enhance and embolden the connection. As time progresses, novelty, imprinting, and the formation of exclusive preference can become the basis formation of the *apple of one's eye*, so to speak. Eventually love, affinity, and adoration can lead to a more enduring attraction and authentically loving relationship.[4]

SUMMARY | ID 29

Sprint? Or marathon? How long's the honeymoon, dear?

Romantic love is often instrumental in the initiation of new relationships, but it can be fleeting unless it progresses into greater and deeper substance.

Lust and infatuation are like shiny pieces of fruit satisfying a momentous craving. To graduate to authentic love does not necessarily mean losing romantic passion as much as it means keeping that intensity while a much broader root system develops over time.

Authentic love is based in deeper connection; it's the tree that bears abundant fruit season after season while bearing out during winter seasons. Those in an enduring relationship look upon stress, disagreements, strains, fallings out, or trauma and are not easily shaken. As time progresses, novelty, imprinting, and the formation of exclusive preference can become the basis formation of the *apple of one's eye*, so to speak. Eventually love, affinity, and adoration can lead to a more enduring attraction and an authentically loving relationship. This applies to enduring love in all relationships, not just one's significant other.

ID 30: Craving | Clinging | Attachment | Addiction

Love is like oxygen
You get too much, you get too high
Not enough and you're gonna die. ~Sweet

Cravings are intense desires that are fixated on a particular person, object, or experience. There is a tightness, rigidity, or must-*ness* about them—as in the addict who craves a fix; the overeater, a binge; the miser, more wealth. Satisfying a craving leads to transitory pleasure, but as the pleasure fades, more craving ensues. Left unchecked, simple cravings, whether for a food or for a person—have a way of attaching to us and commandeering our lives, even enslaving us...and down the rabbit hole we go. Craving forges a path to a state of continuing stuck-*ness* in a binge cycle. It is our trying to fill a void within ourselves with something from outside—and, like any impulse generated in this manner, it results in a temporary fix, an endorphin rush that fades before long, leaving exposed the underlying, unfilled void once again.

Clinging has a close association with dependency and holding on. It creates a circumstance where we experience an emptiness, lacking, and yearning if we perceive we have become detached, separated, and/or disconnected from the thing, idea, or person we want.

WHEN AND HOW do things regress to such a state? Clinging can result when a pleasant feeling evolves to a feeling of *need*. Clinging can remain mild, or it can be more extreme. When genetic or chemical predispositions exist, clinging can graduate into addictive behavior. The cycle that can develop on the more extreme end of this spectrum can be debilitating. In these cases, consciousness may not be enough and is not a substitute for intervention.

For much of the spectrum, though, we can illuminate the link of craving and clinging through awareness of when their benefits wane and instead become hazards. We can gain insight about where such transgressions can lead. Elevating consciousness here is recognizing and disrupting the patterns that lead to craving, clinging, attachment, and addiction.

Wait a minute! I love romantic passion, craving, and the deliciousness of love's emotional expression! Are you saying these are bad?

The distinction here is that this question itself is not framed properly. From the CI perspective, desire, passion, clinging, and craving are actually neutral. They are neither good nor bad. The distinction can be misinterpreted to mean "Thou shalt be free from desire and interpersonal relationships," but nothing could be further from the truth. Remember, we are making the distinction about things that are *sourced from love* versus *being sourced from something else*. In Conscious Intelligence, the previous question could be something more like this: *"Does the presence of desire, passion, and craving ground and seat us in our relationship, or are they pulling us under?"*

Serving others, experiencing and sharing joy, being an involved and present lover, spouse, parent, friend, or neighbor—these are catalyzed by copious helpings of desire and passion. But when desire and passion are fueled by scarcity, desperation, or an internal, perpetual void that seems never able to remain filled, something else is at play—something driven more by afflictions, dependency, and attachment rather than inspiration. Making the distinction facilitates recognizing and addressing the ordeal.

SUMMARY | ID 30

Ah yes, those passionate cravings...

Cravings are intense desires that are fixated on a particular person, object, or experience. Satisfying a craving leads to transitory pleasure, but as the pleasure fades, more craving ensues. Craving forges a path to a state of continuing stuck-*ness* in a binge cycle.

Clinging can result when a pleasant feeling evolves to a feeling of *need*, a condition that has a close association with dependency. It creates a circumstance where we experience an emptiness, lacking, and yearning if we perceive we have become detached or separated from the thing we desire. When amplified by genetic or chemical predispositions, it can graduate into addictive behavior.

So, what's wrong with romantic passion, craving, and the deliciousness of love's emotional expression? Absolutely nothing—we are making the distinction about things that are *sourced from love* versus *being sourced from something else*. Conscious Intelligence makes the distinction: *"Does the presence of desire, passion, and craving come from abundance that grounds and seats us in our relationship, or are they sourced from scarcity that pulls us under?"* Are we cultivating our surrounding environment or bingeing, trying to fill a void *within ourselves* with a temporary fix from something outside that, before long, fades, leaving a perceived, unfilled void once again.

ID 31: Attachment versus Deep Connection

THE DISTINCTION BETWEEN deep connection and attachment can be made this way, as put forth by Dzogchen Ponlop Rinpoche:

Love is a way of thinking, "How can I make you happy?"

Attachment is a way of thinking, "Why aren't you making me happy?"

"How can I make you happy?" comes from love and is associated with deep connection. "Why aren't you making me happy?" comes from scarcity and the misconception that something outside us is supposed to fill the insatiable void inside.

Having a deep connection with someone is not the same as having an attachment to someone.

If we are struggling inside this misconception, it makes no difference how much we claw, clutch, and grab for stuff *out there*. It will never be enough because the void is not caused from anything *out there*. It is a product of our own creation. The need to fill a void carved from scarcity and fear has us gravitating away from our access to Conscious Intelligence.

If we are to elevate consciousness in this set of circumstances, it would involve our becoming more self-aware in locating the true sourcing of what is forming the void within, so we can apply the appropriate measures to eradicate it. Interesting how actually shedding or losing something can be the answer to fulfillment. Otherwise, we remain attached to a fictional outcome that can never be resolved. If we remain dependent upon something outside of ourselves to feel whole, the affliction of attachment becomes the anchor that both drags us down, and those to whom we attach.

Affection, love, care, and compassion live and germinate among the essentials of deep connection. They are sourced from a place of collective contribution, interdependence, and love, not etched from scarcity, fear, and despair.

Heartbreak and Loss: Proof of Love

> *The fog cries for me, it silently weeps, consoles me,*
> *hides my sadness with its own. . .cradles me.*
> *If all my tears were bound on a string,*
> *pearls of sadness so precious and rare,*
> *One falls to the ground and breaks . . . like my heart.*
> *~Michele Marietta (age 15)*

LOVE'S EXPRESSION in all its power, splendor, and complexity can at times result in heartbreak. These kinds of environments, which are super-charged with emotion (and fogged by it) can be mitigated by illuminating the dynamics revolving around loss and heartbreak.

Heartbreak is the visceral experience of pain due to the snatching away of that which we love, whether that absence is actual or perceived. What is meant by "perceived"? Love very well can be present in the circumstance, yet it might not show up the way we want it to, and therefore might not be detected by us or the other. This is illustrated by the absence of, for example, a hug when we want one or a compliment when efforts to please were made.

Heartbreak happens as we perceive in the circumstance that love can be gained or lost. CI distinguishes that we are making this determination operating on the transactional level—where there are *haves* and *have nots*. By now we can suspect that there is another perspective, one where we elevate perspective. For example, consider a breakup of a boyfriend or girlfriend, a marriage, a partner in business, or even the passing of a loved one. While in loving collaboration, the relationship manifests all of the lovely treasures one enjoys while in such a collaboration. If it ends, we indeed experience heartbreak. We can also consider in our grieving that *nothing* of the shared past collaboration *has been lost*; the dividends remain and keep us prospering. All is now a part of who we are in relationships moving forward. The discomfort we experience, not to be brushed aside, is the requisite turmoil and abrasiveness of our transformation as we move through the grieving process.

In the case of the passing of a loved one, we don't stop loving them despite their untimely departure. Rather, the way we sustain our relationship and love them moving forward transforms. The transition that bridges this shift is destined to include heartbreak, but the history is consummated—our eternal love and loving memory is an ever-fixed mark, undisturbed. Moving forward, both our relationship, and way we love, transform.

We live in a temporal reality, a transactional reality where the dynamic of life and death, past and present, gain and loss, love and fear modulate throughout our experiences here on earth. Observed throughout Eastern and Western civilizations alike, this duality of our human circumstance is illustrated:

In Eastern philosophy there exists the notion that: *Born out of the womb of attachment breeds suffering*. We are born into this duality—this temporal, physical, dualistic world, where opposites and extremes define our human condition. This is what is meant by *transactional*: having/not having, gain/loss, empty/full, victim/survivor.

In Western cultural imagery the notion also exists. One prominent example is *Adam and Eve*. They are ejected from Eden, a place of is-*ness* absent dualism, into the duality of the *earthly* world, where they become aware of man/woman, night/day, good/evil, heaven/earth. Both Eastern and Western notions conceptually represent our human circumstance as we struggle to reconcile the powerful distinction between is-*ness* and duality.

When we are attached to a specific way that love shows up and one day it doesn't show up that way, suffering results. The more attached we are to the outcome, the greater the degree of suffering.

Loss and heartbreak are the proof-of-purchase receipt, the seal of authenticity stamped on our heart, for having loved.

While we may not be able to or want to avoid heartbreak, there exists a state, a condition, a realm where the is-*ness* of love is absolute—not was or will be, but *is* in its infinite present moments. It is a place in our hearts where heartbreak is displaced with eternal love and gratitude.

Loss and the Role of Fear

> *Fear is not the opposite of love; fear is the absence of love. Just as darkness is not the opposite of light; darkness is the absence of light.*

MANY OF US HAVE HEARD THE SAYING "Better to have loved and lost than never to have loved at all." The amount that we open our hearts to another is the amount we expose ourselves to potential pain and heartbreak. But here's the thing: The bigger the love, the bigger the loss, the more substantial the grieving. So many people I encounter are plagued with this struggle; they have grown fearful of being hurt and simply decide to stop opening their hearts. Their fear of loss becomes a risk assessment in love as if they are actuaries drafting an insurance policy. They employ the logic that if they don't open their hearts, they won't get hurt. They turn off their projector and cease to gift the world with the light that is the unique expression of their love.

When we choose this scenario, sooner or later we discover that closing our hearts may indeed steer us clear of hurt but not without equally depriving us of the experience of love altogether. Before long, the isolation metastasizes, and a void is created. We become isolated from hurt, yes, but also from love...and eventually from feeling anything at all. When we try to fill the void with other things, it just gets deeper, darker, more desperate, and insatiable. Cultivated by fear, an entire array of ailments develops, manifesting as—you guessed it—attachment, addiction, shame, blame, despair, narcissism, resentment, depression, and worse.

We ask, "Shall I love at the risk of loss, or shall I refrain from love and assure my avoidance of it?" Is it possible to eliminate the aspect of love that has us experience heartbreak, attachment, craving, yearning, sentiment, and expectation? *Not if we wish to remain human.*

> *We cannot gain from love any more than we are willing to risk.*

By recognizing that loss is a natural dynamic of our human experience, we can come to understand it; we can know that we can't gain from love any more than we are willing to risk. Love in its true nature is absent risk, except for our attachment to the transactional part that we can lose. Loss is one possible outcome of following our hearts in this transactional world, but sharing blissful love with another is not possible without incurring it, sooner or later. Boldly opting for bravery, curiosity, and adventure is the only way opportunities of love avail themselves, just as daring to extend our love to another is the only passageway that leads to such opportunities.

When Unconditional Love Opposes Morality

I would do anything for love, but I won't do that.
~Meat Loaf

UNCONDITIONAL LOVE can be deep when it is a promise, a commitment, a pledge. It can be the promise to be there for someone, no matter what, to do anything for someone, *no matter what*.

But *what if* this special someone calls on us for something that, in our deepest, essential Self, conflicts with our inner, moral compass? What if that conflict plunges like a dagger deep into our core values—into our judgment, conscience, and integrity? There we sit, anxious, uneasy, yearning to help, to be there *no matter what*. We want to extend a hand but are competing with the conflicted feelings in the pit of our stomach. We have an awareness that our complicity could prove harmful to this person, to another, or to ourselves. What do we do?

We have a conundrum: On one hand, we have given the deepest, solemn promise to be there, unconditionally, as a friend, parent, partner, sibling, or spouse in sickness and in health, for richer or poorer, even 'til death do us part. Standing in our integrity, *the promises we make mean something*. So, on one hand, we have an unwavering conviction to the integrity of our own moral compass, and on the other, the circumstance situates us diametrically opposed to that compass, risking its betrayal, our principles, and possibly even the law. Something's just *wrong* here. Our integrity splinters into two opposing sides. What do we do?

Sometimes saying "yes" to love means saying "no."

Unconditional love does not equate to providing a perpetual green light. Being fully there for someone requires us to understand the rationale from which that person is operating; we can support the hardware and still question the software and operating system. Are they operating properly, or do they have a virus? Are some files corrupted? We don't throw our computer into the trash because it has a virus, nor do we throw our children, family, or friends into the trash for catching one. We can support the hardware but question, disagree, or be concerned about what software the system is running and how it is functioning.

We can unconditionally love someone and still be allowed to disagree with their choices in conduct at the same time. We can support someone without fueling, enabling, or encouraging that person's current set of behaviors. Sometimes the most loving thing we can do is to say, "No." Remember, if we are being compromised, and we are aware or are made aware that such is the case, we become complicit in fostering the environment of entitlement, and we are prone to perpetuate it. In such a case, sometimes saying "no" becomes our moral obligation. The responsibility is on us, and our integrity actually rides on it.

SUMMARY | ID 31

Filling a hole or building a bridge?

Having a deep connection with someone is not the same as having an attachment to someone.

Love is a way of thinking, "How can I make you happy?" and is associated with deep connection. Attachment is a way of thinking, "Why aren't you making me happy?" and comes from scarcity and the misconception that something outside us is supposed to fill the insatiable void inside. If we are struggling inside this misconception, it makes no difference how much we claw, clutch, and grab for stuff out there. It will never be enough, because the void is not caused from anything out there. It is a product of our own creation. The need to fill a void carved from scarcity and fear has us gravitating away from our access to Conscious Intelligence.

Loss and heartbreak are the proof-of-purchase receipt, the seal of authenticity stamped on our heart for having loved. When we are attached to a specific way that love shows up, and then one day it doesn't show up that way, suffering results. The more attached we are to the outcome, the greater the degree of suffering.

CHAPTER 9

The Shades of Love

LOVE OF SELF

ID 32: Self-Love versus Being in Love with Self, or Narcissism

SELF-LOVE RESULTS when we successfully balance our personal set of values with our compassion for others, and when we successfully equate our perception of our worthiness to the worthiness of others. Self-love is essential for building and maintaining our self-esteem. It could actually be described as the Golden Rule turned onto itself. As the rule states: Do unto others as you would have others do unto you. Turned onto itself, it helps to define self-love: We should treat ourselves as we'd like others to treat us and do unto ourselves as we'd like others to do unto us.

> *Humility is not thinking less of yourself;*
> *it's thinking of yourself less.*   ~C. S. Lewis

A distinction exists between *loving* one's Self and being *in love* with oneself. Self-love is sourced by its nature from love itself. A narcissist's love of self, by stark contrast, is not sourced from love at all; deeply seeded in a realm of scarcity, it is actually sourced from fear and a need to control. A narcissist's over-inflated ego is wrought with self-importance and the cravings of recognition, admiration, and perceived power. Cloaked deeply within a narcissist's subconscious breeds the notion that they are not worthy of love. The fear-centric ego pretends to protect a narcissist from harm, when in reality it inflicts harm by creating a dark void within. This inner void has a constant need to be filled, and because it comes from inside, nothing outside will ever fill it—despite every desperate attempt. This non-resolving predicament fuels the vehicle that drives the narcissist.

Narcissists are often judgmental and critical of others while they draw attention and praise to themselves. They don't care about others; they care about maintaining control and advantage *over* others. Driven by fear, they are hypersensitive, insecure, and terrified of losing control, thereby becoming inconsequential and irrelevant. Their desperation can lead them in a number of directions. Everyone loves acknowledgement and recognition; narcissists *need those attributes to* fill their inner void. Initially, their vanity can appear charismatic, entertaining, and even charming as they pander for reinforcement from others by employing humor, flattery, kind gestures, and the like. If the results to this approach prove insufficient to them, the behavior can regress, becoming more manipulative and scathing, even slipping to hostility and downright aggression towards anyone perceived as a threat to their spotlight.

Dark voids embroidered with scarcity form when one perceives they are deficient or unworthy of love, rather than recognize that they embody an infinite source of love, regardless of stature. When generosity and compassion for others is commandeered by ego and replaced with fear, control, and vanity, chances are narcissism is at play.

In self-love, by contrast, an internal dark void may also be present, but along with it is an affirmative battle, a realization that it cannot be filled with vanity and validation as if these are things to be possessed like a collection of trophies. Self-love is the pathway to eradicating the dark void within in the same way light eradicates darkness. Love is most deeply experienced in its being given away, in its expression, in feeling its radiance. It is experienced through gratitude, kindness, and respect. We are reminded that this also applies to providing these things to ourselves—one of the most difficult acts for many. Regaining a sense of worthiness that is in parity with that which we gift to others is the best indicator that we are trained back onto the scent and that we have stepped back into the light.

Self-Talk

> *There exists only affirmation in this world.*
> *There is no such thing as disaffirmation,*
> *only negative affirmation.*
> *Everything we say, think, and feel is affirmative.*
> *The moment we acknowledge its existence, it has impact.*

IN ORDER TO FORMULATE or create anything, that something, by definition, must be affirmed. Even if we judge something as negative, destructive, or disempowering, it is affirmative because we affirm things into existence. Creation (or destruction) itself requires affirmation. Only afterward do we process it, judge it, and label it in terms of positive or negative.

Whatever we believe about ourselves on the inside is manifested on the outside. When words and phrases become habitual, they embed into our psyche like a program and become unconscious drivers that contribute to what shows up in our lives.

Our Inner Critic (Critical Parent)

SO, WHAT ARE YOU choosing to affirm? The inner critic or critical parent are terms psychologists often use to describe the inner voice that attacks us, saying, "I am bad, wrong, unworthy, stupid, afraid." This is not to be mistaken for our conscience. Our conscience is sourced from our essential Self, fueled by our principles and guided by our integrity.

Our inner critic sabotages us. It is our ego, sourced and fueled from fear. The inner critic consists of misguided programming such as shame and all its siblings. Ego pretends to be protecting us but instead has us getting in our own way. Then, when we fail, it has the audacity to say, "I told ya so."

I learned an important lesson about self-talk and the critical parent many years ago while practicing martial arts. I had just tested for first kyu belt in Aikido, the rank just before black belt (Aikido doesn't really have color belt rankings until black). After the test, I sat in the changing room with my head down, privately going through the test in my head. I didn't execute one technique as perfectly as I'd anticipated, despite my unrelenting training. Although the rest went well, I was milling and simmering over that one particular lapse. I had worked long hours, days, weeks, years. I knew all the techniques and was so attached to the test going perfectly. This was my critical parent telling me, "You suck," and it was very disappointed in me.

While changing out of my sweaty *gi*, a second-degree black belt named Bernard, a man twenty years my senior with whom I regularly trained, entered the changing room. An attorney by trade, Bernard had a very rigid and wise demeanor. He was a man I deeply respected. Bernard extended a congratulatory hand to shake along with a subtle crack of a smile rarely seen in his otherwise stoic carriage. Conspicuously proud of me, he asked in his confident, stern, litigious voice, "How do you feel?" I shook his hand hesitantly, not looking him in the eye, and said, disenchanted, "I sucked."

A silent pause followed; I could feel his whole demeanor shift and his energy change without looking up at him. It was as if I stole something delicate and precious from a child and broke it on the ground.

"What is this you say?"

I went on to express my shame." Well, I screwed up . . . one of the attacks . . . and am so angry at myself for being such an idiot." (Keep in mind, the practice of Aikido follows a very stringent code of conduct, centuries of Japanese tradition rooted in honor and humility. Bernard outranked me; officially, my harsh language was inappropriate and even disrespectful—a testament to how commandeering a critical parent can be.)

Bernard, observing my ample dose of self-punishment, stood poised and dignified while I sat in front of him, broken. His temperance and mentorship was disarming and allowed me to exhale. After several moments, he said, "That's not how I saw it, but you appear compelled to convince me otherwise."

I glanced up, collected myself a bit more, and straightened.

He continued, "Let me ask you. Would you ever look someone in the face and tell him that he sucks..." He meant generally, out in the world, but gestured with a sweep of his arm to the dojo to accentuate where we were. "…or that he's an idiot?" He knew me well and already knew the answer.

"Gosh, no," I replied sheepishly.

"Because if you did, you'd appear to be a completely arrogant jerk, wouldn't you?" Bernard continued.

"Yes, sir," I answered, matching the expression of disgust he had on his face.

"And yet you sit here and tell this to yourself and me, albeit privately." Silence reigned for several moments, then he went on. "That is…*self-arrogance*. You would never say such derogatory things to someone or tolerate hearing them from another because you are not arrogant to others, yet you say them to yourself without any compunction. And I've known you long enough to say, with reasonable certainty, that you say them to yourself not infrequently."

I began to connect the wires. His truth was dead-on right. We can be horrific to ourselves, even if we never speak to others with such disdain and malevolence.

I have never forgotten that light bulb moment and important lesson, the day Bernard earned my even deeper respect and my gratitude.

Incidentally, our Sensei saw it the way Bernard did—an exemplary performance, not as one isolated lapse that didn't go optimally, and promoted me. But the lesson from Bernard that day was far more powerful than any belt promotion.

A Few Words on Self-Deprecation

> *I am so clever*
> *that sometimes I don't understand*
> *a single word of what I am saying.*   ~Oscar Wilde

WORDS MATTER. We've spoken at length about the power of words, the power of thoughts, the power of making distinctions in communication. We have spoken about charged language and how easy it can be to generate negativity from caustic speech and hateful thoughts, whether broadcasted outward or turned inward. But, what of self-deprecating words? What of words intentionally employed as a communication tool, as a strategy to break through barriers of preconception, as an access point to telegraph one's humility as a means to be more accessible?

Self-deprecation is a broadly used speaking style, most commonly attributed to the South and Midwest U.S. It is a phraseology where one belittles, undervalues, and disparages oneself intentionally as a means to be excessively humble and modest. It is a disarming vernacular employed with the intention to invite affinity through creating a bridge of intimacy and familiarity.

> *They all laughed when I said I'd become a comedian.*
> *Well, they're not laughing now.*   ~Bob Monkhouse

Self-deprecation is also one of the most popular and powerful speech techniques used by many prominent figures, from CEOs to presidents of the United States, to authors, entertainers, and comedians. While the delivery is absolutely key, success of the technique depends on the skill of the speaker as well as the content, context, and execution. If the content is inappropriate or simply not funny, it can fall flat and risk having a detrimental effect. On the other hand, well-executed humor that is self-disparaging and even embarrassing, humanizes the speaker. It places them on level footing with the audience and demonstrates vulnerability and humility while inviting their listeners to be receptive and sympathetic.

We are reminded that the most potent power is derived from empowering others. Self-deprecation can empower an audience by positioning the speaker at an accessible level where the audience perceives itself as an equal. It is a tool that can eliminate the sensation of being talked down to, which, in turn, inspires a more casual, familiar, comfortable connection and kinship between the audience and the speaker.

The speaking style relaxes audience expectations while allowing the speaker to show their own humanity in a less formal tone. As a result, it has the ability to be disarming; the audience feels spoken to, not at, and the speaker earns respect, reverence, consensus . . . and a few laughs.

SUMMARY | ID 32

Mirror Mirror on the wall...

Self-love results when we successfully balance our personal set of values with our compassion for others, and when we successfully equate our perception of our worthiness to the worthiness of others. Treating ourselves as we'd like others to treat us, and doing unto ourselves as we'd like others to do unto us, is self-love, in contrast to being in love with self.

A narcissist's love of self, by stark contrast, is not sourced from love at all; deeply seeded in a realm of scarcity, it is actually sourced from fear and a need to control. A narcissist's over-inflated ego is wrought with self-importance and cravings for recognition, admiration, and perceived power. Deep down, they perceive they are not worthy of love. They can appear charismatic, entertaining, and even charming as they pander for reinforcement from others by employing humor, flattery, and kind gestures. If this doesn't work, their behavior can regress to more manipulative, scathing hostility toward anyone perceived as a threat to their spotlight.

LOVE BEYOND SELF

> *I love you not only for what you are,*
> *but for what I am when I am with you...*
> ~Elizabeth Barrett Browning

ID 33: Love | Witness—I See You

Imagine trying to describe in words the uniqueness of a sunset to someone who has never seen one. Could we do it not only so they could clearly imagine what it looked like, but also so they could distinguish it uniquely from any other sunset? Impossible, right? Even if the person sees a photo we snapped, it still wouldn't convey the full experience of being there. Only if we sat side by side with them, witnessing the same sunset, could we share the unique experience. Why? Because our experience is not merely the mechanical components of what makes a sunset.

> **Sunset**: The earth's rotation along its equatorial axis with respect to one's vantage point in relation to the earth's curvature, the position of the sun, and the horizon, as it slowly progresses and impedes one's view.

Our experience also involves the circumstance in the moment as it unravels, our emotions, our state of mind, our memories, and the other amazing elements that constitute the lens of uniqueness that we each peer through. Such *shared* experiences gain value when we and another are present, witnessing each other as a part of the context, as we breathe life into them. Otherwise, the experiences in our lives are just a series of mechanical components like the ones just described.

The tapestries of our lives do not solely involve love as intimacy; they involve a broader spectrum of connection, interaction, collaboration, struggle, and triumph. While shared experiences of love, such as a sunset, the birth of a child, or a kiss, are uniquely ours, they bear little value if not witnessed by those most important to us. Witnessing is constituted inside of the experience and is *not separate*. Unlike observing oneself in the mirror, this is the *window*. Witnessing is the sharing of the view with another as well as sharing a view of each other; it is also seeing ourselves in the other as well as experiencing who we are because of each other.

When we have a conversation about love, intimacy, and the witnessing of another, the span of time is not long before the essential ingredient, *vulnerability*, comes up. Common fears that accompany feeling vulnerable can include a fear of not being enough or having enough to offer; not being strong enough to stand in the truth of who we are fully self-expressed. These are all manifestations that draw us off the beam. We open ourselves to vulnerability when we share with another our passion and love of something, someone, a group, a cause, or a principle. The things we deem important to us involve an investment of ourselves into them. The more important we deem them, the more generous the investment—and the bigger the risk of failure in the eyes of others.

I see you. This element of love—*witness*—requires on occasion another seeing us at our worst, knowing our weaknesses, and not turning away. The act calls for our standing in our human-*ness*, warts and all, successes and failures, quirks and hidden gifts, while, despite it all, the other person considers us sacred, inspiring, and beautiful.

The eyes are the windows to the soul, as the adage goes. Giving another the gift of our vulnerability opens the blinds. Using our eyes and other senses, is to witness another. Sharing the view with another is sharing the view of each other. The tapestries of our lives are painted in part by the brush of everyone that we have met—as theirs is, too, informed in part by having witnessed us.

SUMMARY | ID 33

To witness each other...

"*I see you*" requires another seeing us at our worst, knowing our weaknesses, and not turning away. The act calls for our standing in our human-*ness*, warts and all, successes and failures, quirks and hidden gifts, while, despite it all, the other person considers us sacred, inspiring, and beautiful. The experience of love has value only when shared. Witnessing is the sharing of the view with another as well as sharing a view of each other; it is seeing ourselves in the other as well as experiencing who we are because of each other. Giving another the gift of our vulnerability is to be seen. It is to be witnessed.

ID 34: Love | Recognition—I Feel You

*If you wish to learn a man's true character,
observe how he treats those inferior to him.*
                              ~*J. K. Rowling*

LOVE DRAWS FROM compassion and altruism towards others and has parity in its expression. Having love for, and connection to, our essential Self is compulsory for our personal health, esteem, and productivity. This connection is a key component that informs our relationships with others who are along for the ride. It avails us the ability to experience another's joy, pain, elation, burden, anxiety, and love as if it were our own.

How one treats those they perceive inferior— a stranger, server, janitor, flight attendant, or other service professional—is a sober and honest indication of who they really are. It is a reflection of how they value people, their level of compassion, and how they perceive themselves. It is as much a mirror as it is a window. When love beyond Self and love of Self are in parity, so too is the recognition of love in our consciousness.

Those who apply themselves to participate in another's world by stepping into their shoes, connecting with their heart, and seeing through their eyes do so by habitually elevating perspective and cultivating compassion and empathy. Feeling another's emotions and being present to connecting with them is the powerfully empathic fuel that informs our recognition of another within ourselves.

I feel you engages more inside of us than the singular ingredient of merely feeling another's emotions. It involves seeing into their world with universal perspective and, in the process, offering them a glimpse into ours. It is sharing a picnic blanket and each other's basket of goodies. In this sharing, we create an intersection of our two worlds as they are combined into one. Are you *feelin'* me?

SUMMARY | ID 34

To walk a mile in another's shoes…

"*I feel you*" is the ability to experience another's joy, pain, elation, burden, anxiety, and love as if these emotions were our own.

Those who apply themselves to participate in another's world by stepping into their shoes, connecting with their heart, and seeing through their eyes do so by habitually elevating perspective and cultivating compassion and empathy. Feeling another's emotions and being present to connecting with them is the powerfully empathic fuel that informs our recognition of another within ourselves.

ID 35: Love | Connection — I Am You

> *We.*
> *We together.*
> *One being.*
> *Flow together like water.*
> *'til I can't tell you from me…*
>   ~Terrence Malick, *The Thin Red Line*

To receive love and to love, there is no distinction. Without one there is no other. They are not separate. The act of its giving is inseparable and indiscernible from the act of its receiving. Love in its true essence is simultaneously experienced as both of these. Even though physically we are separate beings, the experience of love requires connection that is either present or not.

Love is neither transactional, dualistic, nor one-sided. Love is beyond dimension—unconditional and boundless. To fully experience, embody, manifest, and share in love—to realize it—we must open ourselves to love and discover we are not alone in this endeavor. We are all connected just as each ocean flows into the other. The only way love flows between us all is to know that there is nothing separating us from each other.

I like to use lightning as a flashy analogy. With electricity, only when the loop in an electrical circuit is closed—meaning the electrical leads connect to each other—will electricity flow. Love follows the same concept. Either the circuit loop is complete, and love is discharged, or it is not.

We think of lightning as a flash of light in the sky. But in order for that to form, several things must occur. First, negatively charged electron particles, called leaders, have to descend from the bottom of a cloud. These are usually invisible without some kind of visual aid, although occasionally they can be seen as faint outlines in the sky prior to the main event.

These leaders are seeking a place to go, something to connect to so that the circuit loop can be closed. Objects on the ground that extend far into the air, such as trees or telephone poles, are great candidates. These objects also possess electrical particles—and in electricity, as in magnets, opposites attract and like repels. So as the negatively charged leaders descend and come into contact with, say, a tree, the negative particles that sit at the top of the tree move down the tree, away from the top, repelled by the negative particles of the leaders. This leaves behind a concentration of positively charged particles at the top of the tree.

At this point, if the pull of the negative leaders descending from the cloud is strong enough, it will draw the positive particles at the top of the tree upward into the air. These *streamers* ascend above and beyond the tree itself, reaching skyward. When an upward-extending, positively charged streamer makes contact with a downward-descending, negatively charged leader, the circuit loop is closed and, BOOM, the electricity stored in the cloud discharges, flowing in a bolt of lightning ranging anywhere from one hundred million to a billion volts of electricity.[1] The result is the huge flash and explosion we clearly see and call the lightning bolt. Now that's LOVE, baby!

> *To receive love and to love,*
> *there is no distinction.*

They are not separate. When we give love, we get love; we see it light up that other person, and in our seeing this, we are lit up. We too are getting something out of it—we are giving, and we are getting; *one and other, there is no one without the other*. It is why love is the most powerful and essential force in all humankind.

So, to return to the initial question—"What's love got to do with it?"—can we elevate our lives without something to love, something we love to do, and something to look forward to, be it in our work, play, family, community? Can we attain fulfillment and a quality of life for ourselves and others without connection? Whether we are trying to guide our organization to leave less of a carbon footprint or guide our five-year-old to consume more green beans, all of it involves connection. All involves plugging in, because love, in its broader sense, in all of its manifestations, does not occur in a vacuum. *No man <or woman> is an island, entire of itself…*

SUMMARY | ID 35

We do not weave the web of life; we are merely a strand in it...

To receive love and to give love, there is no distinction. They are not separate. When we give love, we get love; we see our love light up that other person, and in our seeing this, we are lit up. We too are getting something out of it—we are giving, and we are getting; *one and other, there is no one without the other*. Love in its true essence is simultaneously experienced as both of these. Even though physically we are separate beings, the experience of love requires connection that is either present or not.

THE ELEVATED DISTINCTIONS

DETERMINATION
Something To Look Forward To

ENGAGEMENT
Something We Love To Do

PASSION
Something That Inspires Us

ELEVATED DISTINCTIONS

Introduction to the Elevated Distinctions

The only thing that is constant is change   ~Heraclitus

As we traverse The Conscious Intelligence Paradigm, the scenery is likely appearing different for you at this point. Elevating consciousness is transformative. Illumination is powerful. It gives us perspective. It can also rip us out of our routines, have us feeling exhilarated one moment, then confronted the next—crinkling the eyebrow while saying "Ah-hahhhh,"—then suddenly out of the blue, the rollercoaster plunges, triggering that pit of the stomach feeling.

Our world is dynamic and always in a state of change, all the way down to the cellular level. Billions of cells in our bodies die every single day as billions more are born. Stars die in cataclysmic fashion while others are born in similar fashion. Change is the ONLY thing that is certain, that we can depend upon, that is inevitable. As dynamic as this universe is, our ability to adapt has had us not just survive, but prevail, as we experience what one of my favorite luminaries, Joseph Campbell, called "The Hero's Journey."

It happens on some unparticular, unsuspecting day just like any other. Here you are, embarking on this solemn quest that is the next chapter in your life, the hero's journey that has been set at your feet, placed before you. The train casts off abruptly from the station before you have the opportunity to find your seat or to determine whether you are even on the right train. (Don't worry, you are!) Thoughts flash anxiously through your head. *This is folly, an accident, a misunderstanding*—due to some irresistible force that thrust you here without your permission—or, at least, without your having any idea what you have gotten yourself into. (Don't worry; you have an idea. You just didn't know that fiddling with one domino would start a chain reaction and kick the train into motion.) Whatever the impetus, this doesn't feel like the best timing in your busy schedule. It is inconvenient, and it is downright disruptive.

The journey has no scheduled refueling stops, no transfers or layovers, and not even a conductor announcing… much of anything, at least in any language you understand. But the view out the window—the sky, the clouds, the horizon. You've never seen this landscape so clearly before.

The train ultimately breaks down (it usually does at some point). Perhaps you decide to get out and walk, or maybe you just stay aboard the train, fearful of what stepping off may lead to. Hey! It looks dangerous. So you wait . . . and wait . . . and wait . . . for the train to start up again or for something else to happen.

Eventually and inevitably, someone or something *does* show up—train robbers, a trampling herd of elephants, a sandstorm, or perhaps someone who has been hoofing it for quite a while from a different broken-down train, just outside that last town, over yonder. Imagine *their* disappointment when they arrive, having thought *this* train might be their salvation.

Or maybe the person is *you*. Perhaps *you* left that broken-down train over yonder and, spotting *this* train on the horizon, thought it might be *your* salvation. And it is you who happens upon someone else who hasn't yet gotten off *their* train to venture onward.

The thing is, the journey hasn't stopped just because the train did…and it hasn't stopped even if you think *you* did. Only when the deeper purpose of this train ride is illuminated—and that same brilliant illumination burns away whatever is obscuring your view of the horizon—will your trajectory find its True North and guide you home. Did I mention? Home will appear different now too, if it still even remains in its original location and form (we are speaking in metaphors anyway). Only after you have learned the lessons this journey is meant to instill, after you've slain the dragons, staved off the robbers, avoided the stampedes of elephants, found out why the person from a-yonder came calling to your train will you finally find the passage back home. You may *feel* the same and think home has significantly changed, but the opposite is more likely. Your journey has changed the way you see things, the way you experience things, the way you process things. You are returning transformed, with a new, elevated perspective. With this enhanced illumination, you may discover you are seeking to create deeper meaning in your life... and in the lives of others.

This is the stuff of our human circumstance. This is your own unique, one-of-a-kind, only-one-in-existence, individual human experience. And so we enter the Elevated Distinctions.

CHAPTER 10

The Call To Serve

*Sometimes the answer to our prayers
is to become the answer to someone else's prayers.*
                                    ~Robert Breault

ID 36: Universal Accountability

As humans, many of us feel a calling deep within ourselves to serve others, either by taking on their burdens or by working to secure the well-being for all. We've witnessed this throughout humanity, from the soldier that lays down his life for another, to a company cutting down on their carbon footprint, to everyday people leading the neighborhood watch, attending PTA meetings, holding public office, or rescuing a neighbor from their flooded home. This calling is demonstrated whether a person serves in the armed forces, or serves on the organization's board of directors—whether a person serves in a classroom, or serves hot meals to the homeless. We see it in history with Gandhi, Mother Teresa, Oskar Schindler, Harriet Tubman, and Martin Luther King Jr.

Where does this come from, this call to carry another's load in addition to one's own, to give one's last piece of bread to another, even if they themselves haven't eaten, to seek a spark of goodness even within their worst enemy, to place their own life in peril in order to lift another from peril?

This call is the call of *Universal Accountability*, the heightened consciousness associated with service, either to humankind in general or to those who are not in a position to help themselves.

Universal Accountability serves the collective that spans far beyond oneself. It is a profound expression of Conscious Intelligence and is a perspective that recognizes that everything and everyone is connected. When we bestow upon ourselves the obligation to be in the service of others and to take on the work of serving the vulnerable, we are stepping into Universal Accountability.

The Accountability Doctrine

If not me, then who?
If not now, when?

BEING OF SERVICE is a powerful form of accountability, whether it comes from those well-resourced or those with modest means. Universal Accountability takes up the slack and owns up to the broader collective of circumstances that exist outside of our bubble. It is commonly associated with extending outward, to *serve others*, versus merely looking inward, to *serve* only *one's self*.

In everyday, practical terms, when we step into the shoes of Universal Accountability, the increase in our responsibilities translates into the taking on a greater burden—overseeing more tasks, people, decisions. Basically, we take on bearing the burden required to look after a bigger flock; such an undertaking demands weightier judgment calls and, as a result, fills a role that elicits a broader impact. When we do this, the effort commonly involves higher stakes and greater ramifications.

For example, if I am riding a bicycle and I crash, it is likely that little damage will be inflicted onto others; the damage is probably confined to myself (and the bike). If I am driving a semi-truck and crash, much more damage can occur in a much larger radius and scale, for which I would be accountable. Still greater, if I am piloting an airplane full of passengers, the responsibility is massive and therefore asserts much more accountability should anything go wrong.

Accountability at its highest expression is not merely a linear, one-to-one relationship predicated by the execution of one's punch-list of responsibilities. As in the previous example, comparing riding a bike versus piloting a plane, accountability can reach exponentially further into the realms of universality. Universal Accountability requires elevated consciousness. It is not just something we do; it is also a part of who we are committed to being.

Universal Accountability requires inner initiative and drive as well as outer leadership and engagement. When executed well, it can inspire others to participate and help them realize that they, too, can be of service and find fulfillment.

Being accountable is not the same as giving our power away. Rather, it means that we embrace the extraordinary power that such a solemn act generates. The lens, too, is altogether different. There exists a common misconception between the distinction of *giving our power away* versus *empowering others*. The most elevated form of power and leadership propagates from empowering others. This is not a loss of anything, but rather an exponential gain!

Universal Justice

> *As painful as it is to receive contempt from another,*
> *it is more debilitating by far to be filled with contempt*
> *for another.*
> ~The Arbinger Institute, *The Anatomy of Peace*

ONE DAY, on a mountainous dirt road in the outskirts of Islamabad, Pakistan, terrorists with guns boarded a small school bus carrying twenty young girls returning from a school day. The leader demanded, "Which one of you is named Malala?" When that person was revealed, he walked up to where she sat, his hand trembling as he lifted his gun, and shot her point-blank in the head. Miraculously, she survived—and if you know this brave sixteen-year-old's story, you will only stand in awe of her courage, composure, and conduct following the incident. To this day, she has *never* condemned the shooter; she holds no hate, no contempt, no vilification, and has not uttered an angry or hateful word about the terrorists' beliefs or motives.

How is this possible? How can a young girl of sixteen process such a life-altering event—an act of such evil, hatred, and darkness perpetrated upon her—and reconcile it in such a manner? The girl was intentionally shot in the head! This is an unthinkable, real story, in the real world, about a real sixteen-year-old. It just as well might have happened right outside our own homes to our own daughter, sister, best friend. How can anyone—more astonishingly, a young girl—, possess such composure?

To put this in perspective, I walked into Starbucks this morning and witnessed an enraged patron chewing out the barista, just because too much foam was added to her latte!

What can possibly be more challenging for us than to look at another person who has trespassed against us and caused unimaginable turmoil and not judge, not hate, not resent? While justice should rightfully be served, how can we stand elevated, consciously in non-judgment? How can we simultaneously stand with dignity, without resentment, and find some sort of humanity in the other? Is this possible?

> *It is not only possible; it is necessary.*
> *It is not only a choice; it is a moral obligation*
> *we have to ourselves—*
> *If we wish to elevate our consciousness.*

While Malala's shooting is an extreme example, we all collect various trespasses against us every day: someone cuts us off in traffic, says something unkind, is dishonest to us, or adds too much foam to our latte (kidding). What are our options in such circumstances? One option is to bury our heads and make every effort to ignore the event and forget it ever happened. Naturally, however, whatever happened doesn't simply disappear into the ether; it remains unresolved and repressed. Every time we look in the mirror, we are reminded of the trespasses we stepped over, that are simmering inside of us, and we drift through life mired in that anger, regret, shame, resentment—or, worse, seething hatred. This noxious vitriol corrodes us from the inside and eventually percolates up and oozes out in countless toxic ways. Could this be how a person conjures the twisted notion inside themselves that justifies a heinous act like shooting an innocent sixteen-year-old in the face?

Or, as another option, we might collect all this misguided brute hate and shame and act out intentionally in revenge—but then, we are no different from those who hurt *us*. Such conduct perpetuates and metastasizes the wound, rendering us just as powerless. We become the trespassers we so resent. We also inevitably discover that the choice corrodes us from the inside, consumes us, and ultimately leaves us in pieces, isolated and empty. Even worse is the carnage, destruction, pain, and anguish of others left suffering in the wake.

So, what do we do?

An elevating tide floats all boats. In the transactional world of cause/effect, do this, get that, it is 100% appropriate that justice be served when a trespass occurs. Harm was inflicted and, for society to function, there must be consequences. But let's consider a view that *simultaneously* exists, a view from an elevated perspective, a realm absent judgment. There exists a distinction between the circumstances and us. *The circumstances are not us.* We can be affected by them, but they *do not define us*. The injuries inflicted by the perpetrators are actually inflicted upon themselves, and only they will be able to eradicate them. We can choose to move through the injurious circumstance, to maintain our own personal sovereignty, and to remember who we are committed to being. With the choice comes the conviction to maintain course while focusing on elevating ourselves and others.

The perpetrators are compelled to act as they do, having been shaped from their environment. This universal connection affects us all. In the same way that people in our environment can bring out the joy and best in us, we can also inhabit an environment that brings out the worst in us and drives us to darker things. The emotion that incites anger, resentment, and revenge devolves to become the deepest part of what we ultimately resent about ourselves.

We cannot solve problems with the same kind of thinking that created them in the first place. ~Albert Einstein

While taking revenge may bring us momentary elation, giving in to the urge, this mutated form of anger, is a fleeting panacea. It does not and will not fulfill us ultimately. Exacting revenge is a temporary, short-lived, false remedy, like the drug addict getting a fix. Unchecked, the fix will actually propagate a larger, festering internal hole and result in further suffering. By cultivating such a toxic environment, revenge and retaliation actually embolden those seeking any excuse to escalate. The flames of destruction are fanned, the fire proliferates, and the circumstance devolves, spiraling into darkness.

Does this mean we should do nothing about it? Ignore it? Not seek justice? Of course not. It guides us to step into any circumstance understanding that if we are not being part of the solution, then we are part of the problem.

> *He who fights with monsters*
> *should look to it that he himself*
> *does not become one.*   ~*Friedrich Nietzsche*

If what makes us feel better is reveling in the pain we can inflict back on the perpetrator, then such a choice does little more than metastasize the toxic environment within us. From there it corrodes us from the inside and expresses itself in one toxic form or another. We *become* the monster we wish to destroy.

We are all connected. Reminding ourselves of this is the only thing that cultivates healing and keeps us from descending into the swamp of vitriol. If the way we wish to dispense justice is through the infliction of pain upon the other while we revel, make no mistake—that pain will persist and continue to afflict *us*. To be Universally Accountable, we are called to find a path to healing—to hold the space for the other as we seek our own path to healing. They may never get there, but the space we hold for them, in the case that they do, is the one that releases *us* from the chains of suffering. Our capacity to invite and cultivate compassion around the circumstances that led the other to make the misguided choices—even while we are in great pain—is the measure by which we access Conscious Intelligence.

Universal Grace

UNIVERSAL ACCOUNTABILITY INCLUDES a recognition that the perpetrators are connected to our own humanity. If they have perpetrated injury upon us, it is because, in some place or at some time, their environment created the space for this injury to be inflicted upon *them*. What becomes evident is that they had a lack of resources, guidance, and comparative perspective to make different choices—the distinctions remained invisible to them.

Elevating consciousness requires breaking the cycle; illuminating the distinction means disrupting this pattern as we navigate our energies to instead cultivate the presence of an alternative. Universal grace can call us to look inside ourselves in order to heal. It can call us to make the distinction between thinking we *are* the circumstance versus understanding that we are a bystander affected *by* the circumstance. Both call us to account. Both call us to make a sober choice, otherwise we risk looking outside for someone or something to blame, shame, and judge. Distinguishing the difference and making the illuminated choice have everything to do with whether we become part of the sickness or the remedy.

> *We cannot control what the universe serves up.*
> *We can control how we conduct ourselves*
> *within our circumstances.*
> *Doing so while accessing Conscious Intelligence*
> *is to have grace.*

Those who are guided by principles to retain composure in the most trying of circumstances, as Malala did (truly Herculean), have gained mastery in the discipline of Universal Grace.

SUMMARY | ID 36

If not me, then who? If not now, when? Universal Accountability serves the collective that spans far beyond oneself.

In everyday, practical terms, when we step into the shoes of Universal Accountability, the increase in our responsibilities translates into the taking on a greater burden—overseeing more tasks, people, decisions. Basically, we take on bearing the burden required to look after a bigger flock; such an undertaking demands weightier judgment calls and, as a result, fills a role that elicits a broader impact. When we do this, the effort commonly involves higher stakes and greater ramifications.

Universal Accountability serves the collective that spans far beyond oneself. It is a profound expression of Conscious Intelligence and is a perspective that recognizes that everything and everyone is connected. When we bestow upon ourselves the obligation to be in the service of others and to take on the work of serving the vulnerable, we are stepping into Universal Accountability.

He who fights with monsters should be careful not to become one himself. If what makes us feel better is reveling in the pain we can inflict on the perpetrator, then such a choice does little more than metastasize the toxic environment within us. From there it corrodes us from the inside and expresses itself in one toxic form or another. We become the monster we wish to destroy.

ID 37: Acceptance

ACCEPTANCE IS AN ultimatum doled out by nature, as crucial to our vitality as our breath. It is a naturally occurring component of our human experience, inherently fundamental and instinctive. Its reference appears in wisdom, archetypal symbology, religious teachings, and the social sciences, including behavioral psychology as the final of the five stages of the grieving process.[2]

If a loved one dies, for example, we can do nothing to change this circumstance. But we can change our *relationship* to the circumstance by accepting it and evolving our relationship with the person who is no longer living physically among us. We have no choice but to concede that death is simply a part of life. Death is not negotiable; it cannot be sent up for review or be overturned. While we might protest, we either choose to remain attached to the way things were and continue suffering and stagnating, or we surrender our attachment, evolve to a place of acceptance, and move forward. Surrendering our attachment does not mean relinquishing our love for the person. Celebrating them, and who we are today because of them, is to honor and perpetuate a loving relationship with them moving forward. This is a prolific form of acceptance.

Acceptance is part of *any* process that involves change and the challenges associated, not just the passing of a loved one. The phenomenon of acceptance can occur only in the present regarding a circumstance that exists in the past. Unless we are time travelers, we cannot return to the past, so once a circumstance is over, it is simply out of our hands and beyond our realm. What we can do is make choices regarding our present relationship to the past circumstance and discover how we can best be served by it. By evaluating what has happened, we can apply what we've learned, evolve, and move forward.

Let's be clear: *acceptance is not resignation, nor is it condoning*. Rather, it is the end of our stuck-*ness* in dwelling on what has been lost, the cessation of our resistance to inevitable change. Acceptance is a conscious, intentional acknowledgement that the past circumstance, now beyond our locus of control, has brought about unavoidable change.

Change, by its very nature, can be confronting—but it is a necessary component of transformation. Like the molting process of a snake, acceptance has a beginning and a completion. As with the snake, it takes time to shed the former layer and welcome in the new one. The process is complete when any attachment to our old state of being around the circumstance is discharged, allowing a new way of being to emerge and to initiate. Incidentally, the symbolic nature represented by the snake or serpent often receives a bad rap of biblical proportions because it is commonly misunderstood. A snake is confined to its skin size until it is liberated from its old vessel, upon which its body is free to expand and grow into a new skin. This is transformation. Snakes are scary to some (as is being faced with change), but they are a powerful, archetypal symbol whose dynamism is befitting to a universe undergoing constant change. Welcoming change is not only what we are meant to do, it is the most natural and constant part of being human.

SUMMARY | ID 37

Acceptance is a conscious, intentional acknowledgement that a past circumstance, now beyond our control, has brought about unavoidable change.

As the final of the five stages of the grieving process, acceptance is part of *any* process that involves change and the associated challenges, not just the passing of a loved one. The phenomenon of acceptance can occur only in the present regarding a circumstance that exists in the past. Once a circumstance is over, it is simply out of our hands and beyond our realm. What we can do is make choices regarding our present relationship to the past circumstance and discover how we can best be served by it. By evaluating what has happened, we can apply what we've learned, then evolve and move forward. Let's be clear: *acceptance is not resignation, nor is it condoning*. Rather, it is the end of our *stuckness* in dwelling on what has been lost, the cessation of our resistance to inevitable change. Acceptance is a conscious, intentional acknowledgement that the past circumstance, now beyond our locus of control, has brought about unavoidable change.

ID 38: Forgiveness

To err is human; to forgive divine.   ~Alexander Pope

WHILE ACCEPTANCE IS something we *have to* do if we are to progress through change—forgiveness is quite often the instrument. Sometimes a harm, trespass, or tragedy is so profound, it seems the only way we are going to heal and move forward is by supernatural or Divine intervention—but elevating our consciousness can also make it so. By bringing to light our attachment to the circumstance and illuminating perspective to facilitate its release, we can restore our balance and get on leading a more productive, fulfilling life.

> *Forgiveness is the cessation of blame and desire to exact punishment.*
> *It is letting go of being angry and resentful for an offense or fault.*

Forgiveness releases us from the throes of punitive judgment, those unsettling emotions that can lead to transitory desires such as revenge. We soon discover that such short-lived, cause/effect gratification does not cure the persisting injury; it only perpetuates it. Only changing our relationship *to*, and perspective *of*, the circumstance can release us from the cycle of suffering. We spoke earlier of dwelling, mercy, and revenge, to name a few: *we are not our circumstance.* If we remain attached to the circumstance, if our relationship and perspective to it does not change, then we are dwelling in suffering where we will remain indefinitely until we make a different choice.

What does elevating above our circumstances look like with respect to forgiveness? We have an option either to frame a circumstance from a perspective of *right versus wrong* or from a perspective that it just *is*. The former is akin to opposite sides attacking each other from the trenches of the battlefield, while the latter offers elevation *above* the circumstance, where there are no discernable sides to delineate at all—just an ordeal. This is what it means to rise above a circumstance, to elevate consciousness. The forgiveness vantage point is the view from an elevated perspective.

> *Healing doesn't mean the damage never existed;*
> *it means the damage is no longer allowed*
> *to have power or control over us.*

Forgiveness is not in the business of judgment or duality; it's not punitive. There is no opposite of forgiveness. For example, resentment is not the opposite of forgiveness, it is the *absence* of forgiveness, so we are not making the underlying act okay. The act of forgiving does not turn wrong into right or bad into good. It has *nothing* to do with the duality nature of the trespass. If it did, the grieving process would never complete and would carry on *ad infinitum.*

Forgiveness does not release someone of liability or accountability; rather, it releases *us* from the imprisonment that carrying such a burden bears—which is ultimately the only thing that truly matters if we ever wish to progress, evolve, elevate.

SUMMARY | ID 38

Forgiveness doesn't mean the damage never existed; it means that it no longer has power over us.

Forgiveness is not in the business of judgment or duality; it's not punitive. There is no opposite of forgiveness. For example, resentment is not the opposite of forgiveness, it is the *absence* of forgiveness. The act of forgiving does not turn wrong into right or bad into good. It has *nothing* to do with the duality nature of the trespass. Forgiveness does not release someone of liability or accountability; rather, it releases *us* from the imprisonment that carrying such a burden bears—which is ultimately the only thing that truly matters if we ever wish to progress, evolve, elevate.

CHAPTER 11

Charity | Service | Moral Obligation

ID 39: Purposeful Giving and Receiving

*Overcoming poverty is not a task of charity;
it is an act of justice.*   ~Nelson Mandela

THERE EXISTS A POOL infused with compassion and generosity, where acts of contribution can be neither quantified nor depleted. Its benevolent waters are part of something bigger than itself; its source is drawn from the abundance that love is, the stuff from which formlessness becomes form, where drinking from it quenches another's thirst, and where gazing into it captures the reflection of our face amongst the entirety of humanity.

The world is blessed with the many who find deep purpose in the act of giving. Of those, far fewer realize that there is a morality in their allowing others to contribute back to them as well. Receiving is also an act of generosity incumbent upon those who wish to fulfill the role as givers. In allowing another to contribute to us, we are giving that person the gift of contribution and purpose, both as a part of our lives and as a part of theirs.

To give is to receive, to receive is to give; they are sourced from the same authentic and sacred place. One doesn't exist without the other—*not when sourced from a conscious person.*

Then… there are those tormented by the oppression of scarcity. Keeping score (how much do I get versus you; how much do I give versus you) comes from a place of scarcity. If we are keeping score—if giving and receiving become one and other, then the act becomes transactional (*this for that*.) It is likely that something besides generosity and contribution is at play.

We have all encountered those driven by the oppression of scarcity. People with a scarcity mindset are driven by inner programming containing a flawed notion that one elevates by grabbing, trampling, or crawling over others along their ascension to the mountain peak. Their path is that of the ill-fated Sisyphus who, in Greek mythology, was given a curse to forever push a heavy stone up a mountain only to have it topple down the other side again and again and again.

Scarcity is a form of attachment. It conceives a flawed perception that fabricates a rift between those who have and those who have not. Its source is a void from deep within that no amount of receiving, grasping, clutching can fulfill.

SUMMARY | ID 39

When giving is receiving.

To give is to receive, to receive is to give; they are sourced from the same authentic and sacred place. One doesn't exist without the other—*not when sourced from a conscious person.*

Keeping score (how much do I get versus you) comes from a place of scarcity. If we are keeping score—if giving and receiving become one and other, then the act becomes transactional (*this for that*.) It is likely that something besides generosity and contribution is at play. People with a scarcity mindset are driven by inner programming containing a flawed notion that one elevates by grabbing, trampling, or crawling over others along their ascension to the mountain peak. Scarcity is a form of attachment. It conceives a flawed perception that fabricates a rift between those who have and those who have not. Its source is a void from deep within that no amount of receiving, grasping, clutching can fulfill.

ID 40: Receiving versus Expecting | A Gift versus a Debt

WHILE THERE IS NO distinction between giving and receiving from elevated consciousness, there does exist a distinction between *receiving* and *expecting*. This distinction reminds me of a conversation with author Wayne Dyer regarding the act of giving. From a giver's perspective, a distinction exists between a *gift* and a *debt*. If a prospective receiver *expects* something from a giver, they are not providing the giver an opportunity for it to be *gifted*. Instead, they are transforming a generous, charitable contribution into something they perceive that they are owed—and, in doing so, are creating a sense of entitlement.

The distinction between receiving and expecting really has to do with illustrating that there is no such thing as transactional *quid pro quo* (literally, "something for something") in the context of an authentic act of giving and the gracious act of receiving. A gift is not a gift when the receiver expects to get it and already perceives that they are entitled to it. Such a perspective is more suggestive of a debt collector, not a gracious benefactor.

To get a sense of this, we all know that Valentine's Day is a day to celebrate love and affection, but for some, the day incites an environment brimming with anxiety. Often, we bear witness to the massive commercialization that stirs the pot of expectation. Flowers, cards, jewelry, chocolate—capitalism daring us to quantify how much of these things equals the measure of love we have for our beloved. It is no wonder that this can generate tremendous tension on both the gifting and receiving sides. Love is not quantified by *stuff*. There exists no quantifiable standard. To contrive one is a misuse of the true sense of the holiday and celebration of love in general. In the act of giving authentically, there is no debt being paid, no standard being met—and, actually, no transaction whatsoever.

The pool from which benevolence draws is boundless. No pie chart depicts such apportionment. Benevolence is not a currency; it's a way of being that cultivates joy by the means of showing gratitude.

SUMMARY | ID 40

A gift or a debt? When a gift is not a gift.

If a prospective receiver *expects* something from a giver, they are not providing the giver an opportunity for it to be *gifted*. Instead, they are transforming a generous, charitable contribution into something they perceive they are owed—and, in doing so, are creating a sense of entitlement. A gift is not a gift when the receiver expects to get it and already perceives that they are entitled to it. Such a perspective is more suggestive of the giver being a debt collector, not a gracious benefactor.

ID 41: Entitlement versus Deserving

The most fulfilling things in life aren't things.

W E ALL HAVE LIKELY WITNESSED someone acting entitled at one time or another. We might even be guilty ourselves. How do we recognize it? Most of us instinctively employ the same standard used in 1964 by Supreme Court Justice Potter Stewart to distinguish *obscenity from art*: "We know it when we see it."

In terms of the Invisible Distinctions, the key to illuminating the distinctions around entitlement is to identify the *source* of the sense of entitlement and, in doing so, gain perspective.

> **Entitlement** in its purest definition is *actually* neutral. It refers to universal rights we all have, such as the "inalienable rights" afforded by the U.S. Constitution: the right to life, liberty, and the pursuit of happiness.

But, the distinction is necessary when *entitlement* refers to someone who believes they are inherently deserving of privileges or special treatment—or that they have exclusivity and privilege *over others*—that is altogether different. This person carries on presuming that the world is in their debt. Notably and distinctively, such a person *bestows this sense of entitlement upon themselves*—often with the help of enablers.

> **Deserving** in its purest definition is also neutral. It describes a person possessing qualities or demonstrating behaviors that *earn* merit and reward (or punishment) by consensus *from others*.

The distinction is that deserving is *bestowed onto a person by others*. It is misconceived when one incorrectly bestows it upon oneself. In a nutshell, the misconceptions of entitlement and deserving are flip sides of the same coin, where *entitlement* refers to the privilege one thinks they inherently possess while *deserving* refers to the reward one inherently thinks they have earned. But let's dig deeper. This special coin can also be flipped inside-out, where both deserving and entitlement are inverted. I call this "inside-out deserving" and "inside-out entitlement."

Inside-Out Deserving

THERE ARE THOSE who, despite being acknowledged, have the misconception that they are *not* deserving. They deny themselves the right to be celebrated, affirmed, and acknowledged. It is the perception of being undeserving or unworthy of, for example, love, praise, happiness, good fortune... As a result, despite the efforts by others, those holding this misconception disallow themselves permission to receive these gifts.

Additionally, there are those who find themselves blessed by fortunate circumstances but feel *undeserving*. And there are those who persevere through a tragic crisis where others were far less fortunate; these souls suffer from survivor's guilt.[1] All are examples of *inside-out deserving*, where one has the perception of being undeserving of love, joy, happiness, and fulfillment. Even despite others' efforts to shower these people with these affirmations, the natural, sacrosanct state such as living out one's life is disrupted.

People of this mind may misconceive that accepting these gifts would appear indulgent, arrogant, or that others deserve it more than they do, as if it were in limited supply. Accepting these gifts appear to them as self-serving and trigger feelings of guilt or shame. The disconnect is that *all* love, joy, acknowledgement, and happiness exist neither in limited quantity, nor are they even *quantifiable*. They are not measured in portions or amounts at all. Only their refusal deprives them of it.

What of money and material fortune in this discussion? This seems to contradict the quantifiable haves/have-nots conversation. Whether we witness others with these things or are bestowed such fortune ourselves, the vantage point from the Conscious Intelligence perch is not different. Money and material fortune are akin to energy in their true nature. Like energy, both are neutral; when harnessed by us humans, their impact depends entirely on how they flow and are directed. Those who flow wealth towards themselves provide little if any value to others. Those fortunate enough to receive it and share its abundance fulfill its highest potential. Just as energy can be directed and used to enhance productivity, so can material fortune be used to amplify the most important things in our and others' lives. A conscious versus an unconscious mind interprets and employs these things quite differently.

Inside-Out Entitlement

INSIDE-OUT ENTITLEMENT is also seeded in misconception. It happens when a source with questionable credentials and/or ulterior motives tells you that you are entitled to or deserving of something. We are all witness to this in extravagant advertisements for example. They egg us on to indulge, invite us to consume, encourage us to celebrate ourselves, cheer us on to live it up in lavish style, because, hey, "*we deserve it*!" Luxury brands anoint themselves as expert gurus and purveyors to the deserving, promising happiness and fulfillment in life to those who consume their products or services. They go on to suggest that buying their decadent product or service is our reward, and gosh darn it, we deserve that! So, splurge!

This is not to suggest we should live like monks or deny ourselves nice things; remember, we are making distinctions here, not passing judgment. The distinction merely shines a spotlight on a false notion that suggests buying lavish stuff in the name of *deserving* when we feel a lack of fulfillment in our life will *fill us up*. It won't—not because we don't deserve it, but because these things are offered as a panacea for such a claim. The sourcing of such a directive is inauthentic. So, although the strategy doesn't serve the objective, we need not blame those who pursue promoting it. After all, there's a market for these wares, the peddlers are good at hustling them, and they are paid handsomely for convincing us we need them. The intention here is to bring attention to the conflation and to illuminate what is coming authentically from deserving versus from something else.

Another dimension of this inside-out entitlement is *quid pro quo*. Consider, for example, a patron dining at a fine restaurant, living under the pretense that spending a ton of money at such an establishment *entitles* them to be rude to the wait staff; or someone in the community that donates money to charity, but is involved in human trafficking; or someone who buys their spouse fine jewelry and vacations, but smacks the spouse around from time to time.

Just because one spends money or is generous in one or more arenas in life, even in significant ways, doesn't give them a right to be abusive or act immorally towards others. Acts of "good" in one place don't earn a person the allowances to abuse others as if earning "jerk credits" is a *thing*. That's not the way it works. Yet, the boundary is blurred quite often when it is misconceived or justified by the perpetrator as some sort of earned entitlement.

> *Both sides of the inside-out coin are disempowering, each for opposite reasons.*
> *It all comes down to this question: "What is informing the perspective?"*

Inside-out deserving is the product of an innocent, injured psyche misperceiving that it needs to deny itself acknowledgement, or that it needs to feel ashamed for being more fortunate than others.

Inside-out entitlement is the invitation to indulge by a false authority, filled with the endorphin-releasing seductiveness that materialism provides. It suggests we can fill our inner voids by consuming outer stuff. And inside-out entitlement is the misconception that one can treat others abusively, having filled their scorecard with some good deeds to balance out that bad behavior, affording them "jerk" credits they can cash in to mistreat others.

Noblesse Oblige | The Distinction as Charged versus Neutral

Noblesse Oblige was mentioned earlier. Let's expand to apply it here in the Elevated Distinctions.

Being born into fortune or acquiring it, as well as being fortuitous or having a stroke of luck, are neutral states regarding *deserving* and *entitlement*. The term "neutral" simply means no intrinsic value is assigned to this state. When we add a morality perspective to it, we assign duality and thus *a charge* (positive or negative). Taking such good fortune for granted certainly paves the way to a sense of entitlement, turning the neutrality negative. Humility, generosity, and gratitude, on the other hand, elevate our consciousness, inoculate us from the perils of entitlement, and are more attributed to turning the neutrality positive. You've probably met folks on both ends of the spectrum during the course of your life; they are quite different, aren't they?

Elevation can evolve only from the act of elevating others. Taking the gifts that have been bestowed upon us and elevating others is *not intrinsic*, it is something more commonly conceded as noble and sacred. When we are so blessed as to enjoy fortune that has been bestowed upon us, the concept of *noblesse oblige* is the requisite buttress that elevates the plentitudes of good fortune. Translated as "nobility obligates," this term has come to mean the *unwritten obligation of people from a noble ancestry to act honorably and generously to others*. Today, *noblesse oblige* is the recognition by those gifted with much, that much is expected in return. It is the recognition that the world is best served in the sharing of such blessings, and that being in the service of others elevates everyone.

SUMMARY | ID 41

Deserving to be worthy or worthy of deserving, that is the question.

Entitlement in its purest definition is *actually* neutral. It refers to universal rights we all have, such as the "inalienable rights" afforded by the U.S. Constitution: the right to life, liberty, and the pursuit of happiness. But, the distinction is necessary when *entitlement* refers to someone who believes they are inherently deserving of privileges or special treatment—or that they have exclusivity and privilege *over others*. That is altogether different. This person carries on presuming the world is in their debt. Notably and distinctively, such a person *bestows this sense of entitlement upon themselves*—often with the help of enablers.

Deserving in its purest definition is also neutral. It describes a person possessing qualities or demonstrating behaviors that *earn* merit and reward (or punishment) by consensus *from others*. The distinction is that deserving is *bestowed onto a person by others*. It is misconceived when one incorrectly bestows it upon oneself.

Inside-out deserving is the product of an innocent, injured psyche misperceiving that it needs to deny itself acknowledgement, or that it needs to feel ashamed for being more fortunate than others.

Inside-out entitlement is the invitation to indulge by a false authority, filled with the endorphin-releasing seductiveness that materialism provides. It suggests we can fill our inner voids by consuming outer stuff. And inside-out entitlement can also be the misconception that one can treat others abusively, having filled their scorecard with some good deeds to balance out that bad behavior, affording them "jerk" credits they can cash in to mistreat others.

ID 42: Giving and Generosity

> *He who wishes to secure the good of others*
> *has already secured his own.* ~Confucius

WHEN WE THINK of the most generous of people, we typically think of them as unconditionally selfless. But that's just what we, as outsiders, observe.

> *What do generous people think? How do they feel?*
> *What drives them?*

This distinction focuses on *one's personal* inner relationship to, source of, and purpose in the act of giving and being generous. It does not focus on what *other people think* of such actions. Is the giving motivated by an altruistic, inner purpose? Or is it fed by some degree of craving for acclaim, indulging vanity, or seeking admiration from others? The Latin root of altruistic—*atrium*—means "somebody else." Altruism is a belief in the well-being of others that inspires giving. It is a sentiment, not the act of giving itself.[2]

Why is it important to illuminate distinctions about giving and generosity specifically from the perspective of one's inner motivations? Whether driven by deep inner purpose, or an outward drive for admiration, the acts of giving generate impact, just in different ways. These distinctions of giving all constitute acts of altruism, but each to different degrees, motivations, and relative benefits or costs. When is altruism selfless, and when is it something else? Making the distinction can provide perspective into the motivations of others and can inform, inspire, and direct the motivations within ourselves.

Selflessness

> *You don't have to set yourself on fire*
> *to keep other people warm.* ~Unknown

SELFLESSNESS IS simply giving without the expectation of getting anything back. Although we might think of "selfless" literally as "self-*less*," an absence of self, or some sort of self-denial, this is not true. Giving at such a level does not deplete us; it fills us to the brim with a sense of gratification and purpose. Any notion that compels someone to inflict harm upon themselves as a means to demonstrate contribution is not altruism at all. Neither generosity nor contribution are sourced, motivated, or fueled by such things; rather, an act motivated by such a misconception is *vanity*.

When giving is sourced from selflessness, *we* are the beneficiary; it is not perceived as depleting us at all. Rather, it is the light of inspiration we witness when the benefit of our contribution makes a difference to another.

So, wait! Are we truly being selfless if we are benefitting in this way? Absolutely! Authentic giving is receiving; receiving is giving. There is no separation when the act is coming from an authentic place.

Sacrifice

SACRIFICE IS the selfless act of giving oneself on behalf of another, or for the greater good, in such a manner that it depletes us or causes our demise as a result. Well, wait! We just spoke of how, when giving is authentic, we are not depleted in any way. We also noted that intentional self-harm is not altruistic. So, *what's the distinction here*?

The distinction is that when an act of sacrifice is *authentic*, we do not perceive loss or depletion even if harm befalls us. The Latin root of sacrifice is *sacra* (sacred things) and *facer* (to do or perform). To perform a sacred act is to gain, not to lose.

Throughout history, sacrifice has been chronicled across the gamut of civilizations, cultures, and religions, from the Mayans and Romans to Abraham and Christ. In romantic literature, mythology, and the Hero's Journey, the symbolism of sacrifice plays a powerful role in our human psyche.[3] It is the sacrifice of the one to save the many or the ultimate concession of the body, our corporal, earthbound form of which this earthly realm is but transitory. To do so is a *selfless* act. Metaphors and stories depict the death of a hero's corporal form as the sacrifice that earns their worthy transition and entry into the formless, higher consciousness. We hold such heroic acts, and the heroes of today who perform them, to the same esteem.

What's more, death need not necessarily mean of the body. It also refers to the psychological aspects of death. This is the aspect of sacrifice that refers to the splintered psyche we all possess called our *ego*, where our ego has separated from our essential Self. If we symbolically kill off the dark shadow that is our ego, that leads us back to the one-*ness* that is our essential Self. What results is a calibration of our self-navigation equipment, setting us back on course to our True North. This is what is meant by atonement, (at-one-ment) for example, but it has many names.

The symbolic death of ego is typically accompanied by great discomfort, challenge, and physical or psychological pain. We all feel it; the culprits are our old friends *change and resistance*—going on that diet, working longer hours to make the deadline for the new prospective client, losing sleep to care for the newborn, commuting long distances to work, or caring for a grandparent, friend, animal in need. These acts symbolically kill our ego; they pacify it. Ego death is not to be mistaken for the intentional act of inflicting pain, discomfort, or literal death upon *oneself*. That would be vanity. Intentionally harming oneself is simply not a sacred act; it is a malady requiring critical care and treatment.

The message regarding sacrifice is not for us to become a martyr or to degrade or deplete ourselves at all. Rather, it guides us to annihilate our fear-driven ego, a feat that can feel a lot like *hell* when we're enduring it—so we can once again connect to, and be guided by, our *essential Self*, the place where selflessness is sourced.

When we discussed *self-preservation* earlier, we emphasized the necessity of securing our own basic survival first in order to have the capacity to assist another (e.g., on an airplane, putting on your own oxygen mask first before helping others). It's important to note that acts of sacrifice do not test our capacity to harm ourselves in order to elevate *ourselves*; rather, they test our capacity to live our lives in a way that elevates *others*. It is only incidental, tragically incidental, should harm befall us in doing so. We are also reminded that *self-preservation* is neutral.

> *So, if we conflate the distinction between*
> *selflessness and sacrifice*
> *by depleting our well-being rather than*
> *metaphorically annihilating our ego,*
> *we miss the message entirely.*

What about the ultimate sacrifice exemplified by our brave soldiers and heroes who serve in the military or fire and police departments? This is not putting in long hours at work or tending to our newborn at 2:00 a.m.; it's *real* lives being lost, not symbolic ones! Actually, the part that is considered "sacrificed" actually is symbolic, and such an example encapsulates the notion befittingly.

Recall that the distinction does not focus on what others think about the act. The distinction focuses on the hero's inner relationship with, and purpose for, their act. A soldier purposefully places themselves in harm's way, but at no time do they *wish* to give their life. They do not wish or have any intention to bring harm to themselves. In the solemn event that the soldier is injured, maimed, or killed; it is others that characterize the act as sacrifice. While death might be a solemn result of the soldier faithfully executing their service, *it is not the inspiration for it*. The soldier has already annihilated his ego-driven vanity *in principle*, evidenced by their heeding the call to serve. The distinction illuminates where the soldier's selflessness comes from—their inner motivation to serve, not to die. This distinction does not diminish the honor and nobility we bestow onto the brave soldier in the event of an ultimate sacrifice; quite the contrary, it reveres it.

Quid Pro Quo

> *All selfless people are generous,*
> *but not all generous people are selfless.*

LET'S CHANGE GEARS NOW regarding giving and generosity. Let's say that someone wants to give a million bucks that will result in feeding a village for an entire year, but for their generosity, they want the building administering the aid to be named after them. Terrific! Thank goodness for the aid! This is an impactful act.

Today and throughout history, the business and transactional world continues to function on the concept of quid pro quo. This includes deal-making, negotiations, compensation for providing a service or product, and earning progression up the corporate ladder. Quid pro quo in itself is neutral, neither good nor bad; it has no positive or negative charge. It just *is*. How people choose to apply quid pro quo in the world is a question of ethics and judgment, one that determines whether it is a benefit or a detriment.

The purpose here is to make the *distinction* by identifying, not judging, the source of inner motivation of one's giving and generosity, not about the transactional nature that fuels capitalism. In doing so, we can draw our own conclusions as to where both our and others' motivations fit within our personal value system. As is the objective here, what results is that we gain perspective and elevate our consciousness.

In the last section we talked about how the doling out of "good" acts doesn't permit one to act badly with impunity. Recall the "jerk credits" guy who donates money to charity but is involved in human trafficking. In such a case, the act falls short of morality, it brings harm, and is no longer neutral. But what of quid pro quo if the something received back is harmless and benign?

In the "naming of the building" example, the person is both generous and charitable. Is that person *selfless* if they are motivated by enjoying the favor of others, receiving a tax deduction, or in any other way, expecting something in return? Let's look at this: Recall, the distinction is neutral; the act deemed "generous" is an opinion and a judgment doled out by others. We see it all the time in the form of a dinner gala in one's honor, a seat on the board, or our friend's name on a building, to name a few examples.

We are in the Elevated Distinctions section, so we are talking about charity, giving, and generosity in terms of motivation of the giver. While a contributor's motivation may not be completely selfless or altruistic, it can be prolific. So, generous, yes, but can a person be fully selfless when quid pro quo is at play? Perhaps not as much. According to acclaimed philosophers, scholars, and luminaries at least as far back as the middle ages such as *Maimonides*, the attachment to expectations of getting something back *may* go unnoticed by others, but it *does not* go unnoticed within our own psyche.

> **SUMMARY | ID 42**
>
> **You don't have to set yourself on fire to keep other people warm.**
>
> Selflessness is simply giving without the expectation of getting anything back. Although we might think of "selfless" literally as "self-less," meaning an absence of self or some sort of self-denial, this is not true. Giving at such a level does not deplete us; it fills us to the brim with a sense of gratification and purpose. If we conflate the distinction between selflessness and sacrifice by depleting our well-being rather than metaphorically annihilating our ego, we miss the message entirely.

CHAPTER 12

Social Justice and Change

*The arc of the moral universe is long
but it bends toward justice.* ~Theodore Parker

Social Justice

SOCIAL JUSTICE is served when we account fairly for the universal morality of all. It sits at the intersection between the breadth of our capacity to speak for all humanity and the depth of our willingness to do so.

There exists a distinction between dissent and incivility, between disruption and anarchy, and between fighting for versus fighting against. Further, if one is with the majority, it doesn't guarantee that person is right, nor if one is with the minority, it doesn't make that person wrong. At one point in history, the law permitted slavery, burning witches at the stake, segregation, citizens to be locked in internment camps and denied women the vote, the consumption of alcohol, and the same sex to marry.

History has demonstrated time and time again that sometimes the majority can be just plain wrong. At these major junctures, humanity is called to the carpet to make significant shifts and course corrections in order to realign with its core values. Still today, many biases, beliefs, and traditions exist that some people maintain pass muster simply because they have stood the test of time. Social justice and morality bring such pretexts to question.

*We can't solve our problems
with the same thinking we used
when we created them.* ~Albert Einstein

ID 43: Distinctions of Conflict

Dissent versus Incivility | Disruption versus Anarchy

TODAY, PROGRESS IS MOVING at breakneck speeds while our human capacity to evolve, adapt, and keep up often falls out of step and trails behind. It tests and places great strain on the moral fabric holding even the most civilized of nations, communities, and societies together.

Is the distinction talking about *civil disobedience*? Sure, we could definitely include this, but we don't have to be Martin Luther King Jr., Mahatma Gandhi, Rosa Parks, Henry David Thoreau, or Einstein to question the status quo and stand up and advocate for an alternative.[6] Such people understand that dissent and disruption require knowing the rules so well, they know when to break or change them.

Malevolence, corruption, and injustice aren't resolved by doling out more of the same, no matter how seemingly justified. It is why these kinds of methods are not found anywhere within the iconic journeys of the great disruptors just mentioned.

Such disruptors understand that the methods to challenging, overhauling, or even replacing rules cannot be approached the same way they were formulated and imposed in the first place. They understand that social justice cannot be dispensed matching the same violent, immoral means it protests, just as two wrongs don't make a right. And, they understand that change cannot be approached from opposing, adversarial sides, but rather must be approached finding the intersection of collective values and unifying principles.

In wide contrast, those who practice *incivility* and *anarchy* both reject and disregard rules altogether. They pick sides, polarize humanity, employ ultimatum thinking, and seek to bend consensus towards a narrow cause and a select few, rather than the greater good. Commonly rooted in ignorance, these subscribers lack perspective, are absent critical thought, and are often devoid of morality, reasoning, or concern for others.

Is every fight meant to be won?

Sometimes it is prudent to lose the battle in order to win the war. Sometimes it's not our choice. We witness the application of this concept ranging from the popular "Sales 101" adage that "the client is always right" where acquiescing to a client's sensibilities sometimes is the final word—to landmark court cases faltering in lower courts in order to appeal to the Supreme Court. When we remain attached to a certain way of thinking, when we entrench in the conviction that our way is the only way, when we refuse and dismiss another view that seems radically different from our own, we not only place ourselves at risk, we place social justice at risk. Attachment to ideas and bias give rise to resistance, separation, and isolation. These impede the gaining of perspective and disallow space to consider alternatives. The commensurate challenge to let go of one certain way of thinking arises. This is where diplomacy and civility end and where conflict, isolation, divisiveness, and extremism arise.

Must letting go of our attachment to ideas include ignoring and dismissing an entire set of cultural traditions? Of course not. But updating them to reflect the undeniable insights gained from this evolving world, yes!—that is, if we are to approach them with elevated perspective. Inviting and availing ourselves to listen to the most passionate and informed arguments from *all* sides can be powerful and prolific in spawning fresh ideas, alternative solutions, and innovation.

Fighting to Win

WHEN ANSWERING THE CALL to *fight*, we may be best served considering *why*: What do we hope to win? What will it cost us? Where will it leave us? Is this an opportunity where conflict can build character and challenge us to be better despite the outcome—win or lose? Are we considering that the adversary may be challenging us to confront a blind spot, a false notion, a chink in our armor?

Or, is our adversary luring us downward to an environment of anguish, blame, shame, fear, and divisiveness? Such places commonly invite mudslinging, character assassinations, and hate-mongering. While the short-term gratification of taking up these battles are alluring, this kind of indulgence fast dissipates to become an empty victory, leaving in its place a hangover resembling the worst expression of ourselves.

When Winning Is Losing

When we descend down the escalator to the sewer-level to engage in battle, we risk becoming complicit in the very thing we claim to be denouncing—and for what? We *lose* either way, because only two possible outcomes can result. Either we are outplayed and left lying face down in the sewage, defeated with our know-it-all ego hovering as it does, kicking us while we're down and saying, "I told you so." Or, we are victorious! Yay, congratulations! We are crowned the King of the Sewer! Nobody can sling sewage and assassinate character as handily as we can! Bravo!

Perhaps upon further consideration, we determine that both of those options stink. We are defined by where we dwell and with whom. If we dwell in the sewer long enough, we begin to stink, and the world relates to us in that way.

When we commit to not dwell in the sewer or bask with those who do, we discover that the toxic people in our lives either dissipate, lose power over us, or both.

Yeah, okay, but what about the challenge of having toxic people in our lives that we cannot avoid, despite us steering clear of the sewer? Hey, sometimes the toilets get backed up even in the nicest of neighborhoods. Circumstances can arise where these people are fixtures in our environment—they can be family members, a coworker at the office, or, heaven forbid, that perennial guest at the annual Thanksgiving dinner. Or perhaps these are people who, despite the drama, we still value, love, like, or care about enough that we choose them powerfully, warts and all...but grrrrrr, on occasion, they just get under our skin and drive us crazy! Know anyone like that?

If we were to draft a contract with such a person, an elevated narrative that notes how we intend to remain civil, it might sound something like this:

Out of respect for the sacred space we share, we shall also respect the right of each other's processes. While our processes sometimes are not in harmony, they are uniquely ours. We have no right to change each other, but we shall endeavor to discover ways to bring out the best in each other because we both own up to our processes, and we are both better with each other *in* our lives than *without*…

Yeah, yeah, namasté, peace out, and all that…easier said than done, right? But here's what's powerful about this: Even if we are the *only* one who practices this narrative, upholds our side of the contract, and the other person doesn't care at all, *it still works*. It works because we hold the space for the other person to elevate while we simultaneously set boundaries for our own personal sovereignty.

Careful, though—the temptation to roll our eyes in judgment or to retreat to the kitchen to carve the turkey and partake in gossip or feel superior makes us complicit. This is *not* holding space; it is being righteous. If this happens, consider bailing off that descending escalator you just hopped onto. Otherwise, grab the plunger, because the toilets are about to back up and we are about to soil a perfectly good pair of shoes.

What do you stand for?

Elevation is never about one person levitating above another; an elevating tide lifts all boats. It is not just the environment we choose to inhabit while interacting with the world; it also is the platform we constantly cultivate and invite others to share in.

Fighting For versus Fighting Against | Negativity Bias

History ultimately defines us not by what we think, feel, or believe, but by what we do, what we stand for, and how these actions invite connection and draw us closer to others. This reminds me of a favorite quote by *Maya Angelou*:

> *At the end of the day*
> *people won't remember what you said or did,*
> *they will remember how you made them feel.*

Maya understood this distinction well (and lived it). But what if someone said to us: "Are you with us or against us?" We hear this all the time in one form or another, especially today, don't we? "You're either pro or anti; it's us against them, the good guys versus the bad guys." Pretty powerful ultimatum, isn't it? Do you hear the luring away and divisiveness versus the drawing in and connection? A mythical battle is being contrived out of thin air. Instead, what if we pose an inquisitive question that acknowledges differences but seeks to understand, find commonality, and gain perspective?

When circumstances are framed in *us versus them*, it's in our nature to associate our side as being affirmative, or "pro," while we stigmatize the other side being perceived as opposing. As an example, consider the highly charged, emotional battle that pits *right to life* against *right to choose*. In this historical battle, we find both sides insisting on framing their side as being *pro*. Are you *pro*-life or *pro*-choice? Both sides are as contentiously opposite as can be, but both are aligned with a pro-position narrative and both choose an *us versus them* stance. Why?

Here's a quote from Mother Teresa:

> *I was once asked why I don't participate in anti-war demonstrations. I said that I will never do that, but as soon as you have a pro-peace rally, I'll be there.*

Mother Teresa understood the real stigma that negativity manifests. We all do. It can create a bias that is infectious; it can become a contagion that can spread like a pandemic. The stigma sparks a primal part of our brain that is triggered when we are threatened with danger, and the impulse attributed to such a threat is to take a divisive posture and repel.

Negativity bias is a natural tendency to draw our attention to negativity over positivity. We are drawn to it in the same way our eyes are drawn to a car accident we can't look away from as we pass it on the freeway. It is why the vast majority of news reporting is negative. By generating far more viewership than positive news, negative news is the gold standard since viewership numbers are what determine the valuation and pricing of advertising. It is the gold standard in politics and advertising as well as a darker tool for propaganda and exploitation. When negativity is the strategy, influence is the objective and fear is the delivery system—while narrowing the perspective, skewering the facts, or outright misrepresentation are the weapons.

Negativity bias is *real*. When negativity is shaped into a tool and *used* irresponsibly to manipulate, incite, or gain support, it can become dangerous. When under such biased influence, our ability to remain in command of our circumstances is diminished. It activates people to abandon their sense of reason by appealing instead to their emotions, especially the ones linked to *fear*. Such a reaction comes from a primal area of our brain known as our *reptilian brain*. The reptilian area of the brain is hyper-focused on one primal task: *survival*. It does so by simplifying the circumstance to one, binary decision—*fight or flight*.

This trigger-switch is a decision programmed into us since our beginning—*survive or die*—when existential threats were a daily reality and considerably more common. When we are in this mode, we are not thinking critically nor *responding* in gradations of reason; instead, our brain is *reacting* as if it were perceiving a mortal threat. The area of our brain that otherwise grasps perspective, empathy, strategy, consequences, and critical analysis, *the prefrontal cortex*, is switched off by the reptilian brain.

When presented with frenzied, triggering, evocative situations, our reptilian brain takes over, and we will grab for *anything* resembling a life preserver. I witnessed this all the time during the rescues of those drowning. The one drowning will grasp onto *anything* buoyant around them and not let go, including *you*. If you're not extremely careful, they can pull you down and place you in peril. Emotional reactivity is capable of steamrolling straight over reason, leaving us wide open for exploitation to one who knows how to wield the rhetoric. Inciting our inborn, primitive fear is a powerful tool that is easily weaponized, and like anything powerful, when placed in the wrong hands could be dangerous.

Wait! Wait! Wait! What? I've been talking about how we gravitate to a *pro* stance versus an *anti* stance—*for* versus *against*. How does this become "*negativity bias*"? The answer is: these seemingly opposing concepts are actually bedfellows. The bed they lie in is fear and fear mongering, employing tactics such as blame, polarization, and divisiveness. Negativity bias amplifies the chasm perceived between us versus them; it is rooted in very subjective, narrow perspective capitalizing on our most primal, base emotion: *fear*. It is up to us to identify when this is occurring so we can make the distinction, not take the bait, and refrain from slipping into reptilian brain.

Disruption

THE WORD "DISRUPT" has fast become ubiquitous today. When words become ubiquitous, their meanings and distinctions sometimes get lost or become muffled and their edges dulled. Disruption in the 21st century has shifted the Business 101 adage "adapt or die" from being merely a suggestion to an absolute necessity.

Innovation today is not just disrupting the status quo but annihilating it by completely transforming our approach to business, productivity, research, communication, politics, health, the environment, and social justice. Businesses within these fields are receiving sweeping systemic overhauls or they simply aren't surviving. While disruptors such as Steve Jobs, Elon Musk, Richard Branson, and Mark Zuckerberg are household names, a whopping 88% of the Fortune 500 companies that existed in the mid-20th century are gone today.[9] Amidst the ever-advancing capabilities of this age, disruption of the status quo is the rule, not the exception.

Recall the quote from Albert Einstein, "We cannot solve problems with the same kind of thinking that created them in the first place"? Evolution and change are the *only* constant guaranteed us. Time can fray the edges and tatter the fixtures of our environment, often while going unnoticed. The process can go undetected for *years* as we inhabit the space day to day, settled in our regimens. We cruise along, settled in, until one day, the process, habit, product, service, or technology becomes dated, problematic, inefficient, or obsolete. It is our nature to adjust, to create workarounds, and to stick with the way "it's *always* been done."

Having perspective to approach things with an open mind is a discipline that can feel like defying gravity. Elevating consciousness requires breaking the cycle, disrupting patterns, and advocating innovative culture so evolutionary alternatives can materialize. Oftentimes, the powerful choice is the one we don't want to make because it appears to cut against the grain. It is our human nature to be change averse. Here's that other thing we spoke about earlier: *resistance*. Resistance is confronting. But nothing of any importance with true value ever comes easy.

Sometimes we have to *invent* a choice; this is the true definition of disruption. Why is it so often that influencers, thought leaders, and disruptors have little or no direct background in the industry they are disrupting? Have you noticed this? It's true! It takes someone who can approach the challenges *within* an organization from *outside* of it, someone with an external, fresh, often unconventional perspective.

Innovative companies (as of the date of this book's publishing) such as Uber, Sales Force, Airbnb, Amazon, Facebook, Google, Tesla, Apple, and Yelp have changed the game in this brave new 21st century. Despite whether we like these companies or agree with their practices, they are disrupting the landscape. When terms like uber-*ization*, friending, going viral, and the use of the word "Google" as a *verb* become common vernacular, we quickly discover that the word "disruption" has far evolved from merely describing a pesky kid that shoots spitballs at his classmates.

Disruption typically lives hand-in-hand with a landscape changing faster than most consumers' ability to keep up. Next-generation capabilities in this age of technology have brought to light disruption in social, political, economic, scientific, military, and environmental spheres at a level the world has never seen. Good, bad, indifferent—we witness this as we face the conversation around privacy, expediency, dominance, and the law. Entire industries such as transportation, retail, marketing, travel, entertainment, and finance have completely transformed through the phenomenon of disruptive thinking and innovation.

We are witnessing the effects of disruption every day on the news and media. We see it when economic, social, political, and military conflicts around the world are further stoked by access to social media, connectivity to the internet, hacking, data breach, and propaganda. We witness it in the powerful science and technology that invents more potent antibiotics only to breed drug-resistant superbugs. We are witnessing it in extended life expectancy due to medical breakthroughs, causing the need and costs for end-of-life care to skyrocket, bringing up questions about morality, and challenging the costs of treatments, managed care, and litigation. We are running in a race to better care for our earth's ecosystem in response to climate change. We have the serious debates over organic and genetic farming, over conservation with respect to preserving product freshness versus demand for product packaging, marketing and convenience. The list of innovative solutions begets an ever-longer list of new challenges and opportunities.

It is a widely held misconception today that, for every challenge, there exists a *technological* solution. While there exists a wealth of opportunity in this popular viewpoint, fact is, *we cannot solve human issues without humanity, meaning* we cannot succeed by using technology *alone*. Indeed, technology will continue to solve ever-increasing sets of challenges, but, with every singular solution, several new challenges will always emerge (just like *whack-a-mole*). Innovation and technology will always breed new challenges; as a result, the rise of further innovation will always be required to meet them.

How Does This All Fit Together?

THESE DISTINCTIONS OF DISRUPTION speak to our approach to matters that persist but no longer serve us, between breaking things open to innovate, evolve, and thrive versus just breaking things. They beg us to discover the presence of an alternative, to realize that we always have choice, and to regain perspective by clearing the fog of stale routine.

Disruption is change, and change always begets resistance, the natural reaction enmeshed within our human nature. When our reptilian brain engages, we react and impulsively resist as if our survival is at stake. When not emotionally charged or overwhelmed with fear, we are better poised to *respond* rather than *react*. We shift to offense rather than retreat to defense. We operate from a space where we consider consequences, compassionately listen, devise strategies, employ critical analysis—all to create and implement innovative solutions. Rather than just survive, we prevail—not over one another, but rather over the collective circumstances.

Disruption is prolific when it propels the human race forward, promotes progress, and dispels the inefficient and antiquated status quo. Disruption rocks when it addresses limitations, breaches, and failures of things we just...*accept* without questioning. It places us in inquiry about the things we take for granted, replaces processes by offering new alternatives. Disruption is transformative when it addresses obsolescence and dares us to think differently. It will always create new challenges as well as unintended consequences that, yes, disruption will ironically also be summoned to address.

SUMMARY | ID 43

What do you stand for?

There exists a distinction between dissent and incivility, between disruption and anarchy, and between fighting for versus fighting against.

Those who practice *incivility* and *anarchy* reject and disregard rules altogether. They polarize humanity, employ ultimatum thinking, and seek to bend consensus toward a narrow cause and a select few rather than the greater good. Commonly rooted in ignorance, lack of perspective, absence of critical thought, they are often devoid of morality, reasoning, or concern for others. Malevolence, corruption, and injustice aren't resolved by doling out more of the same, no matter how seemingly justified. Social justice cannot be dispensed matching the same violent, immoral means it protests, just as two wrongs don't make a right. Change must be approached finding the intersection of collective values and unifying principles and cannot be approached from opposing, adversarial sides—not by those seeking to elevate consciousness.

Negativity bias is a natural tendency to draw our attention to negativity over positivity. We are drawn to it in the same way our eyes are drawn to a car accident we can't look away from as we pass it on the freeway. When negativity is shaped into a tool and *used* irresponsibly to manipulate, incite, or gain support, it can become dangerous. When under such biased influence, our ability to remain in command of our circumstances is diminished. It activates people to abandon their sense of reason by appealing instead to their emotions, especially the ones linked to *fear*.

Disruption speaks to our approach to matters that persist but no longer serve us. There is an important distinction between breaking things open to innovate, evolve, and thrive versus just breaking things. "We cannot solve problems with the same kind of thinking that created them in the first place." Disruption is change, and change always begets resistance, the natural reaction enmeshed within our human nature. Disruption is transformative when it addresses obsolescence and dares us to think differently.

ID 44: Effecting Change

Earlier, we spoke of true freedom. Remember that true freedom is not the absence of challenge and responsibility; true freedom actually amasses considerably more of those ingredients. The grander the project, the grander its impact, its scale of responsibility, and our newly spawned accountability.

Change draws no distinction between where we are versus where we are going; it is a wave that we can either choose to ride or be pummeled by. Change requires walking in shoes we may not yet feel we can fill. While change can materialize in as many forms as there are ways for us to avoid it, the rub is, we *can't* avoid change. It catches up to us sooner or later. Initially, the grandness of it all can appear overwhelming. The uneasiness caused from not feeling acclimated to what demands a different way of being—is unsettling. However, when we grow accustomed to invite change versus resist it, to walk into change versus flee, we discover that embracing change in one area of our life, transforms several other areas of our life as well. This is not unusual, nor is it an accident; it's simple physics.

Dream versus Fantasy

Taking on endeavors, projects, or relationships of any significance requires more than just a good idea or even a well-drafted plan. Hey, this is following our dream (this time for real). Following our dream is an ordeal, an undertaking with consequences. Many powerful forces stir the ocean and kick up big swells when we are conjuring big things; we can jump on a board and commit to riding the vision to the distant shore…or we can allow the swells to push us back to the beachhead, risk living in regret, and become resentful for the way things *could have been if I had just…*

The reason we handily execute the initial phases of new endeavors, be it a business venture or a personal one, is that they are articulated as a plan, an idea, a concept, a vision, a dream, a spontaneous epiphany, a "back of the envelope" doodle. But the subsequent phases are the real rub. The next phases move the plan from merely an inspirational, conceptual idea to a physical, visible one, out there for everyone to witness and interact with—and this is when it gets real. Execution invites vulnerability, scrutiny, and criticism. Such visibility typically requires *a pound* of commitment, time, money, and resources before it produces *an ounce* of proof. Following our dream can take us only so far if not matched with the focus and conviction it requires to support our effort. If these key components are absent, then it is less a dream and more a fantasy.

For this reason, the scrapheap of uncompleted projects in the world is massive. Most people check out, confronted either by a lack of authentic conviction, or because staying involved would mean facing their fears (of failure or success!)...and of the accountability that it will demand. Because of this, the common impulse is to panic, check out, and pull the ejection handle. Self-sabotage is one way this plays out. It can come from the fear of stepping into bigger shoes when realizing that the vision begins to become real.

Self-Sabotage

THE BEAUTY OF ACCESSING Conscious Intelligence is that it relates to every aspect of our life. Self-sabotage is commonly sourced from feeling undeserving or unworthy. This kind of self-sabotage plays out in relationships as well:

For example: "I get passionate and inspired in my relationship, but then my enthusiasm wanes. I want a partner who listens and respects my input on how they can make me happy, make our partnership work, and make me a better person. But, my partner seems to have little interest in growing with me or changing. What results is that we don't have enough in common and I end up losing interest."

Do you hear it? This example illustrates a sort-of "me-*centric*" view insisting the *other* needs to change. The other needs to transform to fit around *us*, so the relationship can fit *our life* and complete *us*. We often perceive things as lacking in the other in a relationship when in reality the lackings are manifesting from inside *us*—so we draw in the other person to fill the gaps that persist in our own lives. This is the definition of co-dependence. The reality is that no amount of anything from outside will satisfy it. *We* discover we must do it. At first, this may sound counterintuitive: That which is lacking in the other, we must bring, discover, give more? That which is perceived as scarce, dig deeper and contribute?

When we are able to grasp that we see things from the perspective of the way we are, we gain perspective to better see those things as they actually are. Once we make the distinction, it drives us to own the change, conduct ourselves from the driver's seat, and not peddle it to others and blame—nor pull the ejection handle. From there, we can own our accountability, craft the most powerful outcome, and even if the shoes of change are a little big to fill at first, we can fill them, we can get there, eventually.

SUMMARY | ID 44

Change. Are you open to it?

Change draws no distinction between where we are versus where we are going; it is a wave that we can either choose to ride or be pummeled by. Change requires walking in shoes we may not yet feel we can fill. While change can materialize in as many forms as there are ways for us to avoid it, the rub is, we *can't* avoid change.

Self-sabotage is commonly sourced from feeling undeserving or unworthy. We often perceive things as lacking in the other in a relationship when in reality the lackings are manifesting from inside *us*. When we are able to grasp that we see things from the perspective of the way we are, we gain perspective to better see those things as they actually are. Once we make the distinction, that drives us to own the change, conduct ourselves from the driver's seat, and not peddle it to others and blame.

CHAPTER 13

Essential Life Force, the Divine, and Certainty

*It's your path, and yours alone.
Others may walk it with you,
But no one can walk it for you.* ~Rumi

The Universality of Conscious Intelligence

AN IMPETUS THAT COMPELLED ME to frame what would become The Conscious Intelligence Paradigm was the persisting question: "Why is there so much divisiveness in the world?" I knew it was tied to miscommunication that too often fuels the fire of discord, polarization, and isolation. We cannot live, perform, serve in the highest expression of ourselves while communication, a basic vehicle that connects us, remains conflated and misconceived. What pains me the most is how so much of this angst is over the one thing that actually connects us all together: Humans asking the age-old question, "Why?" in our attempt to elevate our consciousness.

The Conscious Intelligence Paradigm adheres to strict parameters—one of which is that it is *secular*. It abstains from the use of religion or spirituality as its vehicle, although we can find the principles woven throughout numerous cross-sections of literature including philosophy, mythology, folklore, and poetry, *as well as* religion and spirituality. This parameter is not in any way to slight religion, but rather to preserve the neutral universality of the Conscious Intelligence Paradigm.

> *Sacred or secular, what is the difference?*
> *If every atom inside our bodies was once a star,*
> *then it is all sacred and all secular at the same time.*
> ~ Gretel Ehrlich

Chi. Ki. Prana. Life Force. Vital Energy…The sacred or secular source goes by many names. Science and religion both attest that there are things that are known, things that are unknown, and things that are *unknowable*. So, where does Conscious Intelligence fit within the context of what we often refer secularly to as *essential life force* or, religiously and spiritually, as the *Divine*?

The purpose of The Conscious Intelligence Paradigm is to elevate our perspective, not prescribe a point of view. It isn't specifically concerned with physics (empirical) or metaphysics (spiritual) or any particular path in between. The distinctions actually exist independently of both the science and the faith traditions, of both physics and metaphysics. They are universal, not derived or contrived from any belief system, opinion, judgment, or point of view. This chapter is not a comparison between the sciences and faith, nor between the faith traditions, but rather an identification of powerful distinctions to assist in broadening and deepening our views along *our own* unique path independent of what it is.[1]

Whether you are a person of faith, science—either, both, or neither—The Invisible Distinctions serve as a light to enhance perspective along the path. Just as the path is yours and yours alone, so too is your choice of how you wish to direct the light. Light facilitates our seeing; it does not tell us where to go, explain, or interpret to us what it is we are seeing.

We are constantly attempting to translate concepts that are beyond our faculties in an effort to pull them into our earthbound perspective. It is our human experience to wonder, struggle, and triumph. We stare up into the skies and ask the big questions. Over the millennia, we have derived language, poetry, and art to tell life's stories in an effort to translate and perpetuate the journeys of those who came before us. It is our predicament to navigate the dynamic between ego and Self, experience inexplicable feats, to love and feel empathy, to sacrifice, atone, and concede that we are all a part of something bigger than ourselves—that we are all connected. We live out our lives discovering that there are more questions than answers, and that with every answer—more questions. We discover that there are some truths that dwell in the realm of the unknown ... and, perhaps, the unknowable.

The Certainty Conundrum

Does the Divine exist?
It is absolutely a possibility.

Can science prove or disprove that Divinity exists?
It is absolutely a possibility.

CERTAINTY ITSELF IS its own conundrum. Like water, we cannot grasp it by clenching it and tightening our grip; we can only behold it by opening our hands and allowing the water to be its own nature. Water has so much power, both in its very essence as well as in its metaphorical and lyrical nature, to teach us about the dimensions of universal wisdom.

While science cannot physically measure anything deemed beyond dimension, the faith traditions reference such a realm all the time. Think about it—by science's own method, measuring something beyond dimension is impossible. The Divine, however, is attributed as being *beyond* dimension. Something beyond dimension cannot be measured—and physics affirms this. It acknowledges that just because something is not demonstrable, such a state neither denies nor confirms its existence. Faith does not claim to measure its references beyond dimension, it merely makes reference to it. Alan Watts worded it this way: "If we cling to belief in The Divine, we cannot likewise have faith, since faith is not clinging but letting go." These two perspectives are NOT at odds with each other; they simply approach their methodology from different directions.

Science's most respected practitioners concur that not everything is known and that almost anything is possible. They respect the scientific process because it is confined to its purely physical, empirical findings. The essential principles constituting the scientific method attest to the fact that *not affirming the existence of something is not the same as saying it doesn't exist or isn't possible.* This has allowed humans to lean on the viability of scientific methodology and discovery while at the same time appreciate and acknowledge its confining limitations. After all, to this point, we humans do not have the faculties to observe the Big Bang from beyond its blast radius, prove the existence of wormholes (let alone travel in one), see dark matter or dark energy, or know what is inside a black hole or where one leads. Still, this lack of observation neither further affirms nor negates the existence or viability of these things. Here's another one from Alan Watts:

> *The only thing that is certain*
> *is that there is no certainty in the natural world,*
> *but the natural world doesn't worry.*

Religion's most respected practitioners concur that there are some who do religion a disservice, misrepresent it, and place at risk the innocent who place deep trust in such institutions. Those respected practitioners who spend a life inspiring trust and safety within religion's sacred space are left battling the contagion of those who misuse the solemn power granted them.

> *We all know some people who claim to be religious*
> *who in reality are some of the most racist,*
> *bigoted people—*
> *But they believe in The Divine. How is this possible?*
> *It is possible because religion is*
> *one of the safest places to hide from The Divine.*
> *~ Franciscan priest Richard Rohr*

One of the safest places to hide... Here it is, said another way: Opening a door by introducing a powerful tool, say splitting an atom, also opens up a new set of responsibilities and discipline choices. There it is again—*noblesse oblige*. Do we use the technology to help humanity—say, to produce electricity and power a city for a thousand years—or do we use the technology to harm humanity—say, produce a weapon and render a city useless for the next thousand years? Splitting the atom is not right or wrong; it just *is*. Such dispositions in their purest forms exist in a perspective of neutrality and non-judgment. The atom *doesn't worry*—it doesn't have a crisis of identity asking itself: "Am I evil or good?" *Humankind chooses.*

In the argument of certainty with respect to comparing religion to science, well, there is no argument. Not regarding certainty, anyway. Neither religion nor science owns certainty. This is not where their differences lie. If anyone conflates the distinction of certainty where faith belongs, then one might as well start the Tour de France in New Zealand or use curry to cook Italian food. Faith has nothing to do with either science or certainty.

ID 45: Religion versus Spirituality

A NOTE ON THE WORD *"DIVINE"*: Throughout this chapter, the term will be used neutrally to refer to the faith traditions where it is referenced as something larger than ourselves, whether it is a God Almighty portrayed with a beard, or one throwing bolts of lightning; or the natural, ethereal energies that bind nature and us all together; or the mysterious stuff of the universe where energy and intention is generated; or just a benign notion that there is a realm where something is bigger than the likes of ...us. ALL, in the context of this chapter, in one form or another, are collectively referenced as the Divine.

Have you ever wondered what it means when someone says that they're spiritual but not religious? How are these things different, right? Both constitute a relationship with the Divine, but how that relationship is structured is where distinctions can be found.

> **Spirituality** is commonly considered the direct relationship of a person with the Divine in any array, form, or manifestation: energy, light, etc., having no formal, religious, organizational structure.
>
> **Religion** is commonly considered a uniform, widely recognized, and formally structured community, culture, and organization bound by its commonly held scriptures, laws and ideals in its relationship to the Divine.
>
> **Religion Historically**
> Let's observe for a moment the world prior to the concept of separation of church and state. This is before the advent of modern-day psychology, spiritual, self-help, and self-realization sections at bookstores, let alone any bookstores at all. There was no Dr. Phil, Oprah, Deepak Chopra, Wayne Dyer, and the rest.

Leaders, monarchs, dictators, emperors, and so on were left to their own devices to control and govern the masses—which they had to do to remain in power and survive being conquered. Whether by tradition or adoption, many of these rulers leaned heavily on religious texts for guidance, even though they themselves were not necessarily religious scholars. Because of this, leaders also interpreted (and perhaps took great license with) religious teachings. The texts doubled as a framework for punitive purposes in an effort to create and maintain law and order as well as to organize and rule. Using religious texts as a means to govern and affect civil punishment is a marked departure from solely pledging gratitude and revering the Divine.

In addition, many rulers were believed to be *ordained* by the Divine (hence the term "Divine rule"), and the slightest air of protest was not looked on lightly.[9] It was not only *treasonous* to speak in opposition about a ruler or, heaven forbid, directly to the ruler; such conduct was considered *blasphemy*, usually punishable by death. Speech was not free; there was no First Amendment to the U.S. Constitution.

Rule by means of interpreting the role of the Divine remains in parts of the world today, even though to do so is subject to interpretation and riddled with human fallibility. Throughout history, those declaring themselves to be a direct conduit to, or embodiment of, the Divine commonly fall short of faithfully executing such an office proficiently. The shortcomings can lead to anything from an execution for a crime, where innocence is later proven, to the end of dynasties, empires, and kingdoms. Plenty of genocide has been inspired by tyrants, totalitarian despots, and clans, as have been mass suicides led by cult leaders pretending to be Divine. All conceived from attempts to play the role of the Divine.

Religion Today

RELIGION OF TODAY has evolved, but still has its challenges and complexities. Providing context helps us gain perspective to more clearly distinguish how conflicts and challenges arise in modern times. Religion is still, at its core, a vehicle meant to organize the masses for the purpose of celebrating and interpreting the Divine. Religion's challenges today are much less about exacting rule and punishment and more about incorporating its community within the confines of today's organizational requirements. What does this mean? Well, celebrating the Divine in organized, modern-day religion requires corporate infrastructure to be woven into its practices so it can run like a business because—it *is* a business; just ask your local parishioner, rabbi, or clergy. They will attest to the fact, typically much to their chagrin, that part of their day's travail requires organizational communication, business practices, management, and navigating the bureaucracy.

Let's unpack this, as it's fascinating to see what this entails and how different it is from the institution of religion of the past. Most religions have a meeting place for worship, such as a church, temple, or synagogue. Someone has to buy the land, build the structure, equip and maintain it, water and mow the lawn, trim the hedges, supply it with required texts, bibles, etc., buy light bulbs, pay the electric bill, purchase wine and bread for the Eucharist or the Kiddush and Hamotzi, buy candles . . . lots of candles. Perhaps there's a marquee out front that someone has to maintain. Don't forget making sure the establishment is wheelchair accessible and has the necessary restrooms and all the requisite supplies and cleaning services required.

It's a nonprofit, you say? *Indeed* it is. Someone needs to file for 501(c)(3) status and file tax returns, apply for grants, and collect membership dues. Also, although it is a nonprofit, there are still bookkeepers, payroll to be done, budgets, bills to pay, and an account where endowments and the funds from the collection bowl can land. There is a staff that organizes and runs the volunteers, a board of directors, likely even an HR department and an administration building where they are all housed. There are socials, group meetings, and events to plan, a website, social media, designers, marketers, information about the upcoming mission trip to Israel, the Vatican, Mecca, Tibet, or the sister church orphanage in El Salvador. There are music teachers with teaching credentials and choir practice and a piano or even a pipe organ requiring tuning and servicing. Someone has to hire all these people as well. The clergy likely emerged from formal education, an accredited scholar program, university, or rabbinic school. Then there is typically political and community outreach as well as press and guest speaker relations. There is a parking lot, stairs, childcare drop-offs that require strict screening of the staff, and attendees with health issues all requiring the establishment to carry insurance for purposes of indemnification.

These are just *some* of today's requirements to assemble the masses for organized religion. It certainly provides perspective, doesn't it? If you attend a church, temple, synagogue, or mosque, the next time you do so, you may be more compelled to add an extra buck or two in the collection bowl and "thank the Divine" for the remarkable miracle that is your place of worship.

Spirituality

COMPARE THE RELIGIOUS ELEMENTS in their entirety just mentioned, to a conversation with a non-religious but spiritual friend. This friend shares a recent spiritual experience or revelation they had while they practiced meditation, were in conversation at the bedside of their grandmother during her final hours here on earth, or while on a long run or swim or nature walk during a retreat in Costa Rica.

With spirituality, the relationship with the Divine remains very personal. Spirituality concerns itself more with the presence of something bigger than oneself, not requiring community, organizational, or congregating elements. It is the presence of a Divine conversation no matter where one's faith is located, where one worships, or what name one chooses to reference the Divine.

Religion's Move Towards More Creative, Spiritual Exploration

FORMAL RELIGIOUS AFFILIATION is declining precipitously according to several research studies. These studies reflect significant decreases in religious membership and identity, and even larger trends downward in affiliation to, and recognition of, the religion one is born into.[101,102]

While this trend cannot be explained simply or completely, it is becoming increasingly clear that some of the decline is due to a growing disconnect. The disconnect arises when traditional, religious views do not evolve to meet the contemporary environments, conventions, and intricacies of the world of today. This era is defined by quite a different set of fundamentals. Its technology, globalization, increased cultural interaction, and evolved views regarding concepts such as equality, inclusion, and tolerance pose just a few of the challenges religion is having in keeping up with the generation of today.

Another headwind is the increased challenge to cultivate connection with the younger generations. Until the religious community as a whole aligns more with the contemporary, unifying, universal sensibilities of the generation, it appears the rift will widen. The realities today show ideas such as equality to be at odds with the interpretation of scripture, be it between man and woman or beyond to include expanded forms of self-identity. There exist antiquated views around equality that compete with tradition. There exist asymmetrical views of acceptance and inclusion regarding the powerful bonds that are love, race, gender, and orientation. These factors have a monumental effect regarding the lens through which stories of scripture are interpreted and propagated. The challenge is that modern generations are drawing less and less connection to traditional ritual and practice because those activities no longer apply to the contemporary narratives of society today. The generation is drawing more contrast based on what they see, what is happening, and what their experience is today in the world. At the same time, they are being fogged by the increased divisiveness, conflict, and scandals that often dominate news and media. If religious practitioners are not connecting to modern generations of the world today in the areas of faith, purpose, and connection, taking into account anxiety, technology, equality, sense of community, and contemporary relevance, they will continue to see an exodus in even greater numbers.

Modern religious scholars are called to the altar to reconcile the elemental threads that weave the fabric of major religions of the world today. Choosing to join a global community that seeks unification over divisiveness is no longer optional if one's religion is to remain relevant. Keying in on the sensibilities, anxieties and afflictions weighing heavily on today's generations, meeting them where they are at, and providing a reprieve, may well serve the cause. Those organizations finding creative means to connect the relevance of the age-old stories and messages to contemporary life appear to be finding success in drawing people back in. Providing the space for the expansion of spiritual exploration over restrictive constraining doctrine dwells among the factors appearing to facilitate the much-needed connection.

When fresh ways are discovered to connect the new generations to the old scriptures, and to each other, forsaking no one, religion can again see results in drawing in those who are feeling disenfranchised. The root principles of love, acceptance, and service, found threaded throughout religious tradition, cannot come with preconditions as to what that looks like in society today—not without seeing religious numbers continue to falter. Until all humans are viewed equally as children of the Divine—one needs to search no further than the scriptures themselves to find this—can religion succeed in bridging its heritages to modernity.

SUMMARY | ID 45

Sacred or secular, what is the difference?

Science and religion both attest that there are things that are known, things that are unknown, and things that are *unknowable*. So, where does Conscious Intelligence fit within the context of what we often refer secularly to as *essential life force* or, religiously and spiritually, as the *Divine*? Conscious Intelligence abstains from the use of religion or spirituality as its vehicle, although we can find the principles woven throughout numerous cross-sections of literature, including philosophy, mythology, folklore, and poetry, as *well* as religion and spirituality. This parameter is not in any way to slight religion, but rather to preserve its neutral universality.

Whether you are a person of faith, science—either, both, or neither—the Invisible Distinctions serve as a light to enhance perspective along the path. The path is yours and yours alone; so, too, is your choice of how you wish to direct the light. Light facilitates our seeing; it does not tell us where to go, explain, or interpret for us what it is we are seeing. It is our personal human experience to wonder, struggle, and triumph as we attempt to translate concepts that are beyond our faculties in an effort to pull them into our earthbound perspective.

Spirituality is commonly considered the direct relationship of a person with the Divine in any array, form, or manifestation—energy, light, etc.—and having no formal, religious, or organizational structure.

Religion is commonly considered a uniform, widely recognized, and formally structured community, culture, and organization bound by its commonly held scriptures, laws, and ideals in its relationship to the Divine.

CHAPTER 14
Distinctions of Absolute

ID 46: Perfection versus Imperfection

Perfection or imperfection, that is the question.
~ (Some 21st century Shakespeare for you)

ONCE, WHILE ATTENDING A CHURCH SERVICE, I heard a favorite minister say something interesting, all in the space of eight minutes, while delivering his sermon. He initially talked about how we are all created in the image of the Divine and therefore we are whole, complete, and perfect, as is the Divine.[4] Then, a few minutes later in the same sermon, he went on to describe us as beautiful, flawed, imperfect beings, warts and all, all in the context of original sin, free will, humans here on earth and the Divine who art in heaven. I understood exactly what he meant and loved it, but admittedly, this conundrum popped into my head and remained. It took me a while to make the distinction.

We've all had a friend remind us, while providing a token of support to cheer us up, to not be so hard on ourselves *because we're only human; nobody's perfect*. And yet, we are also told that we are as perfect as the image of the Divine. Perplexing, isn't it? Perfect or flawed?? Which is it?

As the opening quote from Gretel Ehrlich poetically states, we can be both *sacred and secular at the same time*, both one *and* other, both perfect *and* flawed. If we wish to discuss them separately, then it depends on which contextual plane of reference we are speaking from, the Divine realm or the Earthly realm. The distinction is that we cannot speak as The Divine, we can only speak of The Divine.

If we are referencing a universal perspective, beyond the physical world, then there is no duality, no opposites, no perfect versus imperfect, no right versus wrong, no better versus worse, no separation between the Divine and man. Rather, there just *is*, and we, The Divine and man, just *are*.

If we are referencing our physical, tangible world realm, opposites *do* exist. This perspective frames our human faculties, where we contrive variants that distinguish us from each other. We judge; we observe each other as separate and different, man and woman, greater and less than, haves and have nots, right and wrong, and so on.

Here's another major distinction: In the spiritual and religious traditions, there exists a notion that the Divine dwells in the realm of universal wisdom, when really it is the opposite—*we*, here on earth, employ the ideas and principles of universal wisdom, woven throughout religious literature, to aid us in conceptualizing the realm where the Divine dwells. Sadly, when a translation of such literature attests that the religion itself *owns* these universal principles, we miss the entire point; it is often the end of the unifying principles and the beginning of divisive ones. Rather than humankind finding connection through scripture to reach towards the Divine, humankind finds itself standing at odds, obstructing its connection, between each other and between scripture and the Divine.

When humans try to play the role of the Divine, it usually doesn't bode well. No one person nor any religion owns exclusivity on universal wisdom and universal truth. It is not something one ordains themselves to, as if to procure the role of The Divine. It is something one humbly ennobles, aspires, emulates themselves endlessly *towards*.

> *So, what's the practical application of this distinction out in the world?*

With respect to the essence of religion, its most respected practitioners attest that Divinity takes no sides; *only people do*. Here on earth humankind can only strive to emulate the Divine *who art in heaven*. In doing so, people can find universal connection between all fellow humans and between humankind and the Divine. When one attempts to shape and direct the message of the Divine by adding one's own soundtrack, the act risks becoming an agenda. Rather than retain the essential, universal message intended, it is lost instead. When any institution or individual pretends to claim exclusive ownership to the Divine, it is all but certain that the Divine exited the conversation and relationship long ago.

SUMMARY | ID 46

Are we whole, complete, and perfect beings OR beautifully flawed, imperfect beings, warts and all?

We've all had a friend remind us, while providing a token of support to cheer us up, to not be so hard on ourselves *because we're only human; nobody's perfect*. And yet, we are also told that we are as perfect as the image of the Divine. Perplexing, isn't it? Perfect or flawed?? Which is it?

If we wish to discuss them separately, then that discussion depends on which contextual plane of reference we are speaking from, the Divine realm or the Earthly realm. The distinction is that we cannot speak as The Divine; we can speak only of The Divine.

If we are referencing a universal perspective beyond the physical world, then there is no duality, no opposites, no perfect versus imperfect, no right versus wrong, no better versus worse, no separation between the Divine and man. Rather, there just *is*, and we, The Divine and man, just *are*.

If we are referencing our physical, tangible world realm, opposites *do* exist. This perspective frames our human faculties, where we contrive variants that distinguish us from each other. We judge; we observe each other as separate and different, man and woman, greater and less than, haves and have nots, right and wrong, and so on.

With respect to the essence of religion, its most respected practitioners attest that Divinity takes no sides—*only people do*. Here on earth. humankind can only strive to emulate the Divine *who art in heaven*. In doing so, people can find universal connection between all fellow humans and between humankind and the Divine. When one attempts to shape and direct the message of the Divine by adding one's own soundtrack, the act risks becoming an agenda.

ID 47: Judgment versus Being Judgmental

RECALL THE DISTINCTION between opinions and misconceptions. If I say, "My favorite ice cream is chocolate," this is an opinion. It is indisputably *mine*. However, if I insist, "Because your favorite ice cream is strawberry, you are not worthy, and our community feels *uncomfortable* around people who prefer strawberry," such a statement suggests a deeper fundamental issue, doesn't it?

This example, while perhaps overly conspicuous, makes a distinction between two types of judgment. The first is related to my personal preference of ice cream—a judgment of my preference for chocolate over strawberry. The second is more closely a judgment of another person simply because they do not agree with my preferences or beliefs. This is being *judgmental*, regardless of whether my preferences or beliefs are shared with few, many, or even the vast majority.

Sometimes judgment is even used in reference to *Divine judgment*, implying that, since the Divine is with us, if you are not with us, then the Divine is not with you. The danger is that those taking this position think they are pledging their faith to the Divine and being devout; in reality, they are attempting to play the role of the Divine, albeit extremely poorly. At risk are those susceptible to following such misconceived nobility blindly—those who are vulnerable due to the absence of critical thought, perspective, or perceived choice in the matter. Understanding this distinction illuminates perspective. It allows us to have critical consideration regarding those appearing in leadership roles who suggest their such role is the way it is. This is *not* necessarily the way it is. Being conscious that we have every right to identify what amounts to little more than opinion posing as doctrine, we can make the distinction, gain perspective, better maintain our personal sovereignty, and not squander away our power.

SUMMARY | ID 47

Throwing the baby out with the bathwater.

There exists a distinction between two types of judgment. One amounts to personal preference and a judgment of another person simply because they do not align with personal preferences or beliefs. The second is being *judgmental*, regardless of whether preferences or beliefs are shared with few, many, or even the vast majority. Being conscious that we have every right to own our personal preferences, these preferences are little more than opinion. When one's opinion is conflated to pose as doctrine, this is something entirely different.

ID 48: Right versus Righteousness

MUCH LITERATURE AND EDUCATION are available about ethics and morality, so we will not cut too deeply here, but their mention builds nicely into the context of this next distinction.

Morality and Ethics

SIMPLY STATED, generally *morals* reflect our inner values and dictate honorable conduct. They are commonly spoken of as how we treat people we know. *Ethics* are the outer expression of our values and conduct in society. They are commonly spoken of as how we treat the people we don't know. Both, however, are interrelated and not mutually exclusive.

Morals are what make us a good parent, faithful friend, nice neighbor, honorable businessperson, or a respected statesperson; ethics are how we participate, contribute, and get along in a society. Together, they illuminate the true expression of our higher self: who we are when our inner values are in harmony with our outer expression in recognition that we are contributing to something bigger than ourselves.

In contrast, representations of misguided morality are indiscriminate. They come in all shapes and sizes. They can be religious or secular. If a society or organization is governed by constraining and stringent rules that are repressive and confining in nature, the absence of morality may be the culprit. When governance is guided by one individual or a small inner circle of elites, the environment is isolating, and its constituents are confined to narrow, stringent points of view, then morality is at risk. One may infer that *right* is being replaced with *righteousness*.

> **Right**, in the noblest sense, is based purely in ethics, which is to say it resides on the scales of justice—the duality of right versus wrong. This by definition, at its highest ethical standard, is a form of *judgment* in the objective sense. It stands in stark contrast to being *judgment-al*, a view clouded by a narrowed perspective and sourced from ego.

In the highest expression of right, the ego is absent. Ethical judgment is made with a breadth and depth of perspective that considers all sides, facts, and circumstances. Right is not contaminated, steered, or influenced by the notion of *sides*, where the sides insist upon only their points of view in an effort to pull others in their direction. Rather, it is an elevated marker that guides those who navigate ethical perspective towards True North. In its highest expression, right straddles universal truth and ethical judgment, ideally drawing perspective from the former to best inform the latter. Right doesn't pick sides or fight the battle in the trenches for either side; it invites us to elevate above the circumstance and not get entangled within it. It affords us access to perspective when an ethical decision is called for, instead of dwelling within the circumstance—a clouded, confined perspective that constrains us from having much, if any, perspective at all.

> **Righteousness**, on the other hand, is the commandeering of ethical judgment by the ego. Righteousness is the ego thinking it is *right*. We need not seek further than the front page of today's newspapers for examples of this.

Here's Franciscan priest Richard Rohr again, describing this well in the following way: "Religion is the best thing in the world and the worst thing in the world. When ego gets involved, we are going to witness a very swift path to righteousness. An egocentric person *uses* The Divine as his little commodity." In other words, they use the Divine when it is convenient—"*use*" being the key word here—to proclaim superiority over others for personal gain.

> *He who thinks he knows, does not know.*
> *He who knows he does not know, Knows.*
> ~ *Source unknown, but attributed to Joseph Campbell*

The Secular Righteous

WE'VE ALL MET THIS PERSON at one time or another. They are the *non*-religious example of righteousness observed in the context of quasi-academia. They are the certain sort that has an affinity for self-proclaiming their academic prowess and superiority far too often. They tend towards over eagerness, displaying their academic peacock feathers, frequently reminding everyone of their formal scholastic accolades and pedigree. They believe such accolades grant superiority, clearly marking their higher capacity of knowledge on…just about every subject.

The Weekend Warrior Righteous

AH YES. Those who practice anything for only ninety minutes a week and consider themselves full-time practitioners. We've all witnessed someone exiting their weekly place of worship, a yoga or meditation class, empowerment seminar… and, not even minutes later, are rude to the volunteer attendant on the way out, cut someone off while exiting the parking lot, or ignore pedestrians trying to cross the street. It's as if they think that ninety minutes per week of "practicing" grace inoculates them from being decent the other six days, twenty-two and a half hours in the week. Remember, just because a person performs affirmative acts doesn't earn them jerk credits, exonerating them from being abusive. It is possible that those who believe otherwise may have not fully grasped the *higher* intention and are missing the point.

Bless Their Heart

ON A LIGHTER NOTE, many of us (especially from the American South) have heard this one: If someone is spouting a critical judgment of another and attempts to soften the edge with the tongue-in-cheek phrases "bless their heart" or "I pray for them," behold!! Righteousness is amidst. Any slighting comment that implies a more refined or spiritually evolved perspective than that of the person being referenced suggests the presence of righteousness.

> ## SUMMARY | ID 48
>
> ## He who thinks he knows...
>
> Simply stated, generally **morals** reflect our inner values and dictate honorable conduct. They are commonly spoken of as how we treat people we know. **Ethics** are the outer expression of our values and conduct in society. They are commonly spoken of as how we treat the people we don't know. Both, however, are interrelated and not mutually exclusive.
>
> If a society or organization is governed by constraining and stringent rules that are repressive and confining in nature, the absence of morality may be the culprit. When governance is guided by one individual or a small inner circle of elites, environment being isolating and its constituents confined to narrow, stringent points of view, then morality is at risk. One may infer that *right* is being replaced with *righteousness*.
>
> **Right**, in the noblest sense, is based purely in ethics, which is to say it resides on the scales of justice—the duality of right versus wrong. This by definition, at its highest ethical standard, is a form of *judgment* in the objective sense. It stands in stark contrast to being *judgment-al*, a view clouded by a narrowed perspective and sourced from ego. In the highest expression of right, the ego is absent. In its highest expression, right straddles universal truth and ethical judgment, ideally drawing perspective from the former to best inform the latter.
>
> **Righteousness**, on the other hand, is the commandeering of ethical judgment by the ego. Righteousness is the ego thinking it is *right*.

ID 49: Grandeur versus Grandiosity

Grandeur can be described as the radiance, splendor, magnificence, and impressiveness that reflects a higher order, such as the Blue Ridge Mountains, the Grand Canyon, Monument Valley, or the Milky Way (which, in my opinion, includes the candy bar as well). It is the radiance that reminds us that something much bigger than ourselves is at play here, and we stand in awe.

Grandiosity is grandeur for which the ego attempts to take credit. It is the façade of grandeur, the extravagant, flamboyant, arrogant, exaggerated belief one takes credit for while touting one's own importance. It is a person's attempt to claim ownership of the Divine with the purpose that others will exalt that person as such.

Absolute power corrupts absolutely. ~Lord Acton

IN ALL OF THE DISTINCTIONS of absolute-*ness* mentioned in this chapter, whether religious *or* secular, when authority is bestowed upon someone, or one bestows it upon oneself, it begs the question, "Why does this person feel the need to reach for this particular tool?" Identifying who is speaking a more transparent truth and who is threading falsities throughout their rhetoric requires a discerning ear. Gaining influence over others, an audience, a congregating body is powerful. Using absolute-*ness* as the delivery system is but a strategy, a tool. While the tool is seductive and persuasive, especially to the impressionable and vulnerable, it can sound compelling. Absolute-*ness* simply is not compelling...unless we give power to the one conjuring it. Identifying one who insists on evoking the tool of absolute-*ness* in their speak may be the key indicator that leads to a darker truth about that person's true objective. Identifying the distinction is to shed light so we can choose to steer clear if the exploit proves not to be the path of preference.

SUMMARY | ID 49

Beyond reproach.

Grandeur can be described as the radiance, splendor, magnificence, and impressiveness that reflects a higher order, such as the Blue Ridge Mountains, the Grand Canyon, Monument Valley, or the Milky Way (which, in my opinion, includes the candy bar as well). It is the radiance that reminds us that something much bigger than ourselves is at play here, and we stand in awe.

Grandiosity is grandeur for which the ego attempts to take credit. It is the façade of grandeur, the extravagant, flamboyant, arrogant, exaggerated belief one takes credit for while touting one's own importance. It is a person's attempt to claim ownership of the Divine with the purpose that others will exalt that person as such.

CHAPTER 15

Determination

ID 50: Fate | Destiny | Legacy

> *Destiny is not a matter of chance; it is a matter of choice.*
> *It is not a thing to be waited for,*
> *it is a thing to be achieved.* ~William Jennings Bryan
>
> *The only person you are destined to become*
> *is the person you decide to be.* ~Ralph Waldo Emerson
>
> *It is not in the stars to hold our destiny*
> *but in ourselves.* ~William Shakespeare

FATE AND DESTINY are often used interchangeably with very little distinction. Destiny, a word sharing the same root as "destination," is commonly characterized as where we end up in life, while fate is commonly characterized as what is waiting to happen when we get there. Both commonly refer to the ultimate culmination of our lives at the moment we reach the finish line. They refer to a metaphorical point where our earthly, temporal lives have led like a path of breadcrumbs to a line that separates our lives as we know them from what comes next or lies beyond. Are fate and destiny predetermined by some force greater than ourselves, or, as the previous quotes indicate, do *we* make such a determination?

Because fate and destiny are somewhat similar, the subtleties are open to personal interpretation. As far as the Invisible Distinctions are concerned, there's no major distinction between the two. But when we introduce *legacy* into the conversation, a distinction worthy of deeper discussion emerges. Illuminating the fundamental elements regarding our relationship with these concepts is important in our discussion about them, so before we delve deeper, let's lay some groundwork and discharge a few common misconceptions.

> **Fate** is defined as an unavoidable determinant that ultimately befalls a person in their lifetime.
>
> **Destiny** is defined as the predetermined course of events that a person will experience in the future.

These terms refer to where we conceivably end up...but what about where we *begin*? Is there a converse to fate and destiny—a universal principle by which the order of things meets us at the conceptual beginning, as an initiator of our prescribed path?

Admittedly, I've tricked you a bit in the way I posed the question—not to be devious, but rather to illuminate the distinction. The question is flawed because it asks for an opposite, but the answer doesn't reside in opposites such as beginning/ending (or middle, for that matter). *Neither does the question.* That is because the concepts of fate and destiny do not fit within the realm of *duality*; they are timeless. Simply stated, the concept of non-duality exists absent a literal timeline, absent the actual tick, tick, ticking of time. Despite this, there is a term that references a conceptual beginning: *Entelechy*.

> **Entelechy** is defined as the inherent regulating force that directs the development and function of an organism—the vital, universal life force and impetus that develops a potential existence into an actual, functioning existence.[3]

All three—fate, destiny, and entelechy—beg the age-old questions: Is there an order to things? If so, who or what is driving? Is there design in these determinants? If so, who or what is the designer?

Whether we approach these questions as sacred or secular, the interpretation is ultimately personal to each of us. In religion and spirituality, this *intending impetus* is typically attributed to the Divine, while theoretical physics might refer to it merely as a form of consciousness or organized, activation energy yet to be materially documented. Fate, destiny, and entelechy are simply not demonstrable by scientific method. How does an acorn know to become an oak tree and not a plumeria? How do a human egg and sperm know to become a human baby and not a giraffe? Scientifically, we can observe a process once it has been initiated, as it happens, and then explain the *how* to a major extent. What we cannot explain is the determinant *why*.

What is the impetus that intends an acorn into an oak tree? We cannot journal, in an evidentiary way, the universal life force or spark that determines and initiates its beginning. There are several reasons for this, and although the subject is worthy of a fascinating discussion, it is beyond the scope and intention of making the distinctions here—and for good reason.

The Conscious Intelligence Paradigm does not play the role of interpreting what the all-encompassing, universal force is or why it is. The Paradigm merely brings our attention to this enigma so that we can gain perspective.

Everyone has a unique answer as to whether fate, destiny, or entelechy exist, but here's where we all find real consensus: Whether one subscribes to an active order that directs things or to an all-passive and random order, or hasn't decided either way, *all of us* can concur that the answer with any certainty is out of our hands.

The Concept of Vector

How do we discuss something that isn't in the temporal, physical realm (time and duality) with a language that is? Whenever we try to discuss or define something that is beyond dimension from our physical, temporal point of view, we always run into the same limitation.

Because fate, destiny, and entelechy do not exist in the physical realm, explaining them with language falls short of encapsulating them in their entirety. They are not just end or start points as their dictionary definitions imply; rather, they are *vectors*.

"Vector" is a term from mathematics that represents magnitude and direction, not start points or end points. Simply stated, we can think of a vector as we would the course of an airplane. It has a start point and an end point, but to understand the course path of the trip, we'd also need to understand its magnitude (in this case, velocity) and the direction (its heading). With these pieces of information and any reference point, an observer could plot the vector of the airplane with respect to time to get any specific location point anywhere along its path. This is, in fact, how air traffic control can avoid a collision and predict when you will arrive at your destination, or how we can calculate the exact time of a solar eclipse, ocean tidal readings, or the phenomenon known as Mercury retrograde.

Our lives resemble a course heading of an airplane in that they don't just have a start and end point; they also have magnitude and direction. As with an airplane, an observer could plot our movement on a chart by plotting the points of our lives with respect to time to create a vector.

This is why the conventional, dictionary definitions for fate, destiny, and entelechy are flawed as compared to making distinctions. Their definitions are denotations, marking a spot, while what is required is connotation, a deeper, conceptual understanding. Rather than just being a single point in time or location, fate, destiny, and entelechy contain every step, every point, along the way, because the only way to reach a certain end is to make sure the entirety of the path leads to it.

How do we contain and quantify time (yesterday, today, tomorrow) into one singular, packaged moment? The answer is, we can't... not without wiping out time's essential, defining property—*the passing of it*. So, our fate, destiny, and entelechy are contained within the entirety of our lives, not merely the beginning or end or any single point along it, but rather a vector. We may not see a dog's head, for example, but if we follow its tail, it will lead us to the head. The tail and head are inseparable, not one and other; they are both a part of the whole, a part of the same dog. So too are fate, destiny, and entelechy with respect to our lives.

The progressions of these epochs unfold like bursts of photographs that, strung together, create a movie that is the representation of our life. For example, our four years of high school, marriage, tenure as chairman of the board, life in our first apartment…each are epochs of time, a defined set of collective moments. One isolated moment does not define these epochs of time; rather, the entirety of the moments within the epoch of time are what distinguish it.

Here is an example to really cement the concept: On that fateful day, even though the man and woman lived thousands of miles away from each other and had never met, there they were, trapped in the same elevator during the power outage, destined to meet. It was fate that they met, destiny that they were married, and entelechy that you were conceived a year later to this day.

As you can see, "beginning" and "end" in the context of fate, destiny, and entelechy are relative and indistinguishable. In this romantic example, the meeting was a beginning…but because of the meeting, the couple got married. A marriage is not a single point in life; it is a vector that goes until the end of the marriage if not the end of life ('til death do us part; I prefer happy endings). The marriage is also an end of sorts; it is the end of two separate vectors of the people as individuals and a convergence/beginning of a new vector of a couple. We see this ritualized as metaphor in marriage ceremonies when the couple hold individual candles and proceed together to light a singular one. Same for the birth of the child: another vector was created "that is your life." Then the combination of you with your parents creates a family vector…and so it goes with countless vectors created. Our entire lives are a myriad of vectors, of countless present moments, and we can look at them as both a timeline and culmination of countless present moments.

We cannot physically exist in the past or future; we exist only in the present. So here is an interesting perspective about this distinction: The present is the only conceptual place where duality and non-duality intersect, and the vector that represents it is timeless, made up of infinite present moments.

Legacy

> *What we do in life echoes in eternity.*
> *~The Film: Gladiator; writers David Franzoni,*
> *John Logan, and William Nicholson*

WE'VE ESTABLISHED THAT, based on their true nature, we can't control or create our fates or destinies. But can we endeavor to remove the impediments that hinder our progress?

Having made the distinctions just previously, we can now talk about legacy. Legacy is the part of our future that we *do* have the opportunity to craft in the present. By choosing how we conduct our lives *now*, we can create a future that we will leave for those surviving us. This is our ultimate concession of our earthly form: the realization that we all depart this temporal place, survived only by those who remain after we are gone.

> *If destiny is the flowing river of our life,*
> *our legacy is the boat we row along it.*

> **Legacy** is the ultimate gift we humans bequeath. *It is the essence of who we are after we no longer are,* and it is that which lingers after our life impulse is no longer in the vessels that constitute our physical bodies.

It has been said that when Michelangelo was asked (about his statue, *David*): "How on earth did you accomplish the feat of carving such an inspired masterpiece?" His response was, "I simply chipped away everything that was not David." Indeed, he did, and what resulted was the transformation of a slab of stone into a form that exposed its true radiance as well as his.

The story of Michelangelo's David folds aptly into the shaping of his legacy, both as the statue he left behind and as his articulate, insightful words. He illustrated that our radiance emerges when we access the connection between our essential Self and that which emanates from it in its purest expression. Legacy holds a space in the present moment of time for that which is timeless. In the affirmative sense, legacy is the intent to leave others a contribution that enhances their lives and, in turn, celebrates ours long after our physical departure. A legacy could also represent the opposite—reflecting one who left destruction and darkness in their wake.

The distinction here illuminates the relationship between that which we control and choose in life (legacy) and that which is beyond our control and choice (fate/destiny/entelechy). The distinction also illuminates that while we cannot control our predisposition or what we are born into, our potential is infinite and for us to shape. Our birthright, rich or poor, gifted or challenged, privileged or of modest means, is set in motion at the moment we arrive, but that is independent of our power to shape the trajectory (the vector) of our lives. Our impact on the lives of others is ours and ours alone to craft.

> *You can't connect the dots looking forward;*
> *you can only connect them looking backwards.*
> ~Steve Jobs

The destiny/legacy relationship, like many of the distinctions, draws upon what informs, motivates, and fuels our drive to contribute. We are reminded to check in on the ego versus Self. When it comes to legacy, what are the degrees of influence coming from ego versus authentic, essential Self? Legacy splits both ways. It has degrees of prolific benefit as much as it has degrees of notoriety. So, will our legacy be of a luminary, leading a movement that elevates the human spirit (driven by essential Self), or will our legacy be of a notorious tyrant that leaves suffering and destruction in their wake (driven by ego)?

SUMMARY | ID 50

The essence of who we are after we no longer are.

Destiny, a word sharing the same root as "destination," is commonly characterized as where we end up in life, while **fate** is commonly characterized as what is waiting to happen when we get there. Both commonly refer to the ultimate culmination of our lives at the moment we reach the finish line. How do we contain and quantify time (yesterday, today, tomorrow) into one singular, packaged moment? The answer is, we can't...not without wiping out time's essential, defining property—*the passing of it*. So, our fate, destiny, and entelechy are contained within the entirety of our lives, not merely the beginning or end or any single point along it, but rather a "vector."

"**Vector**" is a term from mathematics that represents magnitude and direction, not start points or end points. Simply stated, we can think of a vector as we would the course of an airplane. It has a start point and an end point, but to understand the course path of the trip, we'd also need to understand its magnitude (in this case, velocity) and the direction (its heading).

We may not see a dog's head, for example, but if we follow its tail, it will lead us to the head. The tail and head are inseparable, not one and other; they are both a part of the whole, a part of the same dog. So, too, are fate, destiny, and entelechy with respect to our lives.

Legacy is the part of our future that we *do* have the opportunity to craft in the present. By choosing how we conduct our lives *now*, we can create a future that we will leave for those surviving us. Legacy is the ultimate gift we humans bequeath. *It is the essence of who we are after we no longer are*, and it is that which lingers after our life impulse is no longer in the vessels that constitute our physical bodies.

Our birthright, rich or poor, gifted or challenged, privileged or of modest means, is set in motion at the moment we arrive, but that is independent of our power to shape the trajectory (the vector) of our lives. The impact we have on the lives of others is ours and ours alone to craft.

CHAPTER 16

Happiness | Purpose | Bliss

Joy is the happiness that doesn't depend on what happens.
~David Steindl-Rast

WE WALK AROUND IN LIFE, simulcasting our personal, melodic anthem. We blend high notes and low notes, choose our instruments, and coerce out of them the sounds and textures that determine the pitch, tempo, harmony, and rhythms of our unique musical expression. Our melodies fold together like a collage that is the symphony of our lives.

Independent of how much we rehearse, we still incur rogue soloists, riffs, and digressions that test us. We undergo disruptive, ambient noise, discordant sounds, and out-of-tune instruments. We bear a broken string, coughs from the audience, unexpected exits of fellow orchestra members, and even meteorites that crash through the roof of our performing arts center. Still, we muster the grit to play on; we endure the tests that scope beyond our circles of influence. These tests challenge us to gracefully navigate our way back on track to the thematic motif[1] that defines who we are out in the world, how we occur to others, and what music we will play tomorrow.

He who is not contented with what he has,
would not be contented with what he would like to have.
~Socrates

What Is Happiness?

THE PURPOSE OF THIS CHAPTER is not to suggest and prescribe some secret path to happiness. The purpose is to illuminate it and provide two things: perspective regarding both the role of happiness along our path and our relationship to it. When we gain perspective around the distinctions of happiness, around what happiness is, and what it isn't, we are destined to discover course corrections, adjustments, and clearings about it as it applies to our own unique life.

Do we have a realistic view about what lights us up? We'll talk more about happiness and fulfillment shortly, but here's a hint: It's less about things and more about our habits, attitude, and conduct. I know a lot of rich people who are profoundly miserable, and I know a lot of people of modest means who are living fulfilling and happy lives.

Next, are we coming from gratitude for what we have, or are we coming from a bottomless void of scarcity for what we think we need. Are we running corrupted software in the form of a cruel inner critic voice? *You know*—the one that pretends to guide us but instead fills us with fear, doubt, jealousy, and denial. *Yes, that voice*—the one that convinces us we are undeserving of praise and good fortune.

> *That which is born out of the womb of attachment*
> *breeds suffering.*   ~Buddha

The belief that the accumulation of *things* will fulfill us, in reality, only begets wanting more things. The more we become attached to something, the more suffering we undergo in the event of its loss. It creates a cycle of peaks and valleys, like an addict who gets high, crashes down, and seeks their next fix to re-up their high, again crashing down, and so on. We all know where such a path typically leads. This is the metaphorical definition of hell and eternal suffering. There exists a distinction between attaching ourselves to the accumulation of things versus directing our energy towards our passions, purpose, and our love for what is truly important to us.

ID 51: Object Happiness versus Authentic Happiness: The Nomad versus the Farmer

> *When a flower doesn't bloom,*
> *You fix the environment in which it grows,*
> *not the flower.* ~Alexander Den Heijer

Object happiness is what it sounds like. Object happiness depends upon a condition outside of us, separate and apart from us, as if it were something to be clung to. It is the notion that something outside of us has the power to equip us with, or deprive us of, happiness. (That thing can be a person as well…with a person, there is still something that they possess of which we are desirous.)

OBJECT HAPPINESS is fleeting and mercurial, dependent on the weather forecast, our luck, or perceived privilege, for example. Incidentally, it is also chemically related to the brain in the same way a drug is to a dependent addict. Object happiness appeals to the pleasure centers of the brain and is the culprit for creating a cycle of highs and lows, the aching need for a fix, and the painful withdrawals when cravings aren't fed. If object happiness becomes the determinant condition of our happiness, then our relationship to happiness is one of clinging, attachment, and need. It becomes a constant, a seeking outside of ourselves, like a nomad constantly on the move, hunting high and low across the land to satisfy an ever-nagging hunger that can never be satisfied.

Let's illustrate this within the context of a nature walk. The framework of object happiness would begin with an established baseline. When seeking object happiness, we let the outer weather determine our circumstances. This weather is constantly gloomy, never-good-enough, and melancholy. Rather than just enjoying the experience of the walk, we are in full career of seeking, and occasionally happening upon, a beautiful flower along the path to brighten our day. When we find one, we *pluck* it, treasure it, and we adore it—even covet it. It distracts us as we savor our temporary fix of joy and alleviation from gloom. This fleeting, momentous occasion appears to brighten our day...but after a bit, the flower withers and dies—and with it, the joy and happiness it brought us. Our attention once again diverts back to the gloomy, melancholy weather, as once again we resume seeking to find *another* flower to break the mood. This is *object happiness*.

> *We are not rich by what we possess*
> *but by what we can do without.*
> ~Immanuel Kant

Authentic happiness, on the other hand, is not separate from us, not outside. It is not dependent upon some external weather forecast or fortunate encounter. Rather, it is our connection with our own internal weather. *We* create the conditions within ourselves, be they sunny or melancholy.

When we create the weather of authentic happiness, something different occurs when we happen upon that same beautiful flower: we can enjoy it without the yearning, desirous impulse to pluck it, to covet it all to ourselves. We have an entire farm in our backyard already, with a wealth and abundance of flowers, so a flower we happen upon can be left to thrive and adorn the trail so it can be enjoyed and celebrated by others passing by. In not consuming the flower by plucking it, we are actually contributing to the joy of others.

Authentic happiness is not dependent upon the fortunate encounter with a flower that we pluck; it is the baseline internal weather we *cultivate* that results in the flower garden in our own backyard. It is not a momentous, arbitrary happenstance to which we attach; it is an environment we establish and maintain. It is not separate from us, *out there*; it is a constant we maintain by cultivating it with gratitude, compassion, and generosity and by the sharing of it with others.

When we own our choice to create the weather, we can create any weather we choose—including not choosing melancholy—and we can share that weather with anyone we choose. This perspective is in direct contrast to object happiness, where we allow outside circumstances and other people to control the weather or allow momentous binges to distract us as we forget the weather for a time.

You might say, "Okay, that's a lovely picture being painted, but come on! What happens if a tornado rolls through and wipes out our farm? You make it sound as if we can just choose to be happy all the time, have a lovely farm of flowers, and nothing will ever get us down."

Indeed, we can, but we are required to adjust our perspective—and this doesn't mean self-delude; we are called to adjust to the *actual* realities of our circumstances. Tragedy strikes all of us from time to time, be it an illness, death in the family, financial hardship, heartbreak…

Consider the story of the man who endured more suffering than most could ever imagine—Holocaust survivor, Viktor Frankl. Even in the degradation and abject misery of a concentration camp, Frankl was able to exercise the most important freedom of all—the freedom to determine one's attitude, inner spirit, and character. The Nazis took everything else, every belonging, every family member, every object, and every other freedom from him, but no sadistic oppressor was able to take away his inner attitude, spirit, or character; nobody got to control Frankl's inner life or inner weather. One of the ways he found the strength to fight to stay alive and not lose hope was to think of his wife. Often, he would imagine her hands. He knew every cherished detail of them, every freckle, every wrinkle, every line…because, for many years, he held them; he knew them like the back of his own. Frankl saw clearly that those who had nothing to live for died quickest in the concentration camps.[2]

Authentic happiness cannot be stripped from us unless we allow it to be. We can learn how to nourish and feed it. It is a *habit* that, like a muscle, must be cared for, conditioned, exercised, and held sacred—not just for a day or two, a weekend seminar, a retreat, or a three-day cleanse, but rather a *lifestyle* as routine as brushing our teeth.

What of the tornado? External storms can wreak havoc, leaving devastation in their wakes, but then they pass through. They are fleeting and transitory. When allowed, our inner weather cultivated by our character, attitude, resilience, and inner spirit over time is left unscathed and can reestablish a baseline resulting in the replenishment of the external landscape. The primary cause of unhappiness is not the situation, but rather our attitudes, thoughts, and conduct around it. The universe serves up tremendous challenges on occasion. This defines our human circumstance. We take beatings and are knocked down, are let down, disappointed, heartbroken. *Bad stuff happens*. Loved ones die, marriages fall apart, businesses struggle.

Being down isn't wrong or bad; it is a part of being human. The situation in the universal sense is neutral; we humans create meaning in the circumstance and, from that, assign it either a negative or positive charge. It is why the situation forms a connection to object happiness. If we don't cultivate a strong inner-weather baseline, a challenging situation will destabilize our emotions and typically lead to unhappiness and discontent. Will we reach for comfort food, a tequila shot, meaningless sex, a Xanax? Or, will we remind ourselves that *the weather is not us*? Our circumstances and us are not one and same. *We* get to choose our attitude in how we face our circumstances.

I am reminded of a story that tells of a prominent, wealthy, savvy businessman that one day was kidnapped, robbed, and stripped of all of his wealth, his family, his belongings, his home, everything, and then was transported and dumped in a faraway, remote, barren desert, abandoned with nothing but the clothes on his back. The story continues that within a year, he reestablished himself, built community around him, cultivated new relationships, and emerged as a beloved, prominent, wealthy, savvy businessman once more.

We are all subject to experiences of highs and lows. All of us, without exception. While material things can be pillaged from us, our inner character, compassion, leadership, perspective, and Conscious Intelligence cannot be—nor can our inner weather, fortitude, or content of our character...*unless we allow them to be*. When we strengthen the muscles that mobilize our inner farming equipment to cultivate authentic happiness and establish that as our baseline weather, it makes no difference if we happen upon a beautiful flower or if we happen upon a tornado that knocks us down and wipes out our farm. Like the story of the savvy businessman and Viktor Frankl, nobody and nothing can strip us of our inner character, attitude, and spirit unless we allow it. When we keep in perspective all that constitutes our human experience, our internal weather will remain anchored and navigate us back on course like a compass that finds True North.

One more thing to note: Whether sunny or cloudy, either way, authentic happiness is *contagious*.

What Does It Take to Farm?

> *Happiness is a choice.*
> ~So many people lay claim to this quote,
> it is unknown who actually first said it.

> *Happiness is not a goal. . .*
> *it's a byproduct of a life well lived.*   ~Eleanor Roosevelt

LET'S START WITH an example of that *same flower* and consider the following: What does it take to keep it alive, grow it, harvest its seeds, and from it produce and maintain a habitat of perpetually blossoming flowers? It requires an optimal environment and climate (like the people we surround ourselves with, a job we like, things we enjoy doing); soil, fertilizer, nourishment (like feeding our soul, wellness, education, mentorship), It requires pruning and TLC (like focused attention, discipline, consistency); and it requires gratitude—a reverence for its intrinsic beauty.

Saying thank you out loud every day, counting our blessings, and acknowledging the things we are fortunate to have are powerful components to authentic happiness. It is a debt that is free of cost. It is the *debt of gratitude*. Our expression of gratitude, especially when we are alone when nobody hears us, informs the environment we cultivate. While nobody may be watching—while nobody seems to be within earshot, listening—*we are*. How we conduct ourselves in private, when people aren't watching, exposes our true character, and it has everything to do with how our life plays out.

There's a bigger message here. Rather than our merely chasing happiness, it is much more powerful to carry our happiness around with us. We tend to the garden and celebrate abundance, all of it, not just the blooming flowers, but our prevailing over a lost harvest as well. It is just as important and powerful to tend to the dried-out buds we press into a thick album or that we compost to become the fertilizer for the next bloom. We celebrate the soil, the seeds planted just inches below the surface, stinky manure—ahh yes, there never seems to be a shortage of that in our lives. Manure, literally and figuratively is the fertilizer that soon evolves into the sweet scent of potentiality and promise of the beauty to come. It is the solemn, circular metaphor and truth that there is also gain in loss. Loss is a part of our human experience. We learn from our losses much more than from our wins (incidentally, a lesson all fine athletes know well). These become teachable moments, opportunities for growth, and our hero's journey to triumph over our challenges and adversity.

> But...how can we be authentically happy while others suffer?

Do you feel the unresolving quandary this question can evoke inside? If you do, you are accessing Conscious Intelligence. The question is unsettling and can paralyze some of us. It's clear that even when we have cultivated a consistent lifestyle with a habitual routine harvesting authentic happiness, we inevitably still discover conditions in this world of suffering, social injustice, adversity, inhumane treatment, immorality, abuse, and greed. We witness a lacking caused by ignorance and by the atrophy of education, values, compassion, and basic services, in both under-resourced communities as well as in affluent ones. (The irony is that this atrophy isn't because we don't have the resources; we *have* the resources, but that discussion is for another time, another book.)

Negative Denial

WHEN THIS HAPPENS, what do we do? One option is to look away, walk on past, put our happiness blinders on, and deny the entire thing—yesssss, ignore it away—because *hey*, we are working so hard in our lives to eliminate negativity. We are mightily attempting to conduct ourselves with a consistency of sunlit happiness and joy, and, for heaven's sake, what a *downer* that stuff is! Besides, what can we *really* do about it, anyway? "Let's just think positively!"

That example is the relationship to a circumstance called *negative denial*. We can certainly do all of this—and many do—but if we are accessing Conscious Intelligence, *this doesn't work*. Inaction is an active choice that makes the chooser complicit because *doing nothing...is doing something!* The unresolving quandary remains, along with the torment and unsettling feelings.

Positive Denial

ANOTHER OPTION IS TO turn and face these circumstances, bear witness to them… and say "*no*." We can hold a space for them but not stare. This is another kind of denial—not the kind where we passively pretend something doesn't exist, but the kind where we are accountable; we see what's wrong and approach it head-on, actively choosing not to embolden it. We can say, "I will endeavor to contribute by being accountable and doing my part in transforming the circumstance so that I am *not* complicit. I will not be a part of this in its current state; I will not participate in this or validate this. Although this might be what is happening now, here, today, I do not choose to subscribe to it or accept things as they are. I seek to represent the *presence of an alternative*."

> *We cannot address suffering unless we bear witness to it, understand it, and seek to identify its source.*
>
> *This especially means observing the role, if any, we might be playing in the suffering, what complicity we may have in its remaining status quo, and what we are willing to place at stake to facilitate its transformation.*

When we do this, we recognize the importance of being conscious, of being vigilant, of being accountable about what's happening. Although awareness seeks to understand cause—awareness by itself isn't enough. We are here to elevate consciousness, and elevating consciousness means creating the space that envisions a world already transformed. This is an example of the distinction called *positive denial.* Incidentally, it also constitutes a major attribute of a *disruptor*.

Choosing positive denial can be challenging. How do we bear the enormity of suffering without allowing it to wholly consume us? First, we are well-served to remind ourselves that it's not about *us* or *our* suffering. When we seek the presence of an alternative, we are reminded that we are the conduit through which the electricity flows, not the electricity itself. We do not need to be the answer, but rather a channel for change. And so, we remain dynamic, not static. We neither look away, nor stare, nor dwell. The question here is not "What do we *do*?" Rather, the question becomes, "Who do we need to *be*?"

> *When we consider the circumstance with an elevated perspective, we can cultivate happiness while we actively hold the space for what can be.*
> *We can lessen suffering by being a beacon*
> *for what is possible.*
> *We can by becoming the presence of an alternative.*

SUMMARY | ID 51

Nomad or Farmer? How do you amass happiness?

The most fulfilling things in life aren't things.

Object happiness is the notion that something outside of us has the power to equip us with, or deprive us of, happiness. Object happiness is fleeting and mercurial, dependent on the weather forecast, our luck, perceived privilege, or attainment of desired materialistic things, for example. Object happiness appeals to the pleasure centers of the brain and is the culprit for creating a cycle of highs and lows, the aching need for a fix, and the painful withdrawals when cravings aren't fed. If object happiness becomes the determinant condition of our happiness, then our relationship to happiness is one of clinging, attachment, and need. It becomes a constant, a seeking outside of ourselves, like a nomad constantly on the move, hunting high and low across the land to satisfy an ever-nagging hunger that can never be satisfied.

Authentic happiness, on the other hand, is not separate from us, not outside. It is the baseline internal weather we *cultivate*; it is an environment we establish and maintain. It is not separate from us, *out there*, not a momentous, arbitrary happenstance or material object to which we attach.

What does it take to farm? Cultivation. If happiness were a *flower*, what does it take to keep it alive, grow it, harvest its seeds, and from it produce and maintain a habitat of perpetually blossoming happiness? It requires an optimal environment and climate (like the people we surround ourselves with, a job we like, things we enjoy doing); soil, fertilizer, nourishment (like feeding our soul, wellness, education, mentorship); pruning and TLC (like focused attention, discipline, consistency); and a reverence for its intrinsic beauty. Happiness is a constant we maintain by cultivating it with gratitude, compassion, and generosity and by the sharing of it with others.

ID 52: Self-Actualization | Self-Realization

CONSIDER THIS FOR A MOMENT: Think of the physical, perceivable, observable universe that we live in, in its totality, as if it were a fish tank. Inside this fish tank contains everything, past and present—us, the earth, moon, stars—everything our five senses of sight, sound, touch, taste, smell can perceive. The totality of our perception is confined to and limited by that which can only be observed from within this fish tank. So, is that all there is?

This human condition is confined by this predicament. Our circumstances prevent us from being able to get out of the fish tank, to observe it from the outside in. The condition is called *subject/object*. You are invited to keep this in mind as you reflect upon this distinction.

> **Self-actualization** is performing to our fullest potentiality from within the fish tank. In psychological terms, it pertains to a person's drive to attain their goals, achieve their vision, and fulfill their highest expression and potentiality—planning the work, working the plan, and accomplishing (actualizing) it. Actualization is about doing. Self-actualization is reached when the way we move through the world (fish tank) fully reflects our inner values and reaches parity with our potential.

Continuing the fish tank analogy, we humans, confined to our human condition, are unable to have an objective, outside-the-tank perspective, looking *in*. We simply are not able to get out of the tank—as if we were at an aquarium, for example, just as we cannot observe the Big Bang from beyond its blast radius or peer into (or out of) a black hole to gain any sort of perspective. Incidentally, unless we were able to, this human predicament is the reason we cannot directly observe Consciousness itself. Our abilities are limited by this human circumstance equipped only with our human faculties—sight, sound, touch, taste, smell—in this observable universe that contains space, time, energy, and matter. So, self-actualization is a person performing to their fullest potentiality as sourced from inside (within) the confines of the fish tank.

Self-realization is moving to a perspective outside the fish tank. It is to know oneself and to realize the higher truth of one's existence.[6] This concept (and it can *only* exist as a concept because of the limitations just described regarding us as being inside the fish tank) is also known as our highest *why*; it is about *being* rather than *doing*. It is connection with that which is greater than or beyond ourselves. Those more spiritually inclined may attribute this perspective to linkage with the Divine, but self-realization is not confined to religion or spirituality.

So, *self-actualization* is fulfilling one's potential on the physical, tangible realm, while *self-realization* is the consideration of one's expansiveness in relation to what lies conceptually in the realms beyond (outside of the fish tank). The notion that the physical world intersects with, and is woven within, a realm beyond dimension describes the relationship between self-actualization and self-realization… and *therein lies purpose*.

SUMMARY | ID 52

Potentiality

Self-actualization is fulfilling one's potential in the physical, tangible realm; it is performing to our fullest potentiality and pertains to a person's drive to attain their goals, achieve their vision, plan the work, work the plan, and accomplish (actualize) it.

Self-realization is to know oneself and to realize the higher truth of one's existence. It is the consideration of one's expansiveness in relation to what lies conceptually in the realms beyond. It is also known as our highest why in connection with that which is greater than or beyond ourselves. The distinction is about being rather than doing.

ID 53: Meaning and Purpose

> *The meaning of life is to find your gift.*
> *The purpose of life is to give it away.*   ~Pablo Picasso

WHAT IS THE MEANING OF LIFE? You may be asking yourself, "Is he *really* going to attempt to answer this?"

Yes! I am... well, in a way—by illuminating the distinction here, not by inventing it or giving my personal opinion about it.

I am an athlete, and I love the spirit of competition. However, the objective of life doesn't appear to be a race to the finish line, now does it? This would equate life's goal being an all-out sprint to our deaths. By simple consensus, and by observation of our human drive to survive and thrive on this earth for millennia, it is safe to suggest that such isn't the case...not even close. Something is instilled inside us that gives us the impulse to live, love, learn, connect, overcome adversity, create, thrive, and witness each other.

What's life's meaning? If we search high and low for the wisdom in such a profound question and still come up short of the answer, then it is conceivable the flaw is in the *phrasing of the question*. Are we really searching *out there* to find the meaning of life? Or are we searching *within* to create it? Is this question about something absolute or about something strictly philosophical? Life reveals itself moment to moment, ever dynamic and always in constant flux.

Meaning. What is it really? It isn't something that comes from out there in the Universe; meaning dwells deeply within us. We create meaning about things "out there" from within ourselves. This distinction is no different from that regarding light:

> *It is not in light's nature to create meaning.*
> *We humans create meaning in what light illuminates.*

Light is indiscriminate; it illuminates any path to which it is exposed. Light doesn't create meaning, doesn't take sides or defend one, doesn't have an opinion. It quite simply aids our eyes by broadening and deepening the exposure of the surrounding landscape.

Likewise, the natural world doesn't worry. It carries on in its "is-*ness*." Mother Earth has been here long before we were and will remain long after.

We may think we're driving—and, in some smaller sense, perhaps occasionally we are. But thinking we have control because we occasionally drive is like surfing a wave then thinking we have established mastery and control over the entire ocean. Those who surf have experienced an attitudinal reality adjustment when a periodic sneaker wave comes in, cresting on top of us before we can escape. The result is a colossal pummeling in the Mother Nature washing machine. Oh yes, there exists a wash cycle setting that takes its time—really deluges, agitates, and liberates every misconceived stain of control dripping from the fabric of our mind…long enough to remind us to never forget that we are not ultimately in charge. Life has a unique way, one way or another, eventually, of placing things into proper perspective.

The meaning of life varies from one person to another, as unique to each of us as our own DNA. It changes, evolves, shifts as our individual lives progress and evolve. Meaning draws on our unique value systems as they exist in the present, in real time. Meaning is formed through our interests, sentiments, influences, upbringing, customs, experiences, challenges, and triumphs. We contextualize these factors based on what we most strongly identify with. We can choose to identify with any combination of things ranging from money, power, and influence to love, nature, and service. And the meanings of each of these dynamically vary; they can shift and evolve depending on how we perceive them. For example, money, power, and influence turned outward can shift into enrichment, empowerment, and service to the lives of others.

We often discover that our lives become more meaningful when we aspire to stand for, and contribute to, something bigger than ourselves. Meaning's presence is most felt when its experience is shared with others, when we are surrounded by love, connection, service, community, struggle, triumph, resilience, generosity, and gratitude. We witness this during our most vulnerable moments, while facing the mortality of a loved one—or our own. We witness it with our grandparents in convalescence reflecting on their lives, on their joys and regrets. We witness it as deployed soldiers reach out halfway around the world to say "I love you," or when we sweep up loved ones in a timeless embrace as if the whole world pauses, holding its breath while in that moment, the entirety of it is wholly contained. Life can be only what we make of it.

We create meaning by what our lives illuminate.

What It Is to Be Alive

> *People say that what we're all seeking is a meaning for life.*
> *I don't think that's what we're really seeking.*
> *I think that what we're seeking is an experience of being alive.* ~Joseph Campbell, The Power of Myth

WE ALL SEEK the experience of being alive, don't we? Our individual paths are our own and unique, as are our struggles and triumphs while navigating those paths. This is a defining element of what it is to be human.

Two things exist when we are experiencing being alive. The first is—*we are present*, in the moment, here, now. We experience the moment with every visceral ounce of our body. The second is that *it feels as if someone else is driving*, that they know and have known all along where to go, and that everything is exactly as it should be. It is connection to our essential Self, the inner child—like the one that almost drowned inside of me, both literally and figuratively, in the swimming pool that dark day many years ago. If we are tuned into the voice of our essential Self, our path reveals itself. The Navajos call it the Pollen Path—*Path* with a capital *P*, meaning singular Way. It is true and unique to each of us, laid out in front of us, full of potential that only our essential Self can access—a path dusted with golden, fertile pollen.[9]

Purpose

> *The two most important days in our life are the day we are born and the day we discover why.* ~Mark Twain

THE TRIALS, REVELATIONS, and peak moments during our lives are inflected through us, creating our unique experience of being alive. As we forge forward with each step, our fateful roles are revealed moment to moment. They shape our behaviors, habits, philosophies, and beliefs; they are expressed by us in our unique manners; and they inform the life we live into. They all unfold, blooming like a lotus flower, into what constitutes our substance, purpose, and True North.

When I almost drowned, I allowed the misguided programs inside of me to sabotage my path for a time and to seduce me to the brink of giving up. Something drove me, insisting that I find my way back—in my case, back into the water—so that I could overcome my fear, reconnect to my source, and reenter the sacred place that brings me joy.

We can still get lost following the Pollen Path. In my case, the devastation could have had expansive, impressionable results in my programming, causing me never to return to the ocean again. Such matters can corrode our resolve to prevail in much more significant ways than merely swimming in the pool or ocean; they inform the life we live into, the way we approach life's challenges, adversity, and setbacks. Some check out, lose interest, stop seeking and being curious; they hit the ejection handle in relationships, passions, and curiosity, opting instead for truancy, drugs, and becoming a delinquent.

What is the purpose of life? It matters not whether we approach this answer from the direction of science or faith. Both sit unopposed, concurring that the answer is ultimately beyond our capacity to know. They both conceive that the flaw appears to be in the phrasing of the question, and that we fall short to fully addressing it from what will always be the limiting parameters of our human circumstance (*that fish tank*). We do not possess the faculties or capacity to fully comprehend all that we are or, with any certainty, the source from which we come, who is driving, or where we are ultimately going.

The Invisible "Non" Distinction

WE ARE ENERGY; we are stardust, made of the same stuff as the universe. In the broader perspective, it makes no difference and is independent of whether we refer to this enigmatic protoplasm as the stuff of the stars, atoms and molecules, the image of the Divine, or anything in between.

The marriage of purpose with career, lifestyle, relationships, productivity, our values is commonplace in 21st century consciousness. Today, more than ever before, these things are not separate. You cannot have one without the others. They are all complementary; they all inform and weave into each other and needn't be distinguished from one another. Our job requires relationships and communication with other people. Loving what we do leads us to be more productive. Our relationships and communication with our significant other, children, neighbors, and communities all connect back to our purpose on our journey towards fulfillment. Each require harmony, balance, and cultivation.

SUMMARY | ID 53

The meaning of life…

What's life's meaning? If we search high and low for the wisdom in such a profound question and still come up short of the answer, then it is conceivable the flaw is in the *phrasing of the question*. Are we really searching *out there* to find the meaning of life? Or are we searching *within* to create it?

Meaning dwells deeply within us and varies from one person to another. We create meaning about things "out there" from within ourselves. This distinction is no different from that regarding light: It is not in light's nature to create meaning. We humans create meaning in what light illuminates. Light is indiscriminate; it illuminates any path to which it is exposed. Light doesn't take sides or defend one, doesn't have an opinion. It quite simply aids our eyes by broadening and deepening the exposure of the surrounding landscape.

We often discover that our lives become more meaningful when we aspire to stand for, and contribute to, something bigger than ourselves as doing so draws from our unique value systems in the present as we live moment to moment.

Purpose: Like meaning, purpose has both an intrinsic and extrinsic realm, one that we ourselves formulate and one beyond our capacity and faculties to conceive. It could be said that all of those formulations that we create within ourselves about meaning become the defining mechanisms we assign to ourselves that when actualized, formulate our internal blueprint of purpose. The trials, revelations, and peak moments during our lives are inflected through us, creating our unique experience of being alive. As we forge forward with each step, our fateful roles are revealed moment to moment. They shape our behaviors, habits, philosophies, and beliefs; they are expressed by us in our unique manners, informing the life we live into.

CHAPTER 17
Execution

ID 54: Excellence versus Perfection

Strive for excellence;
Leave perfection for the lunatics.

EXCELLENCE IS NOT A THING. It is a *vector*. Like the trajectory of an airplane we spoke of earlier, excellence, too, has magnitude and direction, velocity and a heading. Excellence is fueled by attitude and conviction, focus and drive, core values and vision. Practicing excellence and making it a part of our daily lifestyle strengthens both our physical muscles and our attitudinal muscles. How we do the small things is reflective of how we do the big things; how we organize our closet is reflective of how we organize our life. When we strive for excellence, our passion, energy, strength, focus, and grace are all indicators of how we show up to the world—and how the world shows up to us. This holds true whether we practice excellence in our career, in feeding our mind, in our relationships, or in our health and fitness and revitalization.

> *We are what we repeatedly do.*
> *Excellence, then, is not an act, but a habit.*   ~Aristotle

The practice of excellence informs the life we live into. Perfectionism is nothing more than fear pretending to have high standards. Excellence doesn't mean being perfect, or that we achieve "perfection." It's a practice—just as we don't "do" or perfect discipline, we practice discipline. We don't do or perfect yoga, martial arts, or meditation; we practice these just as some people practice medicine and law. The Invisible Distinctions are not one and done. They are rungs of a ladder; they define what a ladder is, and they are always present and necessary if we wish to climb. Excellence is a trajectory, a vector, an accretion of skills, knowledge, and experience that we cultivate. Among those most successful in achieving such cultivation additionally seek an experienced practitioner, teacher, mentor, guide, or sensei from whom to learn. The word sensei means *one who has walked the path before*—not a bad idea to seek such a luminary for guidance when we hope to pursue excellence.

When we practice anything, it is incumbent upon us to maintain consistency. We don't diet only once in a while if we expect to maintain long-term physical or physiological health. We don't brush our teeth once in a while if we expect to end up keeping all of our teeth. Attending church, temple, or mosque ninety minutes a week doesn't assure one's devoutness the other six days, twenty-two and a half hours a week, just as going to the gym or walking around the block once a week doesn't necessarily secure a spot on the Olympic team.

Why do we practice excellence? We are more prone to remain centered, focused, balanced, calm, stable, and intellectually primed when a challenge arises. We practice in order to create a solid bedrock of habits so that outside the office, home, laboratory, studio, dojo, church, ashram, or kitchen—we remain grounded when the universe serves up an assortment of adventurous surprises. We practice sharpening our mind, body, and attitude so that we can perform optimally when we are physically, mentally, emotionally, or psychologically challenged. We practice excellence so that we can gracefully respond rather than mindlessly react.

SUMMARY | ID 54

Practice makes…excellence, not perfection.

Strive for excellence; leave perfection for the lunatics.

Excellence is a pursuit; it's a habit. It is a vector, just as legacy was described earlier. It is cultivated continuously and not some summit you reach and stop—where you spend the rest of your life simply resting on your laurels.

The practice of excellence informs the life we live into. Perfectionism is nothing more than fear pretending to have high standards. Excellence doesn't mean being perfect or that we achieve "perfection." It's a practice—just as we don't "do" or perfect discipline, we practice discipline.

We practice in order to create a solid bedrock of habits so that outside the office, home, laboratory, studio, dojo, church, ashram, or kitchen—we remain grounded when the universe serves up an assortment of adventurous surprises. We practice sharpening our mind, body, and attitude so that we can perform optimally when we are physically, mentally, emotionally, or psychologically challenged. We practice excellence so that we can gracefully respond rather than mindlessly react.

ID 55: Flow | Exemplified Through Japanese Culture

Form follows function

"FLOW" HAS MANY NAMES, and we all have the ability to experience it. One powerful illustration of the practice of flow is woven throughout the traditional Japanese cultural disciplines. Such ancient disciplines are notable in their singular pursuit of excellence and harmony, recognizing that the way we take on one thing is the way we take on everything.

Flow is the actualization of elegant form developed through intention, creativity, and discipline. It is the exposure of an act's intrinsic radiance that results as if capturing lightning in a bottle. The Japanese even have a term for its pursuit: *Michi*, meaning "the Way" with a capital "W." "Michi" is a term that describes achieving the highest degree of expression within a fundamental, underlying principle of an art, a skill, or a discipline. It is a set of cultivated habits refined from constant practice and a code of conduct, rooted in honor, principle, and humility. Of course, we are not required to be Japanese to practice or experience flow, nor are we required to train specifically in the Japanese traditions to develop it.

Michi, or the Way, is not to be mistaken for "path." There are many paths but only one *Way*. While a path is a (w)ay with a lowercase "w"[7], the Way isn't a map to any particular place nor is it the subscription to any particular system. Rather, it is a *conceptual term* that describes a pure form of expression. It is used to describe an entire approach to life, a way of living, and the cultivation of a *lifestyle*, not a trophy that, once attained, sits on a mantle while we rest on our laurels. It is rungs on an ever-extending ladder one constantly climbs to elevate consciousness.

Michi is both the expression of, and the inspiration for, the numerous traditional disciplines known for their fundamental postures, alignment, and body movement. You've probably heard of, seen, or even practiced one or more of these disciplines. Examples include:

Sho-do	– calligraphy
Sa-do	– tea ceremony
Ka-do	– flower arrangement

Bu-do	– the martial Way
Kyu-do	– the Way of archery
Bushi-do	– the Way of the samurai
Aiki-do	– the way of harmony
Iai-do, Ken-do	– the Way of the sword
Karate-do	– the Way of empty hand, martial arts

All of these arts have the suffix "-*do*" (pronounced doe). *Michi* and -*do* are one and the same. (The Japanese use several alphabets—and these two terms are one concept written two different ways.)

The Japanese are but one example of a culture that has devised an elegant set of traditions to illustrate and express the Way through these numerous living art forms, but we can observe humanity all over the world exemplifying—*The Way.*

Michi teaches us that excellence is a habit no matter what discipline one chooses. The discipline we learn is merely its vehicle. The pursuit of excellence cultivates our process in life and all the disciplines we take on in our life. Michi is a vector requiring consistent practice, repetition, and trekking the path to mastery. Malcolm Gladwell refers to this as the requisite *ten thousand hours of deliberate practice*. While this gets us to a point of experience and refinement, the Way actually requires a lifetime journey because it's not just a point, it's a heading. It's not a finish line, it's our finding and cultivating our flow and course towards our True North.

We witness flow and pure expression as radiance, the byproducts of countless, inspired moments—a dance or music performance, a painting, photograph, or film, a sports feat, a blissful taste of umami in a bite of culinary genius, a healing touch from a physical therapist, the wise words of a respected luminary, encouraging words of a parent to their child, a spark of devotion in a lover's eyes. When these fortunate, inspirational, timeless moments are manifested out of impeccable commitment to excellence, they are celebrated masterpieces of the expresser, of the artist, of you, *their creator.*

SUMMARY | ID 55

Excellence is a habit.

Flow is excellence in action. It is the actualization of elegant form developed through intention, creativity, and discipline. It is the exposure of an act's intrinsic radiance that results as if capturing lightning in a bottle. When these fortunate, inspirational, timeless moments, propagated by habit, are manifested out of impeccable commitment to excellence, they are celebrated masterpieces of the expresser, of the artist, of you, *their creator*.

SECTION III

THE CONSCIOUS INTELLIGENCE PERSPECTIVE

The Conscious Intelligence Perspective

Elevated Consciousness
is the perspective we endeavor to access
that catapults us far above our circumstances
without placing us an inch above anyone else.

NOW THAT WE HAVE COMPLETED SECTION II and illuminated all of the Invisible Distinctions, the elements that frame The Conscious Intelligence Paradigm, we are ready to look at the world from this new perspective. As these distinctions have been illuminated for you, does your view of the world appear any different? When we elevate *above* our circumstances to view them with a new perspective, we start to view things we couldn't see clearly while situated from *within* our circumstances.

Your path is *yours*. It is as unique as your DNA. Conscious Intelligence is *not a map*, not an instruction manual to your path; it is a light that illuminates the territory where you've been, where you are, where you are going. It illuminates perspective. Your job is to follow the breadcrumbs your essential Self has laid out in front of you. From here on out it's a lifestyle of accountability, cultivation, and execution. It's about being inquisitive, creative, collaborative, and, at times disruptive. It is about parity in both doing and being—and it is a never-ending quest for mastery over your circumstances.

Moving forward, know that you always have choice in the matter. Consider that sometimes to regain power in our circumstances, we have to take what appears to be a step backwards as a means to advance three steps forward. The feat is never easy; it seldom feels good, but when the undertaking liberates us from stagnation, complacency, and self-imprisonment, we just do it. *We do it anyway*; we are resilient; we are better for it. When confronted or challenged, we are reminded that we have options—sometimes ones we might not immediately consider—options perhaps not immediately gratifying or pleasant. Sometimes the right choice isn't the easy choice.

It is our human condition to straddle the blurred line between what is unknown and what remains unknowable—between what may become known and what may never be discovered. Whether we believe this life is it, or believe we get re-dos, karma, etc., we reach the same conclusion: The task is to have the experience of being alive, here, now…*in the present*.

It is challenging to conceive that love, hope, faith, connection, consciousness, wonder, compassion, and creativity can be contained solely within the confines of humankind's relationship with the physical, observable world. To know oneself and to realize the higher truth of one's existence is the departure point where our views begin to disburse into areas of possibility, faith, belief, and the unknown.

> *Life is not a dress rehearsal.* ~Rose Tremain

The notion of lying on a deathbed during our last earthly moments and saying, "Oh, for Pete's sake, I just figured it all out," followed by the beep, beep, beep, beeeeeeeeep of the flatline, is an absolutely dreadful notion. The only thing more dreadful would be our epitaph reading: "Died with their profound potential fully intact."

The choice is up to us to open the aperture wide enough—whether our lens is based in physics or metaphysics, is religious or spiritual, agnostic or secular, right, left, or center. The choice is up to us to realize that what we see right next to us, over yonder, beyond the horizon, or in the mirror—is our essential Self peering back at us. With this perspective comes the widest spectrum of choice. We can choose to celebrate our differences, or we can forge them into a weapon that maims and divides us.

The purpose of the distinctions is to identify the characteristics constituted within each unique choice we make. Gaining insight facilitates perspective regarding the questions that ultimately meet us along the way, no matter which path we choose.

Cultivating Conscious Intelligence is not a periodic endeavor; it is the consistent habit of a practitioner—a person actively engaged in a discipline, profession, or practice. We don't elevate our life by participating only in the vital, essential parts of CI *occasionally*. We develop, build, cultivate a life that we *live into*. Our lives today have been shaped by the lifestyle that led us to this moment, whether our habits have held us back or catapulted us forward, deprived us or served us, muted us or elevated us to reach full self-expression. My hope is that you have come to realize that accessing Conscious Intelligence is a choice. It is the most true, real, and powerful choice we can make.

As we close our exploration of Conscious Intelligence here in this text, and you embark on what I hope will be a lifetime of continued pursuit of greater understanding, compassion, and communication, let us review.

CHAPTER 18

Full Circle

THE CONSCIOUS INTELLIGENCE PARADIGM provides a means to illuminate perspectives surrounding the nature, causation, and dynamics of our circumstances. From the biggest decisions of our lives to the seemingly inconsequential, this Paradigm can inform and drive our conduct, how we observe, listen, process, engage, act, speak—essentially, *how we respond*. If assimilated, it can guide us to respond optimally.

The underlying framework of this platform, The Conscious Intelligence Paradigm, is an organized and structured set of elemental distinctions designed to illuminate and access Conscious Intelligence. It provides the behavioral insights and tools that let us cultivate a path to the life we endeavor to live into. Its intention is not to take on the philosophical or literal interpretation of what consciousness is. It merely serves as a conduit to expand our perspective. As a result of the insights we gain, we become better poised to respond optimally to our circumstances.

There exists a distinction between prescription and illumination, just as there exists a distinction between giving someone a map with instructions versus equipping them with a powerful headlamp. Inspiring is a teacher who guides a student in a way that makes the student feel as if they made the discovery themselves. As timesaving as a map might seem, and on occasion can sometimes be, a deeper and lasting understanding comes from making the trip ourselves.

> *The only enduring way to shift consciousness*
> *is to choose powerfully for ourselves*
> *rather than be told what to do by someone else.*

Illumination expands perspective while prescription narrows it.

There is a distinction between taking the path less traveled versus hitching a ride, between making a path more efficient versus cutting corners.

Elevating consciousness takes work, and it isn't a one-time, one-and-done kind of thing. Like trekking to a summit, The Conscious Intelligence Paradigm provides tactics, skills, techniques, insights, approaches that make our trek more efficient and adroit.

Conscious Intelligence is not a shortcut, nor does such a journey want for one when approached from an elevated perspective. Think of it as a lifetime of cultivation. I have spent much of my life aggregating, organizing, and consolidating The Conscious Intelligence Paradigm so that it could be framed in a clear, concise, and organized anthology. Applying its principles is something only you can do. While I will walk the path with you and guide you, I cannot walk it for you. This is *your* trek and *your* summit.

In framing The Conscious Intelligence Paradigm, I set out to illuminate a pathway to how we can experience the world with greater clarity, perspective, and, yes, consciousness. This Paradigm (derived from the *Genome of Elevated Consciousness*, my research, thesis, and body of work) facilitates opening the key channels of communication between one and other and with ourselves. It helps us navigate the world with clearer connection, so that we can approach business, productivity, relationships, communication, and ourselves much more powerfully and purposefully.

The Invisible Distinctions

JUST AS DNA CONSTITUTES the building blocks of the Human Genome, so do the Invisible Distinctions constitute the structure of Conscious Intelligence. The Distinctions are divided into three main categories: *Base Distinctions, Central Distinctions, and Elevated Distinctions.*

The Base Distinctions illuminate everyday concepts commonly conflated, mischaracterized, and misunderstood. They provide the clear parameters critical to our ability to effect clear and sober communication between each other and within ourselves. They illuminate our personal sovereignty, choices in the matters of our life, and introduce us to not only surviving, but thriving and inspiring others to thrive as well.

The Central Distinctions are all about love, reminding us that love provides the only *real* fuel from which we can operate that propagates our course heading towards True North, towards the fullest expression of our true Self.

The Elevated Distinctions represent the aspect of Self that radiates from us when our scope ventures beyond to that which is greater than ourselves.

The Conscious Intelligence Paradigm has two simultaneous flows: Progression and Perfusion.

Progression: As we advance from Base to Elevated, we progress upward along the Paradigm, like rungs of a ladder, illuminating the distinctions and elevating consciousness.

Perfusion: At the same time, Conscious Intelligence is sourced and rooted from its Central Distinctions. It perfuses like oxygenated blood out to the extremities. Just as every grounded movement we make is initiated from our core, the Central Distinctions are the life blood, the connective tissue, and the structural integrity that binds and connects The Conscious Intelligence Paradigm to us and each other.

In symphony, these collective attributes as we ascend Base, Central, Elevated—and we perfuse from Central, outward, to the extremities—constitute the source of vitality, and the fuel that drives Conscious Intelligence.

Our personal maps are formulated and shaped by factors like our thoughts, beliefs, perceptions, conditioning, experiences, memories, and circumstances. These are very powerful, influential forces, so naturally, we occasionally risk their gravitating us away from our true, authentic *Self*.

What Does Conscious Intelligence Illuminate?

CIRCUMSTANCES:

> *Conscious Intelligence is the ability to gain mastery over our circumstances. It is the attainment of clarity and perspective within our circumstances to bring about optimal results.*

Everything we do, everything we are up to, involves circumstances. We are not our circumstances. We are not defined by our circumstances. Our circumstances are not us.

PERSPECTIVE:

> *We do not see the world as it is, we see the world as we are.*
> ~*Talmud / Nin*

We all view life through a lens—*our lens*. There is nothing inherently faulty about this unless we have the illusion that this is not the case. Conscious Intelligence is pure perspective—that is, a view not obscured by a lens.

CHOICE:

There is always more than one way to view or interpret a circumstance.

ACCESSING CONSCIOUS INTELLIGENCE reveals the comprehensive spectrum of choices we have. From broad choice, we are optimally poised to execute informed decisions.

IDENTITY:

*We are as unique as our own DNA.
At the same time, we are 99.9% identical, nonetheless.*

WE ARE NOT DEFINED by our circumstances. Nor are our circumstances defined by others. It is our choice whether to celebrate our differences or forge them into a weapon that cuts us apart, divides us, and isolates us.

CHANGE:

Change is inevitable; growth is optional.
~John C. Maxwell

THE DYNAMIC OF CHANGE is the only constant in the Universe. We can choose to ride the wave or get pummeled by it.

RESILIENCE:

We cannot always control our circumstances, but we can control how we conduct ourselves within them.

OUR BASIC, innate ability to adapt, heal, and evolve has secured our existence on this earth for millennia. Our response to any given situation stems from the way we approach our circumstances.

CULTURE:

> *Neither majority nor consensus necessarily asserts that something is right or optimal.*

Conscious Intelligence is a habit we constantly build and cultivate, endlessly seeking perspective in an effort to broaden our viewpoints, recognize others, and invite inclusion.

PATH:

> *We create the life we live into.*

Elevating consciousness is a course heading set to True North, the highest expression of who we are.

How Do We Leverage the Insights of the Invisible Distinctions in Our Life?

When seeking to elevate consciousness, consider…

> *Fear lacks perspective and shuts out access to Conscious Intelligence.*

> *When we lead with transactional thinking, it narrows perspective.*

    A civilization is placed in existential risk when the seeking of illumination is replaced by complacent ignorance.
    When an empty mind replaces an open one, it suspends reason and rationale and replaces these things with incivility, divisiveness, and ignorance.
    In society, when constructive discourse is replaced with empty rhetoric that appeals to hate, fear, and blame as a means to unify its people, it is a society that ceases to be, and an empire destined to fall.

When collective conscience is replaced with misleading, inflammatory, divisive language meant to appeal to primal fear, a culture of decency ceases, and a culture of barbaric incivility begins.

We are all connected…

> *Man did not weave the web of life;*
> *he is merely a strand in it.*
> *Whatever he does to the web,*
> *he does to himself.*
> ~Chief Seattle (attributed) / Ted Perry

CONNECTION IS BOTH A FUNDAMENTAL and qualitative key reality in our experience of being alive and in the elevation of consciousness. We need only look at our human circumstance and at humankind's relationship to the universe, Earth, and to each other to see that we are all connected.

When we demonstrate ownership and accountability both for universal love and universal suffering, we are able to gaze deeply into the eyes of our fellow human and see ourselves staring back. We recognize ourselves in others. What we experience as a result is connection. And it is this intersect point that facilitates the flow from which we elevate our consciousness.

Playing It Safe Is Not Safe

> *A ship in harbor is safe,*
> *but that is not what ships are built for.*
> ~John A. Shedd, *Salt from My Attic*

WE BLINK, and it's next week. We blink again, and it's another year. Blink again, and our hair has grayed. The entire time, we are obsessed about trying to get it *right*, get it *perfect*, know for *certain*. We risk discovering too late that right, perfect, and certainty are all myths, mis-phrased conundrums we spend our entire lives trying to unravel. We risk discovering too late that reaching the end of the rope is not the point—and that figuring that out only while crossing the finish line, rather than *here*, *now*... results in our missing out. The powerful, meaningful, impactful moments that propagate from our experience of being alive, right now, right here, in the present are what make all the difference.

It is up to us to make distinctions that illuminate perspective and broaden our array of choices so that we are optimally poised to make powerful decisions and, when necessary, have the courage to course correct.

It is up to us to seek illumination along our path and, by our own radiance, participate in and contribute to what becomes the confluence of our path with others—and, in the process, discover the experience of being alive.

It is up to us to fulfill what it means to elevate consciousness, to periodically step back in reflection, ask ourselves if we are in harmony with our purpose—with our "Why."

How will you choose to live out the remainder of your life? Will you live in the myth of certainty, in the prison cell of predictability, control, and fear, where you believe what you are fed, dwell in your past circumstances, and seek no alternatives to what appear to be just the way things are? Or will you extend your mind beyond your circumstances when seeking elevation, change, and joy. Will you be accountable rather than complicit and seek the presence of an alternative when the circumstances are called for? Will you elevate your consciousness in an effort to expand, grow, evolve, pioneer, create, and be a luminary, for yourself, for others, for posterity?

CHAPTER 19

Afterword—My Final Thoughts

Pierre Teihard de Chardin said:

> *We are not human beings having a spiritual experience, we are spiritual beings having a human experience.*

As you now likely know, I question pretty much everything. So…Are we spiritual beings having a human experience??? I have no idea whether this is true, but I smiled the first time I read this and thought: "How fun!" You see, I began to ponder what that might look like *literally*—how would this mesh into one's lifestyle? It invites us to the carpet to play even bigger. It inspires us. Whether true or not, either way, why wouldn't we cultivate a lifestyle of health, love, adventure, curiosity, an occasional bowl of ice cream (for spirit's sake, of course!), and play huge?

So, just in case…
> *Why not have a duty to our spirit inhabiting the vessel that is our body, to honor it as a guest in its effort to have a human experience?*

Think of it like this—when welcoming someone to your home, you prepare, don't you? You treat guests like royalty. In many cultures and communities, when one is invited into a home, it is a great honor and quite an ordeal because the home is an intimate, sacred place. The host cleans, organizes, prepares, straightens up, pulls out the famous family recipes, dusts off the good china, silverware, and crystal, pours the good wine. Ahhh, this is gonna be truly special! Great emphasis is placed on putting one's best foot forward.

What if we treated our bodies like this? Fed our minds nutritional food. Honored our sacred guest into our home, the temple that is our body—into our life, our community, our *stuff*? What a fun way to approach this experiment with our spirit—ya know, the one that won the lottery (or drew the short straw) and got stuck with us, assigned to have our human experience. So, why wouldn't we give that spirit a beautiful experience, an enchanted journey?

To honor it and its sacred visit to our home, why wouldn't we endeavor to maintain a healthy life, mentally, physically, emotionally, spiritually, passionately. Living mindfully by association would also honor other vessels entertaining their guests and help them be good hosts as they would inspire us to do.

If I were my spirit, a spirit that strives to see the world without limitation, I would want to enjoy the ride from within the best, high-performance vehicle I could find. Being a good host for our spirit, perhaps we'd endeavor to give it a body vessel that can take it anywhere it wants to go freely and give it the best experience of what it is to be alive. Perhaps this means traveling the world, exploring art, cinema, literature, history, culinary creations, and wine. Perhaps it's finding meaningful connection with others, with animals and nature, solving our world's challenges, service, and advocating for social justice. Yes to all! Personally, I run, swim, fly, explore, love, share, serve, fall down, screw up, learn, triumph, and always strive to juice the nectar out of life in an effort to experience life to its maximum potential. I can only do this because I've made a conscious effort to explore every corner of this life adventure with an open mind, an open heart, an incessant hunger to learn, and boundless curiosity. What would your conscious effort look like?

> *So I tell him: "Fasten your seatbelt, because you are in for one hell of a ride!"*

Climbing to the Summit

Follow your bliss ~Joseph Campbell

GETTING TO THE SUMMIT of Everest for the epic view is challenging. It is a long-term commitment. The travails of elevating our consciousness can often feel as equally confronting; but the view once you get there…is extraordinary.

Every day, every moment, we are afforded the opportunity to start on page one. Our every breath anchors us to the countless present moments of our lives, this web of life that tethers us in connection with the earth, with nature, with each other, and with the essence deep within our Self. All of these elements culminate together and constitute the symphony that is our life.

As one human to another, trying to be a good host to my spirit, I invite you to do the same. Whatever role you play in life, it is your choice—*choose powerfully*. Live a life that doesn't just speak to you; live a life that *sings* to you. And in the times when you feel stalled in your self-motivation, consider your guest. Do it for that spirit who has specially chosen *you* to have a unique, human experience. I strongly believe they will not only be grateful; I believe they are the key to your bliss.

APPENDIX

CONSCIOUS INTELLIGENCE PARADIGM

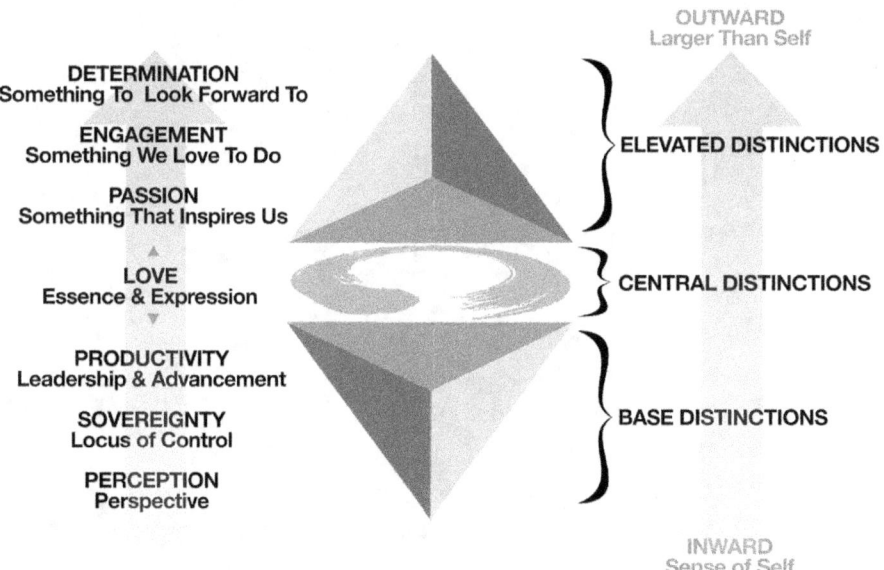

ENDNOTES

CH 3

1. UN Millennium Project, The Faces of Poverty http://www.unmillenniumproject.org/resources/fastfacts_e.htm.

   http://news.mit.edu/2000/mindseye, https://www.nfpt.com/blog/using-visualization-techniques-for-peak-athletic-performance, https://www.psychologytoday.com/blog/flourish/200912/seeing-is-believing-the-power-visualization.

2. Gottman Institute /40 years of research. /Lifestyle poll of 100 mental health professionals. https://www.huffingtonpost.com/2013/11/20/divorce-causes-_n_4304466.html

3. While there are, of course, mental illnesses that can impact our understanding of fact versus story, for the purposes of these distinctions we are talking more lightly about the non-clinical versions, the everyday imaginary conversations many of us have all the time.

4. While some of Reagan's policies were viewed as polarizing to some, he was instrumental in the fall of the Berlin Wall, the reunification of Germany, and the end of the Cold War, significant milestones for the history books in the 20th Century.

CH 5

1. KJB: Matthew 7:1-5. KJB: John 8:7. KJB: Luke 6:37-42. "And why beholdest thou the mote that is in thy brother's eye, but considerest not the beam that is in thine own eye?"

Proverbial idiom, Spanish origin, first half of the seventeenth century. Earliest appearance of the idiom is in Thomas Shelton's 1620 translation of *Don Quixote*.

2. Rescue Tube, Can, Buoy, or Torpedo: A rescue buoy, rescue tube or torpedo buoy is a piece of lifesaving equipment used in water rescue. This flotation device can help support the victim's and rescuer's weight to make a rescue easier. It is an essential part of the equipment that must be carried by lifeguards. It further can act as a mark of identification, identifying an individual as a lifeguard. https://en.wikipedia.org/wiki/Rescue_buoy

3. Personal sovereignty refers to our personal sensibilities and preferences in our acts of giving, generosity, and healthy interactions. These are not to be mistaken for, and are in stark contrast to, the implied and expressed boundaries all people are afforded both legally and morally under protection of the law whereby, when violated, the bad actors are subject to criminal prosecution. These include blatant acts, like grabbing someone inappropriately, assault, and other forms of documented abuse.

CH 7

1. Contributing source: Feeling Our Emotions, Antonio R. Damasio, https://www.scientificamerican.com/article/feeling-our-emotions/.

CH 9

1. National Severe Storm Laboratory. A single lightning bolt can have one hundred million to one billion volts, and it contains billions of watts, depending on whether it is positive lightning or negative lightning. Lightning strikes ground in the United States approximately twenty-five million times each year.

2. The Greek words for love, https://en.wikipedia.org/wiki/Greek_words_for_love.

3. Research article Helen E. Fisher, http://www.dana.org/Cerebrum/Default.aspx?id=39351.

4. Other research includes dating sites eharmony.com and match.com.

5. Research on inherited, genetic addiction and chemical pathways pre-disposition.

6.
   1. This perspective has been recognized in cultures and civilizations by peoples all over the globe since recorded history. They are illustrated in expressions such as Ubuntu(southern Africa), namaste (Sanskrit), and the web of life (Native American). This is the recognition of you in me, me in you, us to the community, the earth, trees, oceans, "the wind that gave our grandfather his first breath that also received his last sigh," to something bigger than our Self—of us all as the collective fingerprint of the Divine—or to the non-spiritual, the collective, shared, elemental stardust of the universe constituting all that is, has always been, and will always be.

   2. Quantum Tethering, Enanglement, Spookiness: Einstein, https://en.wikipedia.org/wiki/Quantum_entanglement,https://www.scientificamerican.com/article/entangled-photons-quantum-spookiness/. Chaos theory and butterfly effect: https://en.wikipedia.org/wiki/Butterfly_effect. Mirror Neurons: Neurolinguistic programming, empathy, compassion, https://en.wikipedia.org/wiki/Mirror_neuron. Ubuntu: "I am because you are" is the affirmation of one's humanity through recognition of another in which the other becomes a mirror for one's subjectivity. A person is a person through other people.

This idealism suggests that humanity is embedded in a person not solely as an individual but as part of a connected whole; therefore, humanity is a quality we owe to each other, https://en.wikipedia.org/wiki/Ubuntu_(philosophy). Namaste: "The light in me recognizes and honors the light in you" is an affirmation that at a deeper level, we are all part of the same light; we are connected, https://en.wikipedia.org/wiki/Namaste.

CH 11

1. Merriam-Webster, Cambridge, Oxford Dictionaries, Wikipedia.

2. Merriam-Webster, Cambridge, Oxford Dictionaries, Wikipedia.

3. Merriam-Webster, Cambridge, Oxford Dictionaries, Wikipedia.

4. Cambridge, Oxford Dictionaries, Wikipedia.

5. In the temporal perspective, our lives consist of past, present, and future. Time exists only in our temporal, physical world experience, and the timeline is the way we, as an observer, plot the progression of our life. In the ultra-dimensional perspective, there is no timeline because time is absent. The only way to represent the same life being (as it is impossible by definition to physically observe) would be from the temporal realm—plotted as infinite present moments rather than a timeline or what conceptually might be an infinity vector (https://en.wikipedia.org/wiki/Dimension_(vector_space)). It would appear as a point (the present), and the point actually consists of infinite points representing infinite present moments. A point has no measure, no length, width, height; infinite points in the same location do not change that.

    Conceptually, fate, destiny, and entelechy in relation to the ultra-dimensional realm are not represented by separate intersect points because, in the ultra-dimensional realm, everything intersects in the present instant. The concept of time is absent, and its passing and future are absent. The concept has no beginning or ending, only the present. Since distance requires time to get from A to B, absent time, there is no distance either; there is no linear distinction connecting A to B, which is why such a concept is deemed ultra-dimensional, beyond dimension. If I lost you for a second with that, don't worry. I'm sort of a geek and include this added description for the enjoyment of my fellow geeks.

6. Thoreau's civil disobedience suggested that the judgement of an individual's conscience is not necessarily inferior to the decisions of a political body or majority, and so "it is not desirable to cultivate a respect for the law, so much so <as to suspend one's own good, independent judgement>. When the government was producing injustice it was the duty of conscientious citizens to be "a counter friction" (i.e., a resistance).."[2]

Law never made men a whit more just; and, by means of their respect for it, even the well-disposed are daily made the agents of injustice."[5] He punctuated the point of hypocrisy of the political body of the time by pointing out: "I cannot for an instant recognize as my government [that] which is the slave's government also."[6] Mahatma Gandhi could be appropriately situated in this conversation about civil disobedience with his own satyagraha.[3]

Mahatma Gandhi : Satyagraha (/ˌsætɪəˈɡrɑːhɑː/; Sanskrit: सत्याग्रह satyāgraha)—loosely translated as "insistence on truth" (satya "truth"; agraha "insistence" or "holding firmly to") or holding onto truth[1] or truth force—is a particular form of nonviolent resistance or civil resistance. The termsatyagraha was coined and developed by Mahatma Gandhi.[2] He deployed satyagraha in the Indian independence movement and also during his earlier struggles in South Africa for Indian rights. Satyagraha theory influenced Martin Luther King, Jr.'s campaign during the Civil Rights Movement in the United States.

The term originated in Sanskrit words satya (meaning "truth") and Agraha ("polite insistence", or "holding firmly to"). Satya is derived from the word "sat", which means "being". Nothing is or exists in reality except (T)ruth. In the context of satyagraha, Truth therefore includes a) Truth in speech, as opposed to falsehood, b) what is real, as opposed to nonexistent (asat) and c) good as opposed to evil, or bad. This was critical to Gandhi's understanding of and faith in nonviolence: "The world rests upon the bedrock of satya or truth. Asatya, meaning untruth, also means nonexistent, and satya or truth also means that which "is". If untruth does not so much as exist, its victory is out of the question. And "T"ruth being that which is, can never be destroyed. This is the doctrine of satyagraha in a nutshell." [5] For Gandhi, satyagraha went far beyond mere "passive resistance" and became strength in practicing non-violent methods.[6] In his words:

Truth (satya) implies love, and firmness (agraha) engenders and therefore serves as a synonym for force. I thus began to call the Indian movement Satyagraha, that is to say, the Force which is born of Truth and Love or non-violence. He gave up the use of the phrase "passive resistance", in connection with it, so much so that even in English writing it is often avoided, instead using the word "satyagraha" itself or some other equivalent English phrase.[7] –Wikipedia.

7. Shoshin (初心) is a concept in Zen Buddhism meaning "beginner's mind." It refers to having an attitude of openness, eagerness, and lack of preconceptions when studying a subject, even when studying at an advanced level, just as a beginner in that subject would. The term is also used in the study of Japanese martial arts.

8. As applied also to a child's mind, the metaphor of a sponge could be likened to the brain not being fully developed, matured, at full capacity, yet able to function and absorb material as can an adult's.

9. The Fortune 500 is an annual list compiled and published by Fortune magazine that ranks the five hundred largest US corporations by total revenue for their respective fiscal years. The list includes public companies, along with privately held companies for which revenues are publicly available. The concept of the Fortune 500 was created by Edgar P. Smith, a Fortune editor, and the first list was published in 1955.

   1. Survivor's guilt involves one or more of the following three variations: feeling guilt about staying alive while others died; feeling guilt about the things one failed to do, like saving more people who perished; feeling guilt about what one did do to survive, as in contemplating the cost to others as when one benefitted to survive. Wikipedia.

   2. In narratology and comparative mythology, the monomyth, or the hero's journey, is the common template of a broad category of tales that involve a hero who goes on an adventure, in a decisive crisis wins a victory, and then comes home changed or transformed, https://en.wikipedia.org/wiki/Monomyth. The concept was introduced by Joseph Campbell in The Hero with a Thousand Faces where he described the basic narrative pattern as follows: A hero ventures forth from the world of common day into a region of supernatural wonder; fabulous forces are there encountered and a decisive victory is won; the hero comes back from this mysterious adventure with the power to bestow boons on his fellow man.

   3. According to the Invisible Distinctions definition and the distinction between self-ish and self-serving.

CH 13

1. From a secular perspective

   The reference of "essential life force" refers to the source of energy or impulse that inhabits all matter, life, things. It is a guiding life force beyond which we are yet to empirically understand because we cannot gain context or step outside it to observe it objectively; consciousness itself is included.

2. From a religious / spiritual perspective

   The reference of the "essential life force" is the Divine. Faith in the Divine or metaphysics,2a organized or not, is defined and commonly referred to as relying on belief rather than empirical science. It is the notion that faith is enough, and all that is required. Navigating the path of spirituality and religion, as 84 percent of the world does, is a personal journey.2b Identifying distinctions within faith traditions as is done here, is different from the distinctions being about the traditions themselves

   2a. Definition of "metaphysics" combined from Merriam-Webster Dictionary, Oxford Dictionary, and Wikipedia.

   2b. Pew Research Center 2010 study The Global Religious Landscape, http://www.pewforum.org/2012/12/18/global-religious-landscape-exec/.

3. A waterman or waterwoman is a person whose lifestyle identifies with the water by way of vast experience and participation in a multitude of ocean and water sports and activities. Historically the term referred to those who make their living from the water, such as professional surf-lifesavers, commercial divers, fishermen, and sailors. It has evolved to describe those who take part in a variety of water activities, such as wave-riding sports that include swimming, surfing, kayaking, and bodysurfing. In surfing terminology, "waterman" refers to a versatile athlete who can engage in various forms of water sports depending on conditions. One early

person given this title was Duke Kahanamoku. Adapted from https://en.wikipedia.org/wiki/Waterman_(sports).

4. Genesis 1:27, KJB.

5. From https://en.wikipedia.org/wiki/Subject_(philosophy).

6. Smithsonian Institute and National Human Genome Research Institute.

7. The use of psychological archetypes was advanced by Carl Jung in 1919. In Jung's psychological framework, archetypes are innate, universal prototypes for ideas and may be used to interpret observations. A group of memories and interpretations associated with an archetype is a complex (e.g., a mother complex associated with the mother archetype). Jung treated the archetypes as psychological organs, analogous to physical ones in that both are morphological givens that arose through evolution.

8. "Collective unconscious," a term coined by Carl Jung, refers to structures of the unconscious mind that are shared among beings of the same species. According to Jung, the human collective unconscious is populated by instincts and by archetypes: universal symbols such as the great mother, the wise old man, the shadow, the tower, water, the tree of life, and many more.

   https://en.wikipedia.org/wiki/Collective_unconscious.

9. The divine right of kings, divine right, or G_d's mandate is a political and religious doctrine of royal and political legitimacy. It asserts that a monarch is subject to no world authority, deriving the right to rule directly from the will of G_d, https://en.wikipedia.org/wiki/Divine_right_of_kings.

10. In discussing human nature and behavior with respect to certainty, we can view certainty as a linear equation with respect to human nature. The inversely proportionate manner

reflecting common public tendency. Take the two statements below:

Person A. "The evidence so far suggests to me X, but, of course, I could be wrong."

Person B. "I am absolutely certain, beyond any possibility of error, of Y."

The public then weighs Person A's hesitancy over asserting X with Person B's certainty of asserting Y. Commonly, certainty trumps uncertainty, and Person B's Y is adopted.

Further insult to injury often occurs in debate, as Person B exploits A's humble acknowledgement he could be wrong and offers contempt to A's supposedly audacious and arrogant suggestion claiming X without knowing for sure, all the while Person B is pretending to be sure himself of Y.

So, common nature leads the public to adopt certainty, arrogantly asserted as fact, over an observation submitted with a qualification that it is the best supported position based on available evidence to date.

An even more common transgression occurs when people listen, absorb, and assimilate the certainty stated by a person of influence and proceed to assert their own influence by passing this along on social media, on television, or in front of a large mass of people, all because the person of influence said so with certainty. All the while, what has happened in the process? The media look for soundbites and take excerpts out of context, and often the public is left with this incomplete and misleading information. First to be eliminated are context and sourcing. Sourcing! Remember the person or doctrine that suggested this was known for certain? And this is what progresses.

What is the remedy to this? Should the people in Person B's camp pretend to have certainty in something they know to be unfounded as a way to convince others? Besides being dishonest and/or ignorant, this completely ignores the moral responsibility to consider the possibility of error.

When they are lacking information or are ill-informed, people are prone to follow just about anything.

101,102

Jewish Journal- https://jewishjournal.com/rosnersdomain/224032/study-finds-half-young-jews-no-religion/

Pew Research Center: https://www.pewforum.org/2015/05/12/americas-changing-religious-landscape/

CH 16

1. A motif is the smallest structural unit possessing thematic identity. For example, Beethoven's Fifth Symphony has the four-note "fate" motif (dah, dah, dah, dahhhh).

2. From https://en.wikipedia.org/wiki/Man's_Search_for_Meaning.

3. Matthew 7:3-5, King James Bible.

4. Buddha.

5. From https://en.wikipedia.org/wiki/Maslow%27s_hierarchy_of_needs, https://en.wikipedia.org/wiki/Self-realization, https://en.wikipedia.org/wiki/Psychosynthesis, https://en.wikipedia.org/wiki/Advaita_Vedanta.

6. The secular definitions of "epiphany" are (1) a usually sudden manifestation or perception of the essential nature or meaning of something, (2) an intuitive grasp of reality through something (as an event) usually simple and striking, and (3) an illuminating discovery, realization, or disclosure.

7. From http://www.city.kanazawa.ishikawa.jp/dentou_e/way/waye.html.

8. Alan Watts, The Wisdom of Insecurity. "There is no certainty in the natural world, but it doesn't "worry."

9. *Joseph Campbell*, The Power of Myth, with Bill Moyers. "The Navaho have that wonderful image of what they call the pollen path. Pollen is the life source. The pollen path is the path to the center. The Navaho say, *"Oh beauty before me, beauty behind me, beauty to the right of me, beauty to the left of me, beauty above me, beauty below me, I'm on the pollen path."*